Virtue Hermeneutics

Virtue Hermeneutics

New Horizons in Textual Understanding

Robert M. Eby

PICKWICK *Publications* · Eugene, Oregon

VIRTUE HERMENEUTICS
New Horizons in Textual Understanding

Pickwick Publications
An Imprint of Wipf and Stock Publishers
199 W. 8th Ave., Suite 3
Eugene, OR 97401

www.wipfandstock.com

PAPERBACK ISBN: 978-1-6667-1279-7
HARDCOVER ISBN: 978-1-6667-1280-3
EBOOK ISBN: 978-1-6667-1281-0

Cataloguing-in-Publication data:

Names: Eby, Robert M., author

Title: Virtue hermeneutics : new horizons in textual understanding / by Robert M. Eby.

Description: Eugene, OR: Pickwick Publications, 2022 | Includes bibliographical references.

Identifiers: ISBN 978-1-6667-1279-7 (paperback) | ISBN 978-1-6667-1280-3 (hardcover) | ISBN 978-1-6667-1281-0 (ebook)

Subjects: LCSH: Virtue epistemology. | Bible—Hermeneutics. | Virtues. | Hermeneutics.

Classification: BS476 E29 2022 (print) | BS476 (ebook)

02/28/22

This work is dedicated with love and appreciation
to my best friend and devoted wife, Lori

Contents

Acknowledgments

SPECIAL THANKS TO DR. Brandon Schmidly for his friendship and invaluable assistance and insight in the development of the ideas contained in this research. I would also like to extend appreciation to Rachel Moore whose diligent attention to details helped to make this work ready for publication.

Introduction

IF A MOUNT RUSHMORE of twentieth-century Western Christians were ever to be carved upon the rockface of some majestic mountain, most evangelicals would likely find a prized location for British writer C. S. Lewis. For many, if not most, he would be honored in this way for his widely popular *Chronicles of Narnia* series of books, which present multiple biblical and theological themes in a fantasy world of allegorical imagery. For others he would be recognized as a popularizer of theology and apologetics for the average person through his non-fiction writings, the most popular of which is his bestselling *Mere Christianity*. While these are noteworthy and sufficient reasons for Lewis's inclusion, they do not speak to his day job. For his daily occupation, he was a scholar in the field of English literary studies, first, as a fellow at Magdalen College, Oxford, and then as the Chair of Mediaeval and Renaissance Literature at Cambridge. In short, he was a professional critic and interpreter of texts. In one little-noticed sentence buried in the first book in the *Chronicles of Narnia* series, *The Magician's Nephew*, he combined his skills as a fiction writer, an amateur theologian, and a scholarly interpreter of texts to give expression to the central tenet of the following two hundred pages.

As a select group of the animals of the newly-created Narnia were endowed with the power of speech, a peculiar scene unfolds when they rush with enthusiasm to speak to one of the two primary antagonists of the story, Uncle Andrew. Though the other characters in the scene, Aslan, Digory, Polly, and the cabby and his wife have all engaged in dialogue and wondered at the speech of the animals, not so Uncle Andrew. "When the Beasts spoke in answer [to Aslan], he [Uncle Andrew] heard only barkings, growlings, bayings, and howlings."[1] In describing how some characters heard language and intelligence while Uncle Andrew heard nothing, Lewis's narrator explains, "For what you see and hear depends a good deal on where you are standing: it also depends on what sort of person you are."[2]

Writing in the waning days of modernity with all of its emphasis on rationalism's pursuit of certainty and objectivity in all epistemological endeavors, including hermeneutics, the idea that what one sees and hears, and consequently knows and understands, is shaped by the location and character of the interpreter was a dramatic break from the orthodoxy of the preceding centuries. Rationalism, historicism, liberalism, and structuralism all employed methodologies to attempt to reach an objective certainty of a text's meaning unaffected by conditional or agential interference. Yet, Lewis seems to imply that an interpreter's location and personal character, both intellectual and ethical, affects what can be perceived and understood by an agent. While anticipating elements of the soon-to-emerge postmodern critiques (rejection of a view from nowhere, certainty, and objective interpretation), Lewis differed from later theorists in still believing that the speech of the animals was objectively present as a meaningful expression and could be understood by other agents depending on their location and character, what Joseph Kotva identifies as, "the need to become the right sort."[3] This position exists in the middle between the untenable modern hopes of objectivity and certainty and the postmodern despair of the very existence or possibility of a durable form of textual meaning. In this particular example, the subjective (not relativistic) component was the interpreter whose own character limited his ability to understand what was genuinely present in the voices of the animals. This is the central idea of the following research.

Virtue Hermeneutics as a Stable Center for Hermeneutical Inquiry

The effectiveness of a hermeneut to come to a better understanding of a text involves many things including skills, giftings, and methods, but the deeply-habituated intellectual character of the interpreter is of

---

1. Lewis, *Magician's Nephew*, 137.

2. Lewis, *Magician's Nephew*, 136.

3. Kotva, *Christian Case for Virtue Ethics*, loc. 1461.

foundational importance. Many contemporary frameworks of hermeneutical inquiry begin with skepticism at the hope, and even desire, to come to know an authorially-established meaning within a text (i.e., hermeneutical realism), ultimately replacing the classical *telos* of interpretation with forms of projection, play, or existential synthesis. By applying the model of Responsibilist Virtue Epistemology (RVE) in an agent-centered approach, Virtue Hermeneutics (VH) can provide legitimacy and stability to the hermeneutical realist's endeavors, even in a postmodern context, and with the addition of a pneumatological element, the approach becomes especially fruitful in the special case of biblical hermeneutics.

Over the course of the research, several key elements must be established if VH is to find a place in the current hermeneutical discussion. After briefly establishing the contemporary context of hermeneutical thought as it has developed since the period of Enlightenment, the remainder of the discussion moves progressively toward a defense of a pneumatological approach to hermeneutics built from the starting point of RVE. Each chapter is a step in both the theoretical and practical expression of the main goal of offering a useful and theologically valid perspective on discovering and extending meaning found within texts. Chapter 1 explains the rise and theoretical underpinnings of RVE as it can be applied in textual inquiry. Chapter 2 attempts to translate this understanding into a programmatic approach to developing virtuous hermeneuticians. Chapter 3 approaches the task of VH by detailing those virtues which form the nucleus of a virtuous interpreter. This detailing of the virtues is not intended to be comprehensive but an attempt to place a foundational description of what a virtuous interpreter might look like. In the final chapter, the transition to a theological frame of reference is brought into view by arguing that VH must possess a spiritual component to overcome limitations within RVE and that this pneumatologically-attuned VH aligns with the historic Christian doctrine of illumination of the Holy Spirit in both the epistemological and hermeneutical disciplines.

The Goal of Virtue Hermeneutics within the Context of Contemporary Hermeneutics

Very little agreement can be found in reference to any element of the task, or even nature, of hermeneutics. The word is employed across almost every contemporary domain of knowledge. In its most expansive form, *hermeneutics* has become the all-encompassing term for the *telos* of cognitive activities. Hermeneutics is looked at, "not only as a discipline in its own right but especially as an aspect of all intellectual endeavors."[4] Because of this, the Modern Era's goal of contact with, or understanding of, reality in an objectively ontic sense, has been dismissed as the desiderata of epistemology. This has left only varied individualized or community-bound interpretations as the highest-grade product possible for all forms of inquiry. This expansive, and potentially irrealist, condition stands in stark contrast with the simplistic and classical definition presented by Grant Osborne, which defines hermeneutics as, "That science which delineates principles or methods for interpreting an individual author's meaning."[5] The divergence of these two definitions is not defined by methods or hermeneutical models, but by shifts in the underlying epistemological frameworks that have variously exerted influence on the task of interpretation.

At least as ancient as Plato, the questions of what constitutes knowledge or those practices, faculties, or habits most conducive to its acquisition have been the topic of philosophical debate. In Plato's record of Socrates's interrogation of Theaetetus, the discipline of epistemology takes its classical form. It is not so much the body of information or skills that characterize a specific art or science (e.g., shoe making or carpentry), but the generalized conception of what makes knowledge, in any field, uniquely, *knowledge*. It is, "The nature of knowledge in the abstract."[6] While Plato leaves the question, "what is knowledge" ultimately unresolved in the dialogue, the third definition offered by Theaetetus has exerted lasting influence. He submitted that, "True opinion, combined with reason (λόγος), was knowledge, but that the opinion which had no reason was out of the sphere of knowledge."[7] From this point, which characterizes knowledge as justified true belief, epistemology has served as a constant interlocutor, either explicitly or implicitly, with all forms of human cognitive activity including the historically defined task of ascertaining textual meaning.

For much of the history of thought, epistemology served as the underlying framework that informed progressive developments in textual

---

4. Vanhoozer, *Meaning in This Text?*, 19.

5. Osborne, *Hermeneutical Spiral*, 5.

6. Plato, *Theaetetus*, loc. 1423.

7. Plato, *Theaetetus*, loc. 2441.

interpretation. As philosophers sought to establish precisely what a justified true belief was and how to acquire it, the similar task of discerning a justified accurate understanding of the intentional meaning of the author within a text and what methodologies are best attuned to achieve this goal developed in a parallel fashion. The ongoing emphases of the various permutations of epistemology through the centuries are recognizable in the subsequent priorities of the hermeneutical schools of thought that developed in their shadow. Some philosophers developed epistemological frames that also attempted to articulate a corresponding hermeneutical agenda (e.g., John Locke, Baruch Spinoza, and Wilhelm Dilthey), while others, like René Descartes, saw their philosophy applied into diverse disciplines by others. The epistemological priorities are often recognizable in a latent sense within the specific methodologies that emerge within the interpretive community during the contemporary and immediately subsequent eras of a major epistemological theory's sway. An early modern example of this is seen in the rise of rationalism as an epistemological system in the aftermath of Descartes, Spinoza, and Gottfried Leibniz, with the corresponding historicism that emerged during Enlightenment-era hermeneutics. Even further, the priorities of rationalism-initiated responses gave rise to the classic theological liberal hermeneutics of Friedrich Schleiermacher. This tendency of hermeneutics to reflect the broader epistemological agenda of its milieu continues until the Postmodern Era, where the flow from epistemology to hermeneutics is reversed, so that epistemology itself is critiqued in its pursuit of what has been deemed an illusory objective form of knowledge and now takes its lead from hermeneutics in seeing all declarations as mere interpretation.[8] Kevin Vanhoozer labels this reversal of hermeneutics and philosophy as the "literary turn" within philosophy. He accurately expresses the ascendency of hermeneutics over epistemology (and philosophy more generally) in the Postmodern Era: "For it is one thing to say that philosophy reflects on principles that undergird literary interpretation, and quite another to suggest that philosophy itself is only a

---

8. Thomas Kuhn's investigation into *The Structure of Scientific Revolutions* (1962) exposes this reversal as it relates specifically to scientific knowledge. For most of the period of Modernity, scientific inquiry was viewed as the most objective form of inquiry and knowledge. Kuhn's discussion served to demonstrate that even the presumed objective realm of the natural sciences is beholden to frameworks of understanding that shape or limit possible solutions to scientific questions. In this way, theories are less objective expressions of reality and more interpretations that possess explanatory abilities as they exist within broader paradigmatic structures.

kind of interpretation."[9] The literary nature of this movement is seen in its origination in the writings of continental thinkers that come from literary, philological, and semiotic backgrounds (e.g., Jacques Derrida, Roland Barthes, Michel Foucault, Jean Francois Lyotard, Umberto Eco, and Ferdinand de Saussure).

This bi-directional, sometimes symbiotic, and occasionally combative relationship between epistemology and hermeneutics is observable at every stage of development. Consequently, many of the problems that have plagued hermeneutics since the seventeenth century are either the result, reflection, or reaction against underlying epistemological commitments and problems. Epistemology exists as a discipline for many reasons, but its most constant companion and foil is the specter of skepticism. For Descartes, skepticism was, somewhat paradoxically, both the adversary to be overcome and the foundational principle in his epistemological framework. How can a knowing subject properly claim to *know* anything? This same grappling with skepticism emerges as interpreters seek to understand what a text means. The contemporary skepticism directed toward any form of stable meaning in the text among many theorists is jarring to those who have been trained by common sense to believe that a text means something, which is generally aligned with the intended meaning that occasioned the text's writing by its author, and that this meaning can be reasonably understood by a reader. The journey from a premodern naïve realism that sees an indivisible and persistent unity between the words of a text and their self-evident and universal meaning to postmodern statements that eliminate the possibility of a durable text which carries any internal sense of meaning[10] is the result of a progressive movement toward textual irrealism and skepticism toward meaning that has been fostered by the underlying epistemological commitments developed over the last several hundred years. The contemporary revival of virtue theory holds a potential answer to the epistemological problems of both the modern and postmodern varieties.

9. Vanhoozer, *Meaning in This Text?*, 19.

10. Stanley Fish is an example of those who dismiss the meaning-bearing capacity of a text. In his seminal work, *Is There a Text in this Class?*, 13, he contends that, "The text as an entity independent of interpretation and (ideally) responsible for its career drops out and is replaced by the *texts* [emphasis mine] that emerge as the consequence of our interpretive activities." This is ultimately a refuting of the historically defined nature of interpretation in favor of a view of texts as simply the impetus for the multiplication of new texts by each reader. Interpretation is replaced by new forms of authorship.

ONE

Responsibilist Virtue Epistemology as a Necessary Contributor to Hermeneutical Inquiry

Introduction

ONE CAN EASILY ENVISION a scenario where a brutish husband, call him Brutus, victimizes his wife by means of angry and violent physical and emotional assaults whenever the couple disagrees about expectations within the marriage regardless of whether household, financial, or relational expectations serve as the presenting conflict. Brutus's abusive actions are readily evaluated as being morally wrong rather than being an epistemic issue, but there is a potentially relevant way in which his thinking could be examined in reference to epistemic and hermeneutical considerations. Suppose Brutus used the Bible as the justifying source of his behaviors. He is confident in the vindication of his actions based upon the words of the Bible. More precisely, he is confident in the vindication of his actions based upon *his interpretation* of the words of the Bible. The interpretive question requires an evaluation of his use of the biblical text. In this scenario, the question becomes, is Brutus's interpretation or understanding of the text a justified reading of the meaning of the text? Are we condemned to go no further than Miguel A. De La Torre's thoughts in evaluating individual interpretations of a text when he makes the observation that, "All biblical interpretations are valid to the one who

1

is doing the interpreting"?[1] Is this form of solipsistic interpretation the highest-grade understanding available when attempting to critique textual interpretations?

Ephesians 5:22–24 (ESV) states, "Wives, submit to your own husbands, as to the Lord. For the husband is the head of the wife even as Christ is the head of the church, his body, and is himself its Savior. Now as the church submits to Christ, so also wives should submit in everything to their husbands." From this verse, Brutus claims justification for his violent actions toward his wife since she violated clear biblical teaching and disrespected his patriarchal superiority, which is proportionate to the Bible's ascription of sovereign status to Christ over the church. Various epistemological approaches have prioritized differing foundations in order to identify stable points of connection to either justify or disallow the interpretation offered by Brutus (e.g., linguistic considerations, intra-text context, socio-cultural context, historical background, or emotional/spiritual reactions to the interpretation). Well-founded, coherent, and cogent arguments can likely emerge from many, if not all, of the preceding perspectives, which, in many cases, would deem Brutus's interpretation as unjustified while others have been offered that would presumably justify his interpretation.

However, the failure of Brutus's particular interpretation is likely related to something more fundamental than grammatical-historical, etymological, or deconstructive literary skills. It is possible to see this act of interpretation as being something worse than unjustified; it could be correctly classified as a vicious treatment of the meaning of the text. All the well-reasoned arguments of the previously mentioned systems could be marshalled and explained to Brutus, and yet, he could easily dismiss them as irrelevant as he holds to his interpretation of what the text means *to him*. Many contemporary models of interpretation have no viable recourse to challenge this understanding of the text. As a result, he could remain closed to new information because he was ultimately not seeking to understand the meaning of the passage; he was using the words on the page to justify himself, not to increase his knowledge and understanding of the ancient text with the expectation of some relevant insight that could beneficially affect his thoughts, actions, or values. It is likely that Brutus's poor interpretation is the result of approaching the text with a selfish agenda, closed-mindedness, and a laziness that resists reading the

---

1. De La Torre, *Reading the Bible from the Margins*, loc. 118.

passage with attentiveness. He is blinded by the need to justify himself rather than understand a text, and as a result, he offers an illegitimate interpretation of the text because of his lack of virtue when interpreting.

By deeming this interpretation less plausible because of deficiencies in the intellectual habits of character within the husband, this example surfaces another way forward in justifying interpretation. The emergence of Responsibilist Virtue Epistemology (RVE) offers hermeneutics a new starting point, namely, the core intellectual habits of the interpreter's cognitive character. The nature of the virtues as being deeply held and practiced habits of intellectual excellencies has long been extolled for its abiding stability. From Aristotle through nearly all contemporary theorists, the relative stability of the virtues, both internally within the agent as well as externally as a generally agreed upon body of desirable excellencies which enable a person to optimally perform their intended function, stands in contrast to the rapidly shifting realms of frameworks, models, skills, faculties, and talents. It is the contention of this research that RVE and the hermeneutical priorities that are entailed within its domain establish the intellectual character of the thinking/interpreting agent as a more reliable measure of the likelihood that an interpretation will be justifiable than appeals to skills or methodological frameworks in isolation from the agent who employs them. It avoids the illusory idea of Modernism's supposed objectivity and Postmodernism's rejection of hermeneutical realism.[2]

Previous modern hermeneutical models have emphasized the skills or ideological starting points, but this has led to the multiplication of hermeneutical approaches that generate diverse and often contradictory interpretations, all claiming some form of objective accuracy. Even more complicating is the reality that many mutually exclusive interpretations of biblical texts originate from within the same hermeneutical school.[3] Skills and ideologies are malleable tools whose usefulness and

2. A helpful definition of hermeneutical realism is offered by Steven Mailloux in his article, "Rhetorical Hermeneutics," as the theoretical position that, "Meaning-full texts exist independent of interpretation. From this perspective, meanings are discovered, not created."

3. The conflict between the hermeneutical products of F. C. Baur, E. P. Sanders, and Wilhelm Bousset aptly illustrate this point. Each of these scholars is embedded within the historical-critical method of interpretation and arrives at incompatible interpretations on the basis of their framework. Baur, writing in *The Church History of the First Three Centuries* (1879), frames a Hegelian model of understanding church history. The thesis of Jewish Christianity led by Peter is confronted by the antithesis of the gentile

interpretive products are, to a great degree, dependent upon the agent who wields them. There is no objective frame from which to interpret a text. Robert Roberts and Jay Wood succinctly demonstrate the failure of the most prominent epistemological theories to secure objectivity, "Our empirical observations are theory-laden and susceptible to error, our reasoning depends on unprovable assumptions, our criteria for dividing justifier and justified are unclear, and our standards of evidence and argumentation contested, to cite a few of the problems."[4] Disillusionment at the pseudo-objectivity of modern approaches and their resultant interpretative conclusions has ended in the more reader-centered and more radically skeptical postmodern approaches that have dominated the discipline since the latter part of the twentieth century. Steven Mailloux defines these theoretical commitments as "hermeneutic idealism" which holds that, "interpretation always creates the signifying text, that meaning is made, not found. In this view, textual facts are never prior to or independent of the hermeneutic activity of readers and critics."[5] At the same moment that the field of hermeneutics was dealing with the aftermath of these epistemological inheritances, philosophers were looking for a new center to hold the epistemological project together beyond skills and rules. Guy Axtell explains the hope of the new approach, "To attribute an action or belief to the workings of an intellectual virtue is to identify its ground with an attribute of the agent that is still more stable and less fleeting than is a skill."[6] The reliability of methodologies or skills is ultimately dependent on the intellectual character of the one implementing them. RVE begins with a different starting point, the deeply embedded and consistently expressed intellectual characteristics of the thinking/interpreting agent. In this way, it offers new perspectives for hermeneutics as well as epistemology.

Christianity of Paul, resulting in a synthesis of Catholicism. In this model Paul is leading a Christianity shaped by gentile worldviews. E. P. Sanders contradicts this in *Paul and Palestinian Judaism* (1977), which locates Paul as being significantly aligned to traditional Judaism rather than gentile frameworks of understanding. Bousset claims the extreme that Paul not only was more influenced by gentile frames but that he utilized Greek mystery religions as the primary method of shaping his proclamation in *Kyrios Christos: A History of the Belief in Christ From the Beginnings of Christianity to Irenaeus* (1913).

4. Roberts and Wood, *Intellectual Virtues*, 5.

5. Mailloux, "Rhetorical Hermeneutics," 622.

6. Axtell, "Introduction," xvi.

The following introduction to Virtue Epistemology as a new and potentially liberating starting point for a fresh view of hermeneutical inquiry will accomplish several goals. An introduction and definition of RVE with an emphasis on its reversal of the movement of justification and the mixed nature of the justification factors (J-factors), encompassing both internally and externally relevant factors, in the task of gaining knowledge is necessary before explaining its relevance to the task of interpretation. After establishing this foundation, intellectually virtuous characteristics are shown as a more reliable point of connection between the author, text, interpreter, and interpretive context. The result is a more accurate attainment and communication of textual meaning. A virtuous interpretation is ultimately a justified understanding of the text.

Responsibilist Virtue Epistemology

The fundamental issue in examining the contributions of broader epistemological thought into the discussion of the development of biblical hermeneutics involves the question of common ground or shared starting point for knowledge and understanding. In epistemology, the justification of true belief has been the central matter of discussion since Descartes. It has remained a primary concern in attempting to steady the postmodern and post-Gettier epistemological endeavor.[7] In each iteration of dominant epistemological frameworks through modern history, the act of justifying beliefs is of critical consideration in how knowledge can be certified and consequently communicable between other agents. Even in highly individualized and internal systems of epistemology (e.g., rationalism and romanticism), justification serves to not only meet the individual's threshold of duty in regard to holding to something as knowledge, but also in being able to express it in a cogent way to another. In rationalism, human reason is the shared ultimate criteria that validates knowledge and allows for its dissemination, since reason was viewed as the supra-cultural ether of human cognition.[8] Romanticism identifies the

7. Gettier, "Is Justified True Belief Knowledge?," 121–23.

8. It is significant to note that in two of the most dominant expressions of rationalism, Cartesian and Spinozian, they both eschew a naturalistic preunderstanding to guarantee their individual rational systems. Descartes rests his rational common ground on the nature of a God (either theistic or deistic), and Spinoza espouses what seems most likely to be a form of pantheism as the necessary common ground to establish the work of reason throughout the universe. This stands in distinction to the naturalistic

place of the affective nature of humanity as the shared starting point. For existentialism, the shared common ground is the fundamental human experience of existing as a being within time which unites each discrete cognitive agent. British Theologian, N. T. Wright, sees the combination of the Romantic and Existential views, which elevates individualism and feelings, as being an even more influential justifying influence in the twenty-first century than either were in the early twentieth century when each were at their individual apogees.[9] Epistemology can only be a meaningful philosophical construct if the justifying criteria finds common ground in some shared realm of human community. The only alternative is the deconstruction of epistemology as a discipline, and its ultimate replacement by solipsism or a form of neo-tribalism. This pursuit of a justifying common ground for knowledge is equally central in the related interpretive discipline of hermeneutics.

As each epistemological framework sought a justifying starting point, they embedded into the hermeneutical frameworks that emerged from their shadow a correlated permissible starting point for justifying textual interpretations. Rationalism led to hermeneutics dominated by historicism as the justifying core of interpretation. Romanticized liberalism, as initiated by Schleiermacher, identified the transcendent *gefühl* (the feeling of complete dependence) as the unifying key to divining understanding (*verstehen)*, or justifying the authorially intended meaning of a text. Existential and New Hermeneutic models sought to bypass the diachronic demands of other systems with an appeal to the contemporaneity of all elements of the interpretive task in a distinctly synchronic view of interpretation borrowed from existentialism.[10] It is this common task of justification which allows hermeneutics to naturally exist as a subset of the broader epistemological task. Where the broader concerns of epistemology seek to justify true beliefs (what Zagzebski identifies as "cognitive contact with reality"),[11] hermeneutics is more narrowly concerned with justifying cognitive contact with textually encoded meaning. Vanhoozer borrows directly from Zagzebski in describing this pursuit as, "cognitive contact with the meaning of the text."[12] Before attempting

---

impulses that quickly became the dominant expression of rationalism, especially as it was applied to theology and biblical interpretation during the Enlightenment.

9. Wright, "Simply Lewis."

10. Gadamer, *Truth and Method*, 124.

11. Zagzebski, *Virtues of the Mind*, loc. 146.

12. Vanhoozer, *Is There a Meaning in This Text?*, 376.

to apply RVE to hermeneutics, the matter of how justification is accrued within its approach must be explained.

The Velocity of Justification

In epistemological thought, *knowing* something is more than the mere acquisition of a true belief. Inherent within epistemology is the idea that something more is necessary to claim to the status of *knowledge*. Virtue theorists begin with this question in identifying their framework: "Why is knowledge more valuable than mere true belief, especially if true belief serves well for guiding action?"[13] For most classical epistemological systems, the answer resides in the term *justification*. It is that which a system deems necessary to variously ascribe value, foundation, support, or rationale to why a true belief is rightly, or justifiably, incorporated into a noetic system. For virtue approaches, the question of *value* is especially pertinent. The manner in which value is accumulated and transmitted is central to the framework. If, as the previous question demonstrates, the pragmatic concern of usefulness of true beliefs seems unaffected by justification, then value must be acquired as something distinct from mere effectiveness. Value derived from virtue implies a praiseworthiness and creditability dimension. It is this element of justification that RVE seems most attuned to deliver. Using the terminology of physics to illustrate the unique approach developed by RVE is helpful in establishing the system's distinctive concept of justification as the transference of value to true beliefs from an intellectual agent trained to virtue.

A velocity possesses both movement and direction. When considering the transmission of justification, it necessarily possesses both movement (since it travels between two objects) and direction (since it necessarily flows from one to the other). If true belief (TB) and a subject (S) are the two elements involved in a discussion of the direction of the flow of justification, the direction of the flow could be from (TB)→(S), (S)→(TB), or potentially in a form of bi-directionality (TB)←→(S). Both traditional and virtue-based approaches to justification make justification a property of (TB), but it is the direction of this movement that is distinct in the two approaches. In traditional approaches the status of a belief being justified moves from (TB) to (S). If the belief is justified (whether the acceptable ground of justification is deductive reasoning,

13. Turri et al., "Virtue Epistemology."

inductive inference, or some form of deontological measurement), then the agent is seen to be justified in claiming the true belief as being knowledge. Virtue theorists reverse the direction of justification's velocity by assigning the movement from the virtuous subject (VS), or, at the least, an agent thinking as a (VS) would typically think, to (TB). It is the (VS) who possesses the necessary capacities which extend justification to the belief. Christopher Hookway details this reversal of justification's velocity in this manner, "Justified beliefs are those that issue from the responsible inquiries of virtuous inquirers. It is a mistake to put it the other way around: epistemic virtues are those habits and dispositions that lead us to have justified beliefs."[14] Guy Axtell furthers this understanding in light of John Greco's explanation of Virtue Epistemology as a "change in direction of analysis" by arguing that, "virtue theories make rightness (or justifiedness) follow from an action's (or belief's) source in a virtue, rather than the other way around."[15] Beliefs only accrue justification as they originate from the well-tuned intellectual habits of the (VS).

In this reassignment of the direction of justification, the false dichotomy established by Descartes between the subject and object in epistemology is removed as the inevitably subjective nature of knowing is acknowledged, anchored within the nature of justification. Although knowing and the conditions which justify knowing are located within the thinking subject and are therefore properly subjective, a correct use of RVE stands against the devolving of knowledge into relativism or perspectivism. The value of the knowledge as a justified true belief is established in the intellectually praiseworthy character of the thinking agent. If justification is the primary matter which RVE is tuned to address in the traditional *telos* of epistemology (i.e., justified true belief), then further refinement of how the intellectual character of a thinking agent conveys justification is necessary before illustrating how it can guard against relativism and aid in the interpretive processes.

Why Look to Virtuous Agents as the Source of Epistemological Justification?

Virtue theory first *re*emerged in contemporary philosophical parlance in the discipline of ethics. As early as G. E. M. Anscombe's article,

14. Hookway, "Cognitive Virtues and Epistemic Evaluations," 225.
15. Axtell, "Introduction," xiii.

"Modern Moral Philosophy," in 1958, the struggle to determine an alternative ethical view that evaluated actions by something other than deontological or consequentialist considerations began to give rise to a contemporary definition of virtues. After exposing the flaws in previous systems, she ultimately concludes that, "Eventually it might be possible to advance to considering the concept of 'virtue'; with which, I suppose, we should be beginning some sort of a study of ethics."[16] While Virtue Epistemology is clearly connected to the preceding rise of Virtue Ethics, the rise of RVE as a means of justifying knowledge has become especially relevant since Edmund Gettier's 1963 three-page paper, "Is Justified True Belief Knowledge?"[17]

In two very brief sample cases within his presentation, Gettier injects scenarios in which a subject has a justified (according to classical constructions of justification) true belief that could not be accurately considered knowledge because of some form of double epistemic luck for which the subject could not be accurately credited with having attained knowledge.[18] In the subsequent half century, volumes have been written seeking to answer and either reestablish the pursuit of a justified true belief at the center of the epistemological project or jettison it entirely; each offering a nuanced defense of a particular response to the Gettier problem. Matthias Steup's survey of the contemporary literature from classical epistemological frameworks attempting to resolve the Gettier problem is summed up in his evaluation that, "It would be fair to say that what is conspicuous about the literature on the Gettier problem is, first, the multitude of approaches and, second, the lack of a settled solution."[19]

16. Anscombe, "Modern Moral Philosophy," 15.

17. Gettier, "Justified True Belief."

18. Simple Gettier scenarios can be readily created by the insertion of a form of double-luck condition. A woman knows that her husband is sitting in their living room. She believes this because she believes that she sees him sitting in his chair. This belief is justified on the basis of the evidence she possesses. He regularly sits in that chair. It is customary for him to be sitting in that chair at that time of day in order to watch the evening news broadcast that he faithfully watches daily. Furthermore, she sees what appears to be him in an environment suited for her visual sense's proper functioning (appropriate distance, lighting, and visual acuity). Unbeknownst to her, it is her husband's brother who bears a strong resemblance to her husband that is in the chair, but her husband is sitting in the living room in a location not visible from her vantage point. Her belief that her husband is sitting in the living room is true, and she is justified in believing it. Even in acknowledging this, it is clear that the scenario presented argues against claiming this justified true belief as genuine knowledge.

19. Steup, *Introduction to Contemporary Epistemology*, 5.

This body of literature, attempting to address Gettier, has exposed a sharp underlying divide in the formulation of justification between the internal and external realms. Externalists like those who have come to espouse the various expressions of reliabilism (e.g., Alvin Goldman and Alvin Plantinga) have sought to counter the luck component which has vexed internalist formulations by demanding an external reliability condition. These reliabilist formulations have themselves been critiqued by a revival of a contemporary form of evil demon critique, which allows for the possibility of external manipulations to defeat reliability focused J-factors. In the end, Plantinga is correct in saying that twentieth-century Anglo-American epistemology, "has made much of the notion of epistemic justification."[20] Of course, by saying "made much of," the rest of his book makes clear that he means *much of a mess*. In many ways, it is the mess created by the poles of externalism and internalism and their inability to bring a conclusive argument to resolve the Gettier problem that has caused the rise of newer formulations, including RVE.

The very same confusion between internal or external justification and Gettier style scenarios are represented in contemporary hermeneutical discussions. What justifies a reading of a text: the internal sense of the reader which reflects interpretive frameworks from Schleiermacher to Reader-Response approaches, or the external justification of *objective* historical reconstructions as seen in Historical Critical approaches? Is it possible that potentially accurate interpretations of a text can be arrived at in spite of what could rightly fit either a deontological, evidential, or reliabilistic form of justification by virtue of luck, as in Gettier scenarios? Many potentially good interpretations that have been based upon acceptable forms of justification within historical-critical frameworks may be accurate only because of an unanticipated turn of interpretive luck rather than the internalistic rationalism upon which the justification was established.[21] Does this luck disqualify the interpretation even if it is a justified true understanding?

---

20. Plantinga, *Warrant: The Current Debate*, 6.

21. Individual interpretations of priestly functions that have emerged from schools of thought indebted to Graf-Wellhausen have no doubt been justified within the historical-critical method by means of the embedded Hegelian model of evolutionary religious development even if later research may have discredited important assumptions of the entire model (e.g., the discovery of earlier manifestations of priestly legal materials as evidenced in other ANE documents (Altman, "Role of the 'Historical Prologue' in the Hittite Vassal Treaties," 48.)), thus demonstrating that even when information can be viewed as justified true belief in textual studies, it may still fall prey to Gettier scenarios of double-luck conditions.

According to Gettier and an honest hermeneutical evaluation, the answer is yes in both epistemological and interpretative settings.

The manner in which properly expressed RVE seeks to convey justification has the ability to resolve the current stalemate between internalists and externalists in epistemology, but more importantly for this research, it aligns well to bridge the justification gap that exists between author, text, reader, and justifiable understanding in hermeneutics. While RVE is a viable contributor to the classic discipline of epistemology, it may have greater impact in its application to subdisciplines, especially inquiry-based pursuits like hermeneutics.[22] This is possible because, as the demands upon the thinking agent increase by virtue of the nature of the particular knowledge pursued, the greater the contribution of RVE. In hermeneutics as in higher-level forms of epistemology, understanding and knowledge require more than sensory or purely rational input. The justificatory capacity of a virtuous cognitive agent exists in a direct ratio to the increasing complexity and density of the knowledge being pursued. As Jason Baehr has correctly explained, "The success or failure of an inquiry has a more personal source. This is due to the fact that inquiry has a robustly active dimension. It involves observing, imagining, reading, interpreting, reflecting, analyzing, assessing, formulating, and articulating. Success in these activities is hardly guaranteed by the possession of sharp vision, sensitive hearing, or an impeccable memory. Rather, it requires an exercise of certain intellectual character traits."[23]

Although not conclusive, the tendency to condemn poor epistemological justification with aretaic language is a clue to the character-based center for the ascribing of value or justification, and subsequently for knowledge itself. Consider that the failure of cognitive processes is regularly condemned by the vocabulary of vice and virtue (e.g., "'narrow-minded,' 'careless,' 'intellectually cowardly,' 'rash,' 'imperceptive,' 'prejudiced,' 'rigid,' or 'obtuse'").[24] The example of a jury wrongly condemning an innocent individual for murder is a good case study. If jurors failed to consider contradictory evidence because they had grown weary of the deliberation process, they would be pilloried for being *rash* or, worse in such a consequential task, *lazy*. If they assumed the guilt of the defendant prior to the full consideration of the evidence because of the race of the

---

22. Baehr, *Inquiring Mind*, loc. 2552.
23. Baehr, *Inquiring Mind*, loc. 84.
24. Zagzebski, *Virtues of the Mind*, 20.

accused, they would be guilty of *prejudice, bias, injustice,* and *narrow-mindedness* in their deliberations. Finally, if the jurors returned either a guilty or not-guilty verdict out of fear of public opinion or threats from other parties rather than on the basis of the evidence, their decision would be criticized as being the result of *cowardice.*

The correct verdict may be considered correct by its alignment with the reality of the event being adjudicated [did the defendant actually, in reality, commit the murder (i.e., its truth)], but it is not justified by the uninterpreted evidence. This illustrates well the difference between truth and justification in epistemological processes. It is the matter of justification that RVE addresses. In the case of a murder trial, it assumes that there is a reality (i.e., a truth) to be discovered, but it is justification that attempts to certify or lead to the more likely than not attainment of that truth.[25] RVE claims that the verdict's justification is more accurately sourced in the virtuous intellectual character of the agents who handle the evidence. A justified verdict is one that is the result of jurors possessing and acting in line with virtues like: open-mindedness, perseverance, courage, attentiveness, and justice. Evidence, factuality, and internal conditions of intellectual obligation are undeniably important in any right verdict, but these conditions are more likely to be attained and adjudicated properly by a jurist who approaches the task in an intellectually virtuous manner. In this way, the classical epistemological components of true beliefs are not dismissed as irrelevant by a virtue perspective but are more reliably satisfied by their stable sourcing, ideally, in a virtuous agent or, at the least, in an agent inquiring in virtuous ways. "All legitimate epistemic desiderata can be brought together in one conception—that of the excellent epistemic agent, the person of intellectual virtue."[26] Legal history is filled with unjust decisions that fail to possess justification not for a lack of evidence, but because of the lack of intellectual character of the adjudicators in assessing the evidence in their deliberative process. The judicial frame is a helpful context in understanding the justificatory power of intellectual virtues because the task of deliberation, inquiry, weighing of evidence and witnesses, imaginative mental reconstructions

25. This reliable capacity of RVE to *lead* to the accumulation of true beliefs is the defining difference between strictly analytical forms of epistemology and RVE's status as a regulative form of epistemology. A regulative epistemology is more concerned with developing a system of epistemology which fosters the attainment of knowledge; whereas analytic forms are more attuned to defining what is or is not knowledge.

26. Roberts and Wood, *Intellectual Virtues,* 42.

of scenarios, and the general complexity of many cases is specifically attuned to the type of knowledge that virtues are trained to acquire. Many of these same contextual matters of the judicial frame are mirrored in the hermeneutical frame as well.

How the Virtues Source Justification

Virtue Epistemology, in its various forms, sees a class of innate human excellencies that can be trained by ongoing habituation as a long neglected but increasingly more important answer to the current epistemological dilemmas. In appealing to Aristotle, they argue, "that our cognitive powers cannot function as they ought if they are not appropriately connected with emotions and concerns that have been trained to virtue."[27] The *Nicomachean Ethics* identifies virtues as, "being of two kinds, intellectual and moral."[28] Rather than a series of analytical rules to be obeyed or duties to which one is obligated, the work, or end, of the intellectual virtues within the individual is naturally the attainment of truth.[29] This fits within the broader teleologically attuned Aristotelian framework of living the highest life of human flourishing (*eudaimonia*): self-sufficient happiness. For Aristotle, many things are necessary to attain human flourishing, and the acquisition of a variety of types of knowledge is, not surprisingly, included. Thus, he identifies both ethical and intellectual virtues as being at the heart of the task. The virtues are simultaneously inherently good but also effective in their specific function, which for Aristotle was *eudaimonia*. "Every virtue we choose indeed for themselves (for if nothing resulted from them, we should still choose each of them), but we choose them also for the sake of happiness, judging that by means of them we shall be happy."[30] It is this dual nature of virtues that is important in how RVE conveys justification. They are both inherently good (and consequently, make the person a better qua person on the level of motivational intent), but they are also effective in attaining their desired end (in this case, the reliable accumulation of more true beliefs than false beliefs). In this way, the value of a subject's life, including their intellectual life, is directly related to the development and embodiment of virtues

27. Wood, *Epistemology*, loc. 2561.
28. Aristotle, *Nicomachean Ethics*, loc. 648.
29. Aristotle, *Nicomachean Ethics*, loc. 1978.
30. Aristotle, *Nicomachean Ethics*, loc. 447.

since they are necessary, even if they are not sufficient, for the *telos* of the *eudaimonistic* life both ethically and intellectually.

Not all proponents of RVE advocate for this Aristotelian dual nature of the intellectual virtues. Heather Battaly classifies the two major streams of RVE according to their relationship with the desired end of the epistemological task. Each classification corresponds to one of the two points to which Aristotle alludes (the inherent internal goodness of the virtues and the external attainment of the desired *telos*).[31] In dividing responsibilism into two primary categories, Battaly exposes the contemporary dilemma between externalism and internalism. On the side of internalism are those like Baehr, who describes his approach as a "purely internalist account."[32] He advocates for the priority of virtuous intellectual habits simply because they contribute to the "personal worth" of the thinking subject without reference to the attainment of the external goods of justified true beliefs since these can be so easily thwarted by conditions beyond the control of the cognitive agent (e.g., luck, external manipulations). The contrary externalist position is held by Julia Driver, who critiques the internalist view because, "It dispenses with any connection between the agent and the world."[33] The externalist view makes much of the truth-conducive nature of the virtues, but it also allows for the possibility of morally and intellectually reprehensible traits to count as virtues if they consistently deliver epistemological goods. For Driver, if selfishness, cruelty, or closed-mindedness reliably attained true beliefs then they should be counted among the intellectual virtues. While likely not empirically accurate that any of the preceding qualities could longitudinally be seen as reliable truth-discovering qualities for a thinking agent, it is even more a violation of intuition and all classical understandings of the nature of the virtues to credit bad intellectual character qualities as being virtuous simply by virtue of their ends.

Batally includes Zagzebski in the consideration of the externalist view along with Driver, but it seems likely that both Driver and Zagzebski would disagree with this overly generalized joint classification. Zagzebski is more accurately described as being of a third category, which should be labelled a "mixed account." Even though she ultimately distances herself

---

31. It is worth recognizing that even though many contemporary virtue epistemologists employ Aristotle's focus on a *telos*, few are pointing at *eudaimonia* as the target but choose various other ends: truth, knowledge, or personal intellectual worth.

32. Baehr, *Inquiring Mind*, loc. 161.

33. Driver, *Uneasy Virtue*, 80.

from the mixed approach of Zagzebski, Driver acknowledges its intuitive appeal.[34] Zagzebski offers one of the earliest and most ambitious attempts to formulate a comprehensive approach to RVE as a necessary amendment to the classical epistemological discipline in *Virtues of the Mind*. Her perspective is especially useful as a template from which to evaluate RVE as a viable system for the epistemological considerations of hermeneutics because of its thoroughness as well as its unique "mixed approach." Zagzebski stands out among virtue epistemologists as she redefines knowledge in terms of virtue but does so by holding to both the internalistic and externalistic conditions. As will be explored in greater detail in the following chapter, this mixed approach shares an affinity with the self-understanding of intellectual virtues embedded within the biblical text.

Aristotle's definition of the intellectual virtues is aligned differently than nearly all of the current iterations of Virtue Epistemology as he identifies "philosophic wisdom and understanding and practical wisdom" as being the intellectual virtues, but Zagzebski's formulation extends the consistency with which Aristotle treats the moral virtues into his less consistent treatment of the intellectual virtues.[35] Throughout his treatment of the moral virtues, Aristotle offers a mixed approach to virtue. To the internal nature, he says, "Virtuous actions must be in themselves pleasant. But they are also good and noble, and have each of these attributes in the highest degree."[36] In reference to the external, he explains that, "The virtue of a thing is relative to its proper work."[37] In other words, a virtue is a virtue because of "its success in attaining good ends or effects, many of which are external to us. This success need not be perfect, but it must be reliable."[38] It is the dualistic approach that acknowledges the inherent goodness which springs from a motivation to attain a specific end and the reliable attainment of that end which is best suited for epistemology and the subset of intellectual tasks contained in the category of inquiry.

Driver, as previously acknowledged, sees in the mixed approach of Zagzebski and Aristotle something "intuitively appealing because they

---

34. Driver, "Moral and Epistemic Virtue," 125.

35. Aristotle, *Nicomachean Ethics*, loc. 644.

36. Aristotle, *Nicomachean Ethics*, loc. 515.

37. Aristotle, *Nicomachean Ethics*, loc. 1972.

38. Battaly, *Virtue*, 8.

represent a compromise between the two theoretical extremes."[39] For her, this intuitive desire for a compromise that preserves credit by way of motivation (internalism) while eliminating the possibility of systemic failure in its delivery of true beliefs (externalism) ultimately does not succeed, and she abandons it in favor of a strictly external consequentialist view. Her critique is well taken because intuitive appeal does not guarantee the viability of a concept under a more rigorous examination, but the opposite is also true. Condemning the mixed view with the faint praise of intuitive appeal does not mean that it is not plausible, at least as it pertains to the specific expressions of epistemological inquiry (e.g., hermeneutics, jurisprudence, history). Zagzebski directly addresses how the mixed nature of an internal motivation and an external reliability is satisfied by her system.

> Basing knowledge on the motive for truth combines the advantages of reliabilism and evidentialism. Like evidentialism and unlike reliability it does not have the value problem because it identifies a good that knowledge has in addition to the good of true belief. Like reliability and unlike evidentialism it does not have the alignment problem because it explains the connection between truth and rationality/justifiability.[40]

Both elements of the internal and external nature of the intellectual virtues are necessary if RVE is to make a contribution to hermeneutics. While many forms of epistemic goods are so immediately derived from sensory faculties that internal considerations such as accessibility, duty, or motivation are essentially absent or inconsequential, hermeneutics is not of this class of knowledge. The reading of a text requires volition and desire when the concept of reading implies more than a reflexive recognition of a semantic sign (e.g., recognizing the intended meaning of a stop sign without volitional contribution, which seems more akin to recognizing a visual symbol than reading). No genuine literary text can be read by accident. Attention must be focused; the literary piece must be selected, and the complex literary techniques of words, sentences, paragraphs, and sections must be willfully engaged and connected by the intentional purposes of the reader. No textual communication can be understood without a desire to understand. To understand, one must understand that they are understanding because of the significant internal demand

39. Driver, "Moral and Epistemic Virtue," 125.
40. Zagzebski, "From Reliabilism to Virtue Epistemology," 119.

required by understanding.[41] For this type of active agent-centered epistemological pursuit, a purely external construction does not address necessary motivational, volitional, creative, and affective components for proper understanding. For this reason, the interpretation of a text demands some sense of a justifying system that engages with these internal factors.[42] A virtuous agent must also possess other-oriented, or external, virtues like justice, generosity, and open-mindedness. This acknowledges that in a text an *other* is active as a willing and communicating agent. Even more basically, it recognizes that *something* exists external to the interpreter (a stable text, intended meaning, and an active and willing author), so it demands a capacity to engage with these externally existent things in a way that does not deny their pre-interpretation independence from the reader. Just as it is impossible for a text to be interpreted without an active agent willing to read and understand, no text can come into being unless an equally active agent creates the text. This shared active nature becomes the point of connection where the virtues align as the justifying condition in understanding. Hermeneutics attuned to virtue embraces Vanhoozer's belief that "We can come to know something other than ourselves when we peer into the mirror of the text."[43] The text exists as the expression of another, the author, not simply the occasion of seeing oneself. Multiple contemporary hermeneutical formulations dismiss this sense of encountering an other, leaving a reflection of oneself as the only possible outcome of reading. If Vanhoozer is correct, then there is a demand to engage with what the other has rightly embedded into the text, namely, meaning. Without the externally focused contribution of RVE, which seeks to reliably align subjective understanding with a pre-interpretive textual meaning, the possibility of discerning this other-centered meaning will remain unattainable.

In the introductory example, the fact that Brutus attempts to justify his actions by an appeal to the biblical text indicates that he ascribes some value to the Bible as a model or contributor to the idea of healthy marital relationships (whether that is genuine or only an artificial attempt to maintain an image within a certain social context is secondary to this

41. Zagzebski, "Recovering Understanding," 246.

42. It is the further argument of this research that the stable internal motivation component of RVE is precisely the necessary connection point between the author, text, reading community, and ultimately, the reader, which admits the possibility of a viable form of hermeneutical realism.

43. Vanhoozer, *Is There a Meaning in This Text?*, 31.

discussion). RVE can help Brutus by equipping him with internal motivations, dispositions, and conceptual models that allow him to interact with what he already perceives to be the authoritative or, at least, meaningful other who is externally revealed within this text.

Theoretical Expression of Virtuous Hermeneutics

The idea that the task of interpreting and justifying the understanding of a text, in particular the biblical text, is somehow deeply related to something more basic than skills, models, or techniques is not new. Early leader amongst Continental Pietists, Johann Bengel, writes in the preface of his seminal work, *Gnomon Novi Testamenti,* concerning the task of biblical understanding, that, "Scripture teaches its own use, which consists in action. To act, we must understand it, and this understanding is open to all the *upright of heart* [emphasis added]."[44] In his formulation, the chain of understanding and signification of the meaning of the biblical text is somehow dependent upon the disposition, or uprightness, of the interpreter's heart. While the precise meaning of his concept of an "upright heart" is beyond this introductory discussion, it is, at the very least, the employing of aretaic language in reference to the ability to accurately interpret the biblical record. Pietists are often disregarded as being purely experiential mystics who abandon systematic methods of interpretation, but this seems uninformed in the case of Bengel (as well as most of the other early Pietists like Phillip Jakob Spener and August Hermann Francke), who is rightly described as the father of modern textual criticism, modern scientific exegesis, and modern eschatological study.[45] Bengel was not devaluing the importance of careful and well-developed hermeneutical skills and technique evidenced by his prolific and rigorous methods, but he was pointing to the necessity of a certain virtuous character quality within the deepest nature of the interpreter as being at the most foundational level of good interpretation.

While preceding contemporary formulations of RVE by more than two hundred years, Bengel seems to have expressed a concept somewhat related to the premise of this research: the subjectively centered disposition and habits of the internal working of the interpreter has a foundational impact on the quality and justifiability of the interpretive goods. As

44. Bengel, "Gnomon."
45. Helmbold, "J. A. Bengel," 80.

illustrated by the previously mentioned case of Brutus, his poor interpretive work was fundamentally related to intellectual and moral vices that prevented him from accurately employing any other interpretive skills and abilities that he may have otherwise possessed. His intellectual character flaws skewed his ability to attain a justifiable understanding of the text, and this justified understanding of a text is the nearest hermeneutical analog to the epistemological goal of a justified true belief.

Having introduced the epistemological discussion of RVE, it is necessary to detail how this developing philosophical discipline can map closely with the literary task of textual interpretation. This must be accomplished before any programmatic explanation can be offered to explain how RVE concepts can be pressed into the service of interpretation (which is the subject of chapter 3).

It is best to see hermeneutics as a subset of those forms of noetic endeavors that are most demanding of active thinking agents, broadly labelled as inquiry. The complicating problem of distance is what locates hermeneutics in this category. Hans-Georg Gadamer exposed the struggle to overcome this distance with the imagery of horizons. For him, the concept of a horizon expressed the "range of vision that includes everything that can be seen from a particular vantage point."[46] Both the author and the reader are inescapably located within distinct, and often, very distant horizons. This reality of discrete horizons stands in contrast to the starting point of most epistemological examples. The immediacy of most standard epistemological examples makes few, if any, demands upon the knowing subject. It is a matter of significant and appropriate interest to epistemologists to explain whether or not the proposition, "The table is brown," can be rightly accounted as knowledge. This type of proposition is a fitting starting point for an epistemological discussion of what knowledge is, but it does not, of itself, place extraordinary demands on the person who observes the table and integrates her belief about the table's color into her noetic collective. Zagzebski concedes that, "the examples often used as paradigms of knowledge are on the low end of the scale," and as a result, do not go far enough to differentiate between the simple knowing of atomized pieces of knowledge and developing a genuine understanding of a portion of reality.[47]

<hr />

46. Gadamer, *Truth and Method*, 313.
47. Zagzebski, *Virtues of the Mind*, 272.

It is substantially more complicated to unpack the proposition, "The Apostle Paul universally disallows all forms of ecclesial leadership to women in 1 Tim 2:12." There are a multitude of distance inspired complications (horizons) for any agent who seeks to interpret a text like this, and the claim to *know* this proposition requires something more complicated than a propositionally expressed justified true belief. It requires understanding. When thinking of the biblical text, the contemporary interpreter experiences distance in the form of language, semantics, grammar, culture, socio-economic matters, geography, worldview, ethnicity, and time period. Even more, none of these previous points of distance begin to approach the most fundamental distance of the encounter occasioned by the text, the encounter of one mind with the mind of another made a step more distant and less concrete than orality as a now detached piece of written communication. Walter Ong expresses this distance that emerges in the act of writing, "Writing separates the knower from the known and thus sets up conditions for 'objectivity,' in the sense of personal disengagement or distancing."[48] It is this distance assumed in the experience of textual interpretation that inspired Gadamer to claim, "Nothing is so strange, and at the same time so demanding as the written word . . . Nothing is so purely the trace of the mind as writing, but nothing is so dependent on the understanding mind either. In deciphering and interpreting it, a miracle takes place: the transformation of something alien and dead into total contemporaneity and familiarity."[49] This idea of contemporaneity and familiarity are terms more attuned to understanding than simply knowing. Without even commenting on the potential of success, to even attempt to span these distances or hope for this "miracle" of understanding demands of the reader an extraordinarily complex collection of active, willful, and imaginative actions. This is where RVE makes its greatest contribution to hermeneutics. It tunes, motivates, regulates, and integrates the sum of the reader's resources to arrive at a justified accurate understanding of the text's meaning.

RVE as an underlying theoretical model is the most promising approach to attaining justified understandings of a text in the aftermath of previously failed modern and postmodern approaches. "Cultivating and exercising the intellectual virtues are the best we can do voluntarily to

---

48. Ong, *Orality and Literacy*, loc. 1134.
49. Gadamer, *Truth and Method*, 163.

obtain understanding."[50] The theoretical framework that connects RVE to hermeneutics must address at least two important matters. The first matter requires an adapting of the epistemological goal of knowledge as a justified true belief to the corollary hermeneutical desiderata, understanding. Understanding is a special form of knowing that exists as a continuum of deepening explanatory and internally integrated expressions of knowledge. In this study, the emphasis is upon textual understanding, although understanding is attainable in many disciplines. Though related, the goals of atomized knowledge (i.e., epistemologically defined knowledge) and understanding are meaningfully different. Beyond defining the task, the manner of how justification is transferred from the virtuous agent to the hermeneutic goods must be explained.

The Proper Epistemological Goal of Hermeneutics

While the influence of epistemological thought is evident in each iteration of hermeneutical development, the correlation is not absolute. If one establishes the goal of epistemological inquiry to be knowledge, then it must be asked if the type of knowledge pursued is equivalent to the *telos* of hermeneutics. The examination of contemporary epistemology reveals that the species of knowledge most commonly pursued by traditional epistemologists is highly atomized, which is central to the explanation of why RVE has most recently re-emerged. Driver explicitly contends that, "Virtue evaluation should be central, and atomistic evaluation of beliefs as justified or unjustified is not good enough."[51] Virtue theory is an agent-centered philosophy that evaluates by means of a holistic sense of the virtuous agent rather than the purely analytical parsings of justification, which is more common in contemporary epistemology. While this radical atomization of knowledge that currently predominates is not necessarily wrong from a certain epistemological frame, and even more, it is likely inevitable as long as the foundational piece of epistemology is the individual beliefs of the cognitive agent, it is limited in its ability to produce more useful forms of knowledge and understanding. As currently constituted, there is little else that can be developed as long as the standard view of contemporary epistemology defines a belief as "an attitude one can have

---

50. Zagzebski, *Virtues of the Mind*, 272.
51. Driver, "Moral and Epistemic Virtue," 123.

toward a proposition."[52] The factive nature of propositions admits only a very limited spectrum of considerations that are not expansive enough to include all the necessary elements that a good hermeneutical account requires (nor is enough for RVE for that matter).

As the two distinct but related disciplines of RVE and hermeneutics have developed, an interesting shared conceptual priority has emerged within both, which shows promise for the thesis of this research that RVE can help stabilize the contemporary pursuit of interpreted textual meaning. Two of the earliest modern commentators on hermeneutics set the direction for the goal of hermeneutics. Schleiermacher is consistently acknowledged as the father of modern hermeneutics, and he has clearly articulated the goal of interpretation (even if subsequent hermeneuts have rejected his prescribed locus of meaning and his resulting methods of divining understanding). In the opening sentence of his *Hermeneutik und Kritik: mit besonderer Beziehung auf das neue Testament*,[53] Schleiermacher offers this definition of the discipline, "*Die Hermeneutik als Kunst des Verstehens* (Hermeneutics is the art of understanding)."[54] It is significant that Schleiermacher chooses the word, *Verstehen*, as opposed to the typical German word for knowledge as is used in the discipline of epistemology, *Erkenntnis*. As is the case with much of Schleiermacher, he is reacting against and also coordinating with both Enlightenment ideals and Immanuel Kant's thought. Schleiermacher's use of *Verstehen* contrasts with Kant's heavy usage of *Erkenntnis*, which is the word that he uses throughout his *Critique of Pure Reason*. Kant's introductory chapter explains the difference between "*reinen und empirischen Erkenntnis*."[55] Schleiermacher moves the conversation and clearly intends something different by the idea of understanding. While the full context of the contemporary epistemological developments was two centuries in the future, it is important to see that what Schleiermacher pursued in interpreting a text was more than simply a form of atomized knowledge of propositions about a text but a more accurately described sense of drawing from the text through hermeneutical methods something best labelled as understanding. Extending beyond Schleiermacher, Dilthey expanded on the

---

52. Steup, *Introduction to Contemporary Epistemology*, 7.

53. This is the first collection of Schleiermacher's lectures on Hermeneutics which was published by his student, Dr. Friedrich Lücke, in 1838, four years after Schleiermacher's death.

54. Schleiermacher, *Hermeneutik und Kritik*.

55. Kant, *Werkausgabe*, 27.

concept of interpretation rooted in the idea of *lived experience* in differentiating between understanding (*Verstehen*), which "is a process that employs all our capacities and is to be distinguished from pure intellectual understanding (*Verstand*)."[56] In another place, Dilthey distinguishes between his deeper goal in the human sciences (*Geisteswissenschaft*) of immediate understanding (*Wissen*) instead of the more objectified and conceptualized external form of knowledge (*Erkenntnis*).[57] This concept of understanding does not preclude the inclusion of propositional knowledge but expands the entire domain of hermeneutics into broader realms including affections, experiences, motivations, and necessity of integrating *hermeneia* into internally and externally located systems of belief. In both of these foundational hermeneutical expressions, understanding exists as something akin to, but ultimately beyond, traditionally defined ideas of knowledge. Since these initial formulations that established understanding as the *telos* for contemporary hermeneutics within the evolving modern world, the discipline has failed to articulate a stable foundation from which to develop lasting methodologies. Instead, hermeneutics has been plagued by continual realignments of the grounding of understanding (e.g., feelings, experiences, psychologizing, historicism, formalism, existentialism, relativism, and nihilism).

While not displacing the concept of knowledge at the center of the philosophical discipline, contemporary epistemologists are wrestling with the reality that the narrowest of constructions of cognitive desideratum (i.e., JTB) seems to omit other important products that are related but distinct from knowledge.[58] One of the most commonly engaged and contested para-epistemological goods is, likewise, understanding. Baehr is representative of many other epistemologists (Zagzebski, Kvanvig, Roberts, Wood, and Battaly) when he writes, "While virtually no one would deny that this work falls within the purview of epistemology, few would maintain that understanding as these authors conceive of it is part of the very nature or essence of knowledge."[59] All of these authors see

56. Makkreel, "Wilhelm Dilthey."

57. Dilthey, "Concluding Observations," 228.

58. Under this category of broadly epistemological concerns that exist either apart from or only tangentially connected to knowledge are matters like: justification (which Plantinga argues is separate from warrant, which he defines as the truly necessary part of knowledge), rationality, wisdom, and understanding (cf. Baehr, *Inquiring Mind,* loc. 2557).

59. Baehr, *Inquiring Mind,* loc. 2573.

understanding as part of the broader context of epistemology, related and attuned to many of the same concerns as epistemology proper, but still set apart from knowledge. Roberts and Wood's description of understanding as "a certain sophisticated kind of acquaintance" illustrates the para-epistemological status of understanding as well as setting the stage for how it can be a relevant concept for hermeneutics.[60]

The overlap between hermeneutics and RVE in the area of understanding is substantial and important in the potential contributions that can be made in determining a justified understanding of a text. Among the commonalities in construction are issues relating to its explanatory function, its integrative nature, and its aspect. While non-virtue epistemologists are producing some literature concerning understanding,[61] the unique contribution of RVE to the broadly epistemological category of understanding is immediately recognizable, as almost all monograph-length treatments of RVE contain a significant discussion of understanding. The organic connection between the expected deliveries of the virtues within inquiry-related understanding is evident by its consistent inclusion in the discussion.

Understanding as an Explanatory Concept

Understanding is the primary goal of hermeneutics and a prime product of virtuous inquiry. Epistemology (including Virtue Epistemology) and hermeneutics are not the only disciplines to seek to define the concept of understanding. In the realm of the philosophy of science, Peter Lipton has addressed it in his theory of *Inference to the Best Explanation*. He draws a clear line between knowledge and understanding. For him a causal model of explanation that acknowledges but does not concede fully to David Hume's critique of induction, "provides a clear distinction between understanding why a phenomenon occurs and merely knowing what caused it . . . Understanding is not some sort of super-knowledge, but simply more knowledge: knowledge of causes."[62] For a variety of rea-

---

60. Roberts and Wood, *Intellectual Virtues*, 33.

61. Zagzebski points out, "Few contemporary epistemologists mention understanding except in passing, and even when it is mentioned, it is usually identified with that minimal grasp of the sense of a proposition necessary for believing it. Understanding in this sense is clearly not the major problem in attaining knowledge and so it gets little attention." *Virtues of the Mind*, 45.

62. Lipton, *Inference to the Best Explanation*, 30.

sons, most epistemologists would not accept the loose use of the word *knowledge* that Lipton employs when speaking of understanding as "more knowledge," but his attention to the idea of explanation of causal relationships underlying epistemized propositions is a helpful and recurring theme in discussions of understanding in all disciplines. Stephen Grimm clarifies this sense of understanding even further, "It seems to be a hallmark of having understanding that we can typically articulate (or explain) what it is in virtue of which we take ourselves to understand."[63] This ability to connect, explain, and articulate an understanding has a decidedly internal focus. If one adopts Zagzebski's mixed model of RVE, understanding is the theoretical goal of interpretation that relies most heavily on the internal contribution of the intellectual virtues. "Understanding has internalist conditions for success, whereas knowledge does not . . . Understanding, in contrast, not only has internally accessible criteria, but it is a state that is constituted by a type of conscious transparency. It may be possible to know without knowing that one knows, but it is impossible to understand without understanding that one understands."[64] If this concept of understanding is pressed into the hermeneutical realm, its implications become clearer. In our case of Brutus, he may know that Paul is giving instruction concerning marital relationships within a Christian context; he may even know some general definitions of terms, like head, submit, or love. This knowing may meet valid conditions of justified true belief without his conscious awareness that this is the case (this is more likely if one is working from an externalistic model rather than a deontological or accessibilism approach). To understand the passage, as Zagzebski explains it, requires that Brutus would need to be able to explain the inner-connections of his interpretation of the text with a fuller range of noetic contributions, including: volitional, affective, and cognitive concerns. The simple ability to cogently explain one's interpretation in light of these broad noetic concerns is necessary for the attainment and expression of understanding, and his intellectual laziness, pride, and selfishness all mitigate against his ability to articulate anything resembling understanding.

While there are several necessary components in coming to articulate what understanding entails, none seems as central as the concept of explanation. "The ability to give an explanation of what one believes

63. Grimm, "Is Understanding a Species of Knowledge," 517.
64. Zagzebski, "Recovering Understanding," 246.

indicates understanding, and the better the explanation, the deeper the understanding."[65] When speaking about the complex matters of inquiry present in a field such as hermeneutics, this ability to explain (including exegetically, theologically, and applicationally) the meaning of the text by means of many discipline-relevant capacities (e.g., reason, affective and empirical matters, creativity, and spiritually-attuned sensibilities, etc.) is far more valuable than simply "knowing" a meaning in a detached and atomized manner. Sometimes the causal and explanatory matters that are expressed in understanding may take the form of further propositions, but understanding "differs from propositional knowledge, not in being necessarily non-propositional, but in not being necessarily propositional."[66] This admits important human capacities (e.g., spiritual, affective, and possibly something similar to Calvin's *sensus divinitatis*) that were often excluded from previous epistemological discussions. James K. A. Smith speaks of some of these other faculties to attaining knowledge, "We could say that narrative is a way of understanding the world that draws upon an affective or emotive faculty (rather than a judgment about the world effected by the intellect)."[67] Other disciplines are exploring these very same issues, like Carl Plantinga's view concerning meaning in film which speaks of meaning as related to affectivity. "Affective experience and meaning are neither parallel nor separable, but firmly intertwined."[68] Having explanatory power standing under propositional knowledge highlights the unique capacity of RVE in reference to understanding.

In all models of RVE, the unified and stable center of the virtuous cognitive agent contributes to these underlying explanatory contributions. The agent who is motivated and directed in their inquiry by the steady and habitually ingrained excellencies of intellectual character will pursue the goods of understanding that stand beyond and beneath the mere acquisition of a discrete proposition. While a variety of interpretive intellectual virtues will be addressed in chapter 3, two brief introductions here can illustrate the point. Consider how the intellectual virtues of love and justice could facilitate the attainment of deeper levels of textual understanding.

---

65. Roberts and Wood, *Intellectual Virtues*, 49.

66. Roberts and Wood, *Intellectual Virtues*, 47.

67. Smith, *Thinking in Tongues*, 64.

68. Plantinga, *Moving Viewers*, 3.

The love of truth as a virtuous characteristic motivates inquiry beyond a purely utilitarian attainment of discrete forms of knowledge since in a stable and continual way the agent is motivated to attain fuller understanding because truth is experienced as being inherently valuable and desirable. If the motivation for knowledge and understanding is conditioned upon a strictly utilitarian, pragmatic, or externally coerced foundation, the minimum of knowledge is sufficient to satisfy these conditions, but the one who is fundamentally compelled by a deep and abiding love of truth finds satisfaction, and likely, joy, in the deepening of understanding that underlies knowledge in searching for integrative connections, explanatory causes, and creative extensions of the meaning. "The love of knowledge will be an enormous aid in driving excellence of understanding. Understanding often emerges only with concerted intellectual activities like exploring, testing, dialectical interchange, probing, comparing, writing, and reflecting. These practices require virtues for their best prosecution."[69]

The other-oriented virtue of justice can also illustrate the understanding-conducive nature of intellectual virtues. When a hermeneut is compelled to do justice with textual knowledge, the mere statement of a potential meaning is hardly sufficient. Justice seeks to give the fullest measure due to another which is more than the barest of propositional knowledge. To do justice to an author, a text, or a receiving community motivates an interpreter to seek an understanding that is as rich and textured as the purposes of the author and underlying contributors of the author's context and community. It seeks to not only understand meaning in its original context, but it seeks to be able to relevantly express meaning in a way that possesses sufficient explanatory support to convey that understanding to others.

Applied in the context of biblical hermeneutics one can see the explanatory nature of understanding a text in the example of the Parable of the Lost Son from Luke 15:11–32. Without pretending away the many interpretive issues that have attended the interpretation of Jesus's parables through the centuries, it seems a reasonable and secure statement to acknowledge that, as recorded in the Gospel of Luke, this parable in the simplest of readings can be said to mean, "The forgiveness of grievous injustice (sin) and the resultant restoration of relationship is a matter of great celebration." This can be seen as a propositional attempt to capture

69. Roberts and Wood, *Intellectual Virtues*, 50.

the meaning of this parable, but understanding of this parable would require, or admit, far more than this proposition. The virtuous mind that seeks understanding is drawn beyond simple statements. It is compelled by a love for truth, a drive to integrate, a need to explain, a passion to analogize into diverse contexts, and a hope to experience a "knowledge of" rather than purely a "knowledge about."[70] The understanding of this parable is not contrary to the previously stated proposition but deepened when one understands how radically Jesus redefined the concept of a merciful father (and by metaphor, the nature of God) in his context.

As Kenneth Bailey explains, "Granted, anyone can read the Bible and be blessed by that reading, just as anyone can listen to a Bach cantata and be moved. But at the same time, the trained ear will hear more and be moved on a deeper level by the same music."[71] Bailey continues by saying that the universal appeal and accessibility of parables has been used as an excuse to avoid the "hard work of attempting to discover what Jesus was saying to his audience."[72] This condemnation of the vicious nature of this form of interpretive laziness demonstrates the specific appeal of understanding over simple knowledge which depends on virtues like intellectual perseverance among others. The basic outline of meaning may be discovered in simplistic reading but understanding demands effort and investigation. Specifically, he points to the understanding that can be gained by exploring the context of sociological familial realities of Middle Eastern society. For a son to ask for his inheritance while his father is still living is equivalent to saying, "Dad, why don't you drop dead.' The father is expected to get angry, slap the boy across the face and drive him out of the house."[73] Beyond this sociological context, understanding can be deepened within a reader who brings to the text the powerful empirical and affective experience of having been forgiven a great wrong. Those who may critique these examples as being simply the inclusion of other traditional components of hermeneutics or exegesis without being particularly novel are partially correct. Understanding is not new nor are the skills or domains of potential contributing sources, but the best of traditional hermeneutics are those forms that have demonstrated the

70. In this distinction between "knowledge of" and "knowledge about" as a component of understanding, the definition of Roberts and Wood, which sees understanding as a sophisticated kind of acquaintance, can be clearly perceived.

71. Bailey, *Jesus Through Middle Eastern Eyes*, 280.

72. Bailey, *Jesus Through Middle Eastern Eyes*, 281.

73. Bailey, *Jesus Through Middle Eastern Eyes*, 281.

virtuous demand of deeper explanatory components even if they did not name the underlying virtuous motivation that compelled it. Naming and emphasizing this underlying virtue motivation and its capacity to reliably attain accurate understanding by pressing the agent to go further, support more, and explain more deeply is what stands out in this construction of Virtue Hermeneutics (VH).

The Integrative Nature of Understanding

It is a fundamental flaw of most hermeneutical paradigms to elevate a singular locale as being where understanding is to be gained at the exclusion of all other possibilities and then to devise methodologies that are attuned to maximize the mining of this particular locale. Examples of this are voluminous. John Toland (1670–722), an English Deist, saw reason as the only source of understanding. "We hold that reason is the only foundation of all certitude; and that nothing revealed, whether as to its manner or existence, is more exempted for its disquisitions, than the ordinary phenomena of nature."[74] In contrast, German confessionalist theologian Ernst Wilhelm Hengstenberg counters the pervading German rationalism in interpretation by appealing to the place of religious experience, "In order to understand the Old Testament, philology does not suffice: it requires a disposition, to which the glory of Christ is opened." He goes even further, "human reason is blind to divine matters."[75] In the early twentieth century, Karl Barth located understanding of a text not in reason, history, anthropologically-centered feeling, or experience, but in the divine inbreaking of revelation. After condemning historical criticism as being "no commentary at all, but merely the first step towards a commentary,"[76] he says that understanding requires that the "commentator must be possessed of a wider intelligence than that which moves within the boundaries of his own natural appreciation."[77] If Barth is correct, then interpretation cannot be attained by anything within the capacity of the interpreter, so he looks to revelatory "flashes of insight" as the only sufficient focus. Others may argue as intently for an external and naturalistic locating of interpreting authority without an appeal to divine

---

74. Toland, *Christianity Not Mysterious,* 6.

75. Reventlow, *From the Enlightenment to the Twentieth Century,* 288.

76. Barth, *Epistle to the Romans,* 6.

77. Barth, *Epistle to the Romans,* 8.

activity. Stanley Fish argues for the external influence of an interpreter's reading community as the source of understanding, or more accurately, it serves as the limiting influence on the creation of meaning occasioned by the text. "It is interpretive communities, rather than either the text or reader, that produces meanings."[78] This brief survey illustrative of the reality that each hermeneutical system that pursues understanding has done so by elevating one or another of the internal (e.g., reason, affections, or volition) or external (e.g., revelation or communal) frames to the exclusive source of textual understanding. This exclusivistic tendency can be balanced by an appeal to an RVE-inspired form of understanding and must be in order to integrate a fuller sense of textual understanding in the postmodern context.

The agent-centered focus of RVE allows, and more accurately, requires, a larger set of contributors to be admitted into the interpretive dialogue, both internally and externally. This openness stands in stark contrast to hermeneutic approaches that totalize only one locale from which to mine interpretive goods. An examination of any list of intellectual virtues contains virtues that are both *self* and *other* oriented. One cannot develop the full concept of a virtuous approach to hermeneutics by artificially limiting the locales of contributors to the process. This is implicit in the concept of RVE. It is not possible to have the requisite *other* oriented interpretive virtues if there is not, first, a place for others in the realm of hermeneutics. The others-oriented virtues of justice or open-mindedness require an acknowledgement of something existing apart from the agent with which the virtuous agent engages in an encounter. At the very least, these virtues must be integrated into the interpretive task because of the presence of an external text, the other who authored the text, and the communal environment of the author. In a complementary manner, the concepts of perseverance and love of truth are self-oriented virtues. This underlying ability of the virtues to address the full range of internal-to-the-agent as well as external-to-the-agent contributors to the hermeneutical process allows it to be liberated from the totalizing effects that plague most other systems, while at the same time, being open to using the resources afforded by these previous systems. Rather than demanding the strictures of rationalism alone (e.g., deism), the affective nature in isolation (e.g., theological liberalism), or the control of one's own reading community (e.g., Reader-Response), understanding in an

78. Fish, *Is There a Text in This Class?*, 14.

RVE approach allows, and even invites, the full capacity of the inquiring agent and all the encountered contributors into the process governed by something more than analytical rules: the wise and experienced shared context of the intellectual virtues.

While this holistic and integrative strength of RVE can be condemned by some as too reliant on metaphysical or religious presuppositions concerning the nature of human existence, it seems illegitimate to deny the existence of more than one element to human cognitive capacities. Some, like the Enlightenment-era rationalist, may say that emotions are too erratic and unreliable to be acceptable cognitive contributors, but it is another thing to say that humanity is emotion-free in intellectual processes. Plantinga properly argues that it is plausible to believe that the entire epistemic system of human beings, including both "cognitive and affective systems," when properly functioning, serves the end of gaining, "a certain sort of knowledge, or of morality, or loyalty, or love, or a grasp of beauty, or something else."[79] It is far better to acknowledge and incorporate the properly-attuned virtuous capacities of the affective nature, than to deny their existence or marginalize them as cognitive dysfunctions. The same can be said for volitional, practical, spiritual, and relational capacities. RVE unites, without trepidation, the fullest and widest range of the human epistemic contributors because the deeply-habituated virtues serve as the governing influence that balances and tunes all of the contributors toward the *telos* of deeper understanding. Theistic frameworks integrate the contributors as being part of the "proper function and design" plan, to use Plantinga's phrase, but as he points out, even non-theists can adopt this framework without necessarily positing a divine creator.[80]

Understanding is fully integrative in another sense as well. Rather than attempting the impossible task of a bias-less or objective approach to a text, which existed as the aspiration of modern hermeneutical approaches, a VH need not pretend to have a detached universal view to engage in textual interpretation. To understand a text is to ideally bring the whole of the virtuous self to the whole of the hermeneutical context. This does not imply that a virtuous interpreter comes to the task void of pre-understandings or presuppositions. A truly virtuous approach is one attuned to admitting the exact opposite in humbly acknowledging

79. Plantinga, *Warrant and Proper Function*, 203.
80. Plantinga, *Knowledge and Christian Belief*, 26.

the pre-existing noetic commitments of the interpreter with a genuine and persistent ability to reevaluate and update this structure as deeper understanding is attained.

As previously referenced, Zagzebski points out that understanding has an unavoidable internal component, so that, unlike knowledge which can be held without being internally accessible as to how one knows, understanding must integrate into a broader internal whole within the agent so that they inescapably understand that they understand.[81] This admits that readers understand a text as they connect what they are reading to other existing propositions, feelings, experiences, and intuitions already held within the interpreters, but a virtuous humility moves along the longitudinal axis moving toward greater refinement and openness to having these previous understandings adjusted by new understandings. It is impossible to understand a text without a whole collection of other components of an understanding system. Osborne acknowledges this continual shaping progress in the title and development of his text, *The Hermeneutical Spiral,* but he establishes this escape from an endless hermeneutical circle by means of frameworks and skills rather than the more foundational locus of the interpreter's intellectual character. While his work is excellent in demonstrating how "grammatical-syntactical exegesis and historical-cultural background" can be employed to influence not only the specific understanding of a particular text but also the overall understanding system it engages, it fails to address the much more fundamental virtuous dispositions that are required for these contributors to speak effectively into the process.[82]

Consider how two radically different understanding systems approach a text. One interpreter has been raised to believe and trained to interpret reality as being open to the inbreaking of transcendent power into the natural world, a world that admits miracles (supernaturalism). The other interpreter has accepted and has had reinforced the understanding that all that is is the material universe with nothing or no one who transcends it (i.e., naturalism). When each interpreter encounters the textual relating of the angelic declaration of Matt 28:6, "He is not here, he is risen," they will necessarily have to interpret from a framework that sees this statement as either true or not true. This frame of understanding will shape the potential interpretive products of both readers.

---

81. Zagzebski, "Recovering Understanding," 246.

82. Osborne, *Hermeneutical Spiral,* 324–25.

They will necessarily attempt to fit the idea of Jesus's resurrection within their preexisting system of understanding and, consequently, return irreconcilable interpretations of the passage. The one sees a miracle; the other sees the introduction of either an intentional lie or the expression of a religious myth.

The problem of understanding this text resides at a very different level than grammar or cultural context. Since, as Zagzebski has pointed out, understanding must be internally consistent with one's system of understanding, these interpreters are limited in their ability to understand this text in a compatible manner. If Osborne's emphasis is all that exists, then little can change to reconcile these interpretations, and all that can be hoped for are two disparate readings of the same text. The significant matters of grammatical-syntactical or historical-cultural background are incapable of bridging the understandings of the text. As necessary as the skills of an interpreter may be, they are insufficient to resolve between these competing potential interpretations. Epistemologically one is true and one is false, with little by way of hermeneutical resources to adjudicate between them. A virtuous view of understanding opens a potential third way. If one believes in any form of existential realism, the event recorded in the text, the resurrection, cannot be physically true and not true at the same time. This is where a further component must be connected to understanding. Kvanvig, like Zagzebski, sees understanding as being related, "with the way in which an individual combines pieces of information into a unified body . . . The grasping of relations between items of information is central to the nature of understanding."[83] Yet Kvanvig adds a specific point of emphasis beyond that of Zagzebski, the ultimate facticity of the matters that are to be understood. While he argues that knowledge and understanding both have a necessary facticity, they diverge after this connection. Knowledge then pursues "nonaccidental connections between mind and world," but understanding seeks to grasp the "relations between items of information."[84]

When utilizing a virtuous model of inquiry, evaluators have more recourse without having to abandon Kvanvig's facticity condition. Both interpreters may be able to offer significant points of understanding, but ultimately one will fail and cease to have explanatory power because of the absence of a connection to a *true* understanding of the meaning of

83. Kvanvig, *Value of Knowledge*, loc. 2882.

84. Kvanvig, *Value of Knowledge*, loc. 2888.

the text. In this way, an interpreter may have some useful understanding of historical, cultural, linguistic, or rational elements of the text that need not be wholly dismissed (as one would need to do in a strictly epistemological discussion), but there is a fundamental flaw in the deeper understanding and signification of the text on their part.

Several elements of RVE are helpful in evaluating the depth of understanding between the competing views. First, a virtuous approach can assist in interpretive disputes by, "first of all doing justice to each competing claim on its own terms, and in particular seeing how each account might succeed in offering a way of understanding the other."[85] Intellectual virtues such as patience, open-mindedness, generosity, and justice all afford opportunity to gain from the understanding of others without abandoning the goal and reasonable hope of ultimate facticity. Second, a virtuous approach admits more contributions to the adjudicating process beyond the limited nature of other approaches, giving a greater likelihood to reconciling disparate views including reason, affective, intuitional, and spiritual contributors. Third, the truth-conducive nature of the virtues will in the long term tend to the accumulation of more accurate and deeper forms of understanding, so the more intellectually virtuous the interpreters, the more likely they will attain a deeper and more accurate understanding over time as their pre-understandings undergo continual revision from the broadest epistemological and hermeneutical resources.

The Aspect of Understanding

A primary difference between understanding and knowledge can be usefully illustrated by analogy to a common grammatical concept. In grammatical terms, a verb's aspect speaks to the manner in which a verb interacts with time. A verb that possesses a punctiliar aspect speaks of the action of the verb being located at a specific point in time (e.g., I run). The emphasis is on the action in an unextended relationship to time. In contrast, verbs can also possess a continuous aspect (e.g., I am running). In this continuous sense, the action is seen to be extending through a period of time. The difference between these states is mirrored in the difference between knowledge and understanding.

Knowledge assumes a more punctiliar sense. As epistemologists analyze the nature of a proposition, there comes a moment when the

85. Briggs, *Virtuous Reader*, 97.

proposition is either credited as knowledge, dismissed as not being knowledge, or undetermined as to its epistemic status. When viewing these three options at a specific point in time, the final two possibilities can be reduced to the status of not being knowledge. As a result, at any specific moment, there are only two possibilities for the epistemic status of a discrete proposition: knowledge or not-knowledge. Some may counter that degrees are admitted in systems like Plantinga's form of reliabilism, but this is a confusion between knowledge and its component elements, particularly justification/warrant. While certain forms of justification/ warrant may accrue in degrees as Plantinga implies by his definition of warrant as being, "that property *enough of which* [emphasis added] is what distinguishes knowledge from mere true belief,"[86] this does not change the position that once a true belief attains *enough* warrant, knowledge is achieved in his system. Something can be more or less warranted by virtue of the amount and quality of warranting factors, but once it is sufficiently warranted, it is simply and irreducibly knowledge. Knowledge is a mutually exclusive either/or binary. It is not possible to know a proposition and come to know it more. It is either known or not known. Consider the proposition (P), "I feel pain." This belief is an incorrigible belief that comes to be a justified true belief for the one who possesses it at a particular point. "Knowledge does not come in degrees."[87] This is the unavoidable nature of epistemology so long as atomized propositions are the subject of analysis.

In contrast, the idea of understanding presents itself as more like an extended action as is seen in verbs with a continuous aspect. Understanding does not have a final moment in time that concretizes its status. It has the more linear capacity of being accrued in increasing and ongoing measures. This characteristic lends itself to terminology like "*deeper* understanding" or "*more insightful* understanding." It is possible to understand something but also come to understand it deeper or more fully. Understanding admits to degrees. It is one thing to know (P), but the move to understanding (P) may be related to awareness or acquaintance with the cause of the pain, the awareness of previous experiences of this type of pain, potential remedies to the experience of pain, the intensity in degree of painfulness, or the type of pain (e.g., throbbing, sharp, dull, chronic).

86. Plantinga, *Knowledge and Christian Belief,* 25.
87. Roberts and Wood, *Intellectual Virtues,* 43.

When approaching a complex textual record that is embedded with cultural presuppositions, linguistic distance, and thematic nuances, combined with the unavoidable reality that readers bring with them their own set of biases and expectations, we are confronted with the possibility that knowledge and understanding are related but different. Chief among those differences is the nature of understanding extending beyond a specific point. When approaching the complex nature of textual interpretation, this element of understanding allows for the continual accrual of ever deepening or richly textured understandings of a particular text. Two understandings of a text may be justifiable and accurate, but one may possess deeper connection to explanatory and supporting material and a more fully integrated sense, thus rendering it a better understanding of the text.

Responsibilist Virtue Epistemology as a
Means of Justifying Interpretation

If, in the process of interpreting a text, the goal of understanding, which by Kvanvig's definition must entail a truth condition, is already established in the previous section, then the final necessary component to complete the parallelization of epistemology's pursuit of justified true belief is some form of interpretive justification. With the exception of recent attempts to supplant the term *justified* with the concept of *warrant* within some reliabilistic frameworks, the pursuit of a form of justifying factor(s) in order to epistemize true belief has long been a consistent task of epistemology, and this is mirrored in attempts to certify or justify interpretations of particular texts in the discipline of hermeneutics. The usefulness of the term in an interpretive context is made more complicated by virtue of the diversity of its usage within epistemology. What does it mean to justify an interpretation? What is added to an understanding of a text if the understanding attains some form of justification? Does a justified understanding of a text possess greater value than one that lacks it? Is there any way to evaluate the relative justification of diverse understandings?

The necessity of some form of justification upon which an understanding of a text stands is made clear by a simple illustration. Consider the Apostle Paul's straightforward message in Rom 12:21, "Do not be overcome by evil, but overcome evil with good." The relative simplicity of the sentence does not necessarily equate to a simplicity of genuine understanding. Only the most naïve of interpreters sees no complexity in seeking an understanding of this text. One could easily generate a long list of important matters in the text. What is evil? Whose definition of good is privileged when readers from communities with disparate views of good encounter the text? Is this a command that can be reasonably attained by a volitional agent or simply a statement of an aspirational desire? What does overcoming evil look like in daily life? All of these questions and many more can, or in some cases must, be addressed by a diverse collection of resources, both internal and external to the interpreter and the text if an explanatory and integrative understanding is to be found. Once the understanding is expressed, other hermeneuts can then debate the merits of each potential interpretation that is proffered by tools of evaluation that each deems most salient. Having conceded this multi-layered complexity, what seems incontrovertible is that an understanding of Rom 12:21 that locates its meaning as pertaining to the mating habits of northern white rhinoceros in sub-Saharan east Africa is absurd and not justified. At the very minimum, the intuitive sense that classifies this peculiar interpretation as not justified admits that there must be some qualification upon which justification can be evaluated.

Fish, who sets as his foil the "objectivist" who believes in a form of "determinant meaning" present within a text,[88] almost counterintuitively, in light of his attack upon a determinate textual meaning, acknowledges that some interpretations are rightly ruled out.[89] While the emphasis of this research strongly rejects the approach of Fish's hermeneutical theory, it is not helpful to unfairly caricature his true position. Even within his Reader-Response framework, he would not advocate that Rom 12:21 is about rhinoceros simply because any random reader or reading community says it is. He would read the previous paragraph concerning the rhinocerian interpretation of Paul and agree to the unjustifiable nature of its understanding. But he anticipates the potential inconsistency in his reasoning by redirecting the discussion to, "the real question" which is, "what gives us the right."[90] For him, the standard by which this interpretation is unjustified is not static or unchangeable, but more a description of the current status of allowable interpretive frameworks present amongst the various reading communities. He hedges on the possibility

88. Fish, *Is There a Text in This Class?*, 338.
89. Fish, *Is There a Text in This Class?*, 342.
90. Fish, *Is There a Text in This Class?*, 342.

that someday a framework may gain communal acceptance and credibility that may serve to justify something akin to the rhino understanding. In this way, he is able to presently dismiss absurd interpretations without limiting the radical polyvalence of the text for which he advocates.

Fish's discussion is especially helpful in admitting the possibility of an unjustified understanding of a text since he is one of the leading advocates of the concept of the indeterminacy of textual meaning.[91] This admission is important since it implies the ability to justify an interpretation, but it is his question about what gives us the *right* to make that declaration that is the most important contribution.[92] Fish cannot use the text to justify interpretations because the "text independent of interpretation drops out and is replaced by the texts that emerge as the consequence of our interpretive activities."[93] If the pre-interpretive text does not exist as a meaningful entity, then it cannot be the source of interpretive justification. This is similar in function to the contemporizing emphasis of the school of the New Hermeneutic which pursued "present application rather than simply antiquarian biblical research."[94] While the New Hermeneutic does not entirely dismiss the text as a meaning-bearing entity (which Fish seems to advocate), it sees hermeneutical meaning as a synthesis of the distinct horizons of the text and the reader within the dynamic moment of a "language event (*sprachereignis*)," which functions to create a meaningful *new* text. One of the founders of the New Hermeneutic, Gerhard Ebeling, demonstrates why, in this system, like Fish's, the text cannot be the source of justification when he limits its role to that of being only, "a hermeneutical aid in the understanding of

91. Many examples of evaluating whether an interpretation should be considered justified or unjustified could have been drawn from the full array of modern frameworks of hermeneutics without any contribution to this discussion because they all assume a particular framework from which to attain the true understanding of the text, which immediately establishes a means of justifying the interpretation. In contrast, the postmodern frame does not subscribe to the idea of a stable pre-interpretive meaning of a text. The fact that Fish would admit that even in a framework that does not allow for a stable textual meaning of a text it can rightly be deemed unjustified greatly supports that idea that the concept of justification is inseparable from a discussion of interpretive practices.

92. It is ironic and significant for this research that Fish employs the term "right" instead of ability or capacity. By using this word, he moves the discussion beyond skills and techniques into the realm of obligation and ethics, precisely that realm within which virtue epistemology is most suited to function.

93. Fish, *Is There a Text in This Class?*, 113.

94. Thiselton, "New Hermeneutic", 78.

present experience."[95] The denigration of the text to being an "aid" as well as the focus on "present experience" signal a clear shift away from the text as justifier. Within both of these frameworks, which serve as fitting exemplars for approaches that have the broadest and least encumbered interpretive lenses for justifying readings, the text serves no definite role in the process of justification. The thesis of this research agrees with the necessity to be able to rule out unjustifiable understandings of a text as well as the demand that justification of the understanding cannot be attained by the text itself or by the elements that constitute the expression of the textual understanding without falling prey to a paralyzing form of circularity. The intellectually virtuous character of the interpretive agent allows an escape from this circularity without abandoning the idea that something more than an untethered textual meaning is still possible to be discovered within the task of interpretation.

By putting the interpretive discussion within the framework of RVE, the move to justify the interpretative products of textual understanding are located outside of the rules and methods of exegesis, or even the atomized details of the text. This move outside of these parameters is sensitive to the previously addressed concerns of some twentieth-century systems like Reader-Response or New Hermeneutic, but in sharp contrast, it is not dismissive of a stable, discoverable, and increasingly more understandable textual meaning. An expression of the understanding of the text is the explanatory and integrated meaning of the text, which depends on the fullest array of hermeneutical resources, both exegetical and theological, but the justifying component comes from the deeply ingrained and habituated intellectual excellencies of the interpretive agent. Justification flows from the agent to the deepest and most robust understanding of the text in the same way that justification flows from the agent to the beliefs in virtue epistemology.

Justification remains a stubbornly important element of all interpretive endeavors, including within this proposed model, but it becomes a form of justification shaped by virtue theory. The distinction between virtue based and traditionally defined forms of justification is critical because, as Zagzebski explains, the ascendency of traditional justificatory concepts since Descartes fits a historical pattern which emphasizes justification as a manner to attain certainty in the face of heightened periods

95. Ebeling, *Word and Faith*, 33.

of skepticism.[96] Since the Enlightenment, hermeneutics has wrestled with various forms of skepticism by adjusting the manner of attaining interpretive certainty by differing loci of justification. Most conservative, liberal, and radical interpreters would generally agree that certainty is a chimera in both epistemology and, even more so, in hermeneutics. If, as here presented, the goal of understanding, which includes increasingly more cogent, integrated, and explanatory expression of the textual meaning and application, is accepted, then the concept of reaching certainty is already disallowed by the definition itself.

Unlike propositional statements of knowledge, which are either knowledge or are not knowledge, understanding admits to degrees. This continuum of understanding demonstrates that the binaries of knowledge or not knowledge (i.e., certain or not certain) cannot be possible in the interpretive context, so a concept of justification that seeks some form of certainty is unnecessary, counterproductive, and ultimately impossible. This abandonment of the possibility of certainty is the result of more than definitional matters. The distances of language, culture, time, socioeconomic, and other-mind concerns only serve to further the impossibility of attaining any form of certainty in interpretation, but the inability to attain certainty need not descend into pervasive skepticism at the possibility of pre-interpretive meaning embedded and proximally discoverable within the text. There is a vast difference between acknowledging the inability to assure certainty by some form of justification and disallowing any form of accurate and justified understanding altogether.

Having listened carefully to the past century of skepticism directed at stable textual meaning and corresponding interpretation, Zagzebski's determination concerning the similar phenomenon in epistemology seems relevant: "Many now agree that epistemology is stultified if the issue of skepticism is allowed to dominate epistemological inquiry. It is perfectly legitimate to pursue epistemological issues that leave the skeptical challenge to one side."[97] Applying this to literary communication, skeptics seem to have inflated challenges and played with the complexities of communication in order to serve their broader worldview agenda. This tendency is illustrated by the geometrical game of supposing that an object at a set distance begins to move toward a specific location. In this case, the image of my finger approaching the letter "a" on my keyboard. At some

---

96. Zagzebski, "Recovering Understanding," 236.
97. Zagzebski, "Recovering Understanding," 236.

point, my finger will be half the distance from the starting point to the destination. Continuing with this logic, the distance left to be travelled can always be halved. Since numbers can be infinitely divided in half, it is theoretically possible to state that my finger will never arrive at the letter "a" (which seems a plausible excuse for why this dissertation is taking so long to complete). Though a clever mind game, it bears no correspondence to the commonsense reality of human experience.[98] My finger will eventually reach its destination. The extraordinary ambiguity attributed to verbal communication by skeptics has many similarities to this kind of mind game. On paper it is possible to foster extreme skepticism, but human experience speaks clearly: communication happens all the time, and even when burdened by a myriad of complicating circumstances, it finds a way. It is difficult to conclusively argue against D. A. Carson's declaration that, "Practical experience with the way people actually communicate confirms that accurate communication is possible."[99] Since communication can be seen to be generally efficacious amongst humanity, including in textual form, and that the idea of certainty is a relic of a bygone era, justification must mean something different in hermeneutics.

In a virtuous model, "Virtues are those habits and dispositions that lead us to have justified beliefs."[100] Justification is seen "in terms of beliefs produced or sustained by an intellectual virtue instead of attempting to understand that concept in terms of the concept of adequate evidence for belief."[101] By shifting this emphasis within justification, the intellectual virtues serve to accrue value and credit for the interpreter (i.e., justification), and on account of the general reliability condition of true virtues as expressed by both Lorraine Code and Zagzebski, they are tuned to generate more accurate and deeper understandings of the text over a longitudinal course (i.e., warrant).

Conclusion

Since Brutus's bad interpretive habits served as the starting point for this chapter, it seems fitting that it should conclude with him as well. His poor

98. This argument is derivative of Zeno's dialectic with the Pythagoreans in his paradox expressed in the story of *The Tortoise and Achilles*.

99. Carson, *Gagging of God*, 102.

100. Axtell, "Introduction," xiii.

101. Kvanvig, *Value of Knowledge*, 78.

understanding of Eph 5 and the unjustifiable status of this understanding resulting from an underlying deficiency in Brutus's intellectual character raises the question, can this condition be remedied? From the present vantage point, the answer is likely no. Previous models of hermeneutics that have been built upon their era's contemporaneous epistemological assumptions leave little hope of truly challenging his interpretation in any definitive manner. The days of interpretive hubris that characterized Modernity have descended into the equally unsatisfying Postmodern malaise of solipsistic or communal approaches of Reader-Response or the nihilistic tendencies of deconstruction. Reading as a transformative experience that wrestles with deeper understanding must issue from a new locus if it hopes to mean something more than, "This is what the Scripture means to me" kinds of interpretations void of understanding and justification. If the fault lies at the dispositional and motivational level, it is difficult to hope that the presentation of more data, tools, resources, and models will prod Brutus to any form of effectual change. While other approaches have much to offer, they are insufficient in themselves to justify an understanding, or more importantly, motivate a deeper and more accurate assessment of the text when biases, pre-understandings, or vicious intellectual habits are deeply embedded. Ultimately, all the failings of other systems can be reduced to the motivational or functional level of the agent's intellectual character. The virtues address motive and are specifically attuned to attain the desired end of true belief, or in the specific case of hermeneutics, understanding. RVE and a corresponding hermeneutical program that embraces the goal of interpretation as a justified understanding of the text (as has been defined within the virtuous framework) is the most reliable course to help Brutus not only interpret better but also transform his entire internal understanding system. The description of a programmatic attempt to transform the interpretive project with primacy given to the transforming of the interpreter as a virtuous agent is the subject of the next chapter. In this way, there is still hope for Brutus and his hermeneutical deficiencies.

TWO

Applying Virtues to the Task of Hermeneutics

Introduction

As THE GRANDFATHER OF contemporary virtue epistemology, Aristotle seems a useful starting point in considering how to move beyond the conceptual idea of VH to the implementation of a program that embodies its values and reaps its produce. Having already explained that virtues are expressed in both moral and intellectual varieties, he further divides the intellectual functions into the contemplative (ἐπιστημονικὸν) and the calculative (λογιστικὸν).[1] The former deals with unchangeable matters of logic, both inductive and deductive. The latter deals with variable things, "both things made and things done."[2] Of particular interest to Aristotle in the second category is the concept of phronesis, practical wisdom. The individual who can calculate (deliberate) well and then act in a manner that is productively good, both making and doing things, possesses phronesis. In detailing the science of epistemology in the previous chapter, the analogue is to the contemplative element of Aristotle's theory, but the ultimate goal is the wisdom to employ the deliberative capacity in producing a practical good, namely justified understanding from a text. Unlike Aristotle's category of contemplative reasonings, even the best applications of phronesis, as well as all other calculative

1. Aristotle, *Nicomachean Ethics*, loc. 1971.
2. Aristotle, *Nicomachean Ethics*, loc. 1989.

reasonings, have the potential of fallibility.[3] Consequently, the goal in interpretation, whether viewed through the lens of an Aristotelian, a postmodern, or a postlapsarian theological model, remains beyond the reach of certainty but not beyond the discovery of a justifiable understanding of a pre-interpretive intention and meaning within the text. This particular reality permits reformed epistemologist Nicholas Wolterstorff to advocate for an anti-foundationalist position in epistemology but not adopt an anti-realism in metaphysics.[4] Just because the certainty that foundationalism aspired to convey is lost in the fallible realm of calculative reason does not demand a rejection of metaphysical realism; it simply admits to the potential fallibility of attempts to express it. As this pertains to textual interpretation, it admits to the inability of an exhaustive and infallible interpretation, but this need not mean that meaning existing within the text prior to the engagement of the interpreter is wholly absent or unattainable.

This rejection of the certainty of any foundationalist approach is further complicated as it pertains to hermeneutics by conflating interpretive understanding and the potential metaphysical reality of the justifiably understood meaning expressed by the text. Both of these elements exist as contemplative forms of knowledge beyond the realm of certainty for the interpreter as sought in a foundationalist approach. It is possible to employ VH in a way to attain a justified understanding of a text without necessarily ascribing metaphysical or even epistemological truth to what is justifiably understood. This differentiating between interpretation, epistemology, and ultimately metaphysical ideas of reality is easily illustrated. In the summer of 2017, a controversy swirled around NBA star Kyrie Irving. He unequivocally stated, "This is not even a conspiracy theory. The Earth is flat."[5] His primary evidence to support his conclusion was based on his view of his own sensory perceptions and deep skepticism toward testimonial evidence: "It's right in front of our faces. I'm telling you, it's right in front of our faces. They lie to us."[6] It is one thing to say that a reader encountering Irving's thoughts can properly understand what he means in that statement, and even acquire deeper levels of explanatory understanding of his thoughts by engaging with the broader

---

3. Battaly, *Virtue*, 48.

4. Wolterstorff, *John Locke and the Ethics of Belief*, xii.

5. Gartland, "Is the Earth Flat?."

6. Gartland, "Is the Earth Flat?."

context of his statements, but it is a different matter to embrace the justifiably understood statements as accurate expressions of physical reality. As an interpreter, one can have a justified and textured understanding of the text of Irving's thoughts, which counts as good interpretation, but wholesale reject as unwarranted, unjustified, and ultimately, untrue, the belief he expressed. There is a difference between these two categories, but they have in common that certainty is ultimately unattainable for both. Fallibility remains possible (even if increasingly rendered unlikely based upon the measure of warrant, justification, and understanding) to both interpretive and epistemological understandings. To properly interpret a text does not demand agreement or assent to the understanding gained from interpreting the text. What one does with a justifiably understood text in the context of the interpreter's noetic system depends on a variety of epistemological and metaphysical factors.

Going back to our primary interpreter, if Brutus is to change his defective intellectual ways and become a better interpreter and a better qua person, then the theory needs to be translated into some type of phronetically guided program. The practical wisdom element that must be developed in an effective VH helps someone like Brutus deliberate the many complex matters that confront every interpretive assignment. Practically, a virtuous interpreter will be able to reliably distinguish between a justified understanding of a text and a self-justifying misreading of the text. Brutus, like many, is especially susceptible to the latter error.

The following expression of VH first defines its function and its manner of development within the active interpretive agent. This chapter will demonstrate how the properly ingrained interpretive virtues will serve to expand both the depth of understanding and its justifying factors in the task of hermeneutics. A virtue approach to epistemology and hermeneutics has the capacity to nurture practically wise interpreters who are able to pursue and discover the embedded textual meaning without falling prey to the overreach of Modern approaches or the unnecessarily skeptical challenges of Postmodernity.

Defining the Program

Regulative Versus Analytical

In attempting to express a programmatic method for VH, the demand for the quick return on investment and the continually rising tide of pragmatic expediency makes an emphasis on underlying dispositions and intellectual habits less appealing to a great many individuals who are interested in hermeneutical inquiry across the spectrum of academic, kerygmatic, or devotional readers. A would-be hermeneut shaped by these contemporary goals may likely reply to a call to intellectual character development as a necessarily laborious and time-consuming endeavor that exists at a level prior (certainly in importance if not also temporally) to skills development with the brusque dismissal, "Yeah, yeah, I need to *be* a good thinker, but what I really want to know is how do I *do* interpretation. What are the steps or tools to do it?" As a result, the emphases in textbooks are often focused upon productive systems, tools, and skills that can be broadly and repeatedly applied to a variety of texts in order to generate a specifically and systemically desired herme-neutical outcome. For example, many adherents of *formgeschichte* see the de-supernaturalized and quasi-objective historical and oral backgrounds of the formation of the text and, to use Hermann Gunkel's phrase, the *Sitz im Leben,* as the proper historically attuned goal of hermeneutics, so skills and methods that are supposedly designed to efficiently discover information that attempt to answer these questions are quickly taught in their programs. The same can be said for systems that deconstruct the supposed internal inconsistencies of culturally oppressive structures embedded within the text or those that exclusively emphasize the inter-textuality of meaning as in literary approaches. Much of the literature on developing programmatic approaches to hermeneutics begins with a relatively brief description of the philosophical commitments of the author of the interpretive framework which defines what the analyti-cally suitable outcome for hermeneutical inquiry should be, and then the remainder, often a great majority, of the textbook is then focused on specific methodological steps that will efficiently and effectively guide the interpreter to attain the desired outcome. What is conspicuously absent is any discussion of the interpreter's intellectual habits and character will profoundly shape anything that can be produced by the process of inter-pretation, so the focus remains at a more surface level of programmatic development of skills and techniques.

VH has no such clearly-defined system that has an obvious and ab-solutely repeatable program that accepts inputs from A, B, and C, and generates the immediate product of interpretive goods: D. The emphasis in these more analytical systems is on what should rightly be called an acceptable interpretation, and on analyzing and explaining the methods and skills that produce this outcome. A virtue approach certainly has an element of this analytical describing and defining, as expressed in the previous chapter, but it is ultimately more attuned as a regulative approach that guides *how* the interpreter and the act of interpreting proceeds rather than being limited by a particular method or skill. In many ways, VH as a phronetic program employs scientific (*wissen*) techniques, but at its core, it recognizes what Schleiermacher calls the art (*Kunst*) of the discipline. While Schleiermacher may be right in the unavoidable element of *kunst* in the process of understanding, his overly-optimistic modern expectation of certainty and his suspect system of *divining* understanding as the manner of the practice of the *kunst* is the root of his system's demise.

The virtuous agent is able to draw the best of the skills and attending products from the full range of other approaches since the regulative influence exists, not as a rigid framework of universal rules or a narrow set of particular skills, but rightly tuned intellectual excellencies that issue from proper motivations that reliably attain understanding. VH rejects the one-size-fits-all approaches of other analytical systems, trusting that the stability of the virtues and, by extension, the virtuous agent will appropriately differentiate at times and integrate at others from the vast array of options for understanding. Roberts and Wood make a parallel point in reference to epistemology:

> We have argued that the search for an e-definition of knowledge, which was so dominant in the last decades of the century, is a hopeless and not very interesting project, yet we certainly think that clarification of the concept of knowledge is an important task for the epistemologist, and we regard the task of regulative epistemology as, in a broad sense, an analytic task. The one-size-fits-all concept of justification that analytic epistemologists tended to seek is, again, a chimera, but virtually all the ideas of justification that were proposed have merit as aspects of a concept of justification.[7]

The same could be true for approaches of hermeneutics. The methods, skills, and frameworks of nearly all existing hermeneutical systems originated as potentially useful responses to the perceived deficiencies of other preceding systems. Once the new system emerges, the tendency is to totalize its approach. This only repeats the inescapable pendulum-like instability of the entire discipline that has been witnessed since the end

---

7. Roberts and Wood, *Intellectual Virtues*, 112.

of the Medieval Era. The virtuous agent need not be controlled by this instability but is able to work from the place of a stable center of long-acknowledged intellectual characteristics to guide the process toward meaning and understanding. In so doing, the agent is able to employ practical wisdom (phronesis) to identify and properly employ all the useful aspects of the other systems. Vanhoozer similarly argues that, "Ethical interpreters, therefore, must resist becoming a slave to any single interpretive method while at the same time admitting that every interpretive method may describe an aspect of textual meaning."[8]

Wolterstorff sees John Locke as the pivotal modern philosopher who is responsible for building the dominant regulative epistemology that endured throughout Modernity. His description of analytic and regulative epistemology as seen in Locke is helpful as an analogue of what RVE and VH are most attuned to accomplish. He describes Locke,

> as primarily engaged in *regulative*, as opposed to *analytic*, epistemology. In analytic epistemology one explores the conditions under which one or another merit is present in beliefs. Theories of knowledge and theories of rationality belong to analytic epistemology. They are not meant to offer guidance, except, of course, guidance in analysis for those who wish to pick out knowledge from non-knowledge and rationality from non-rationality. In regulative epistemology, on the other hand, one discusses how we ought to conduct our understandings—what we ought to do by way of forming beliefs.[9]

For Wolterstorff, Locke cannot be limited to the camps of empiricism or rationalism; ultimately, he was attempting something more. Locke was trying to calm the intellectual upheaval that attended the end of the Middle Ages and saw appeals to traditional authorities as the guiding epistemological practices dismantled. The same type of epochal upheaval exists as Modernity has passed into Postmodernity. The same call to a new regulative framework is needed to steady the dislodged and adrift hermeneutical ship. The emphasis on the transforming of the underlying intellectual character of the interpreter as the regulative key allows for the best possible interpretive outcome, rather than solely describing what interpretation is or is not, or what skills and techniques are most important that sets apart a regulative program. Regulative epistemology

8. Vanhoozer, *Is There a Meaning in This Text?*, 402.
9. Wolterstorff, *John Locke and the Ethics of Belief*, xvi.

"tries to generate guidance for epistemic practice."[10] By this definition, VH fits better under a regulative approach to hermeneutical inquiry. Rather than describing and analyzing the specific rules, skills, methods, and frameworks that are characteristic of the analytical approach to hermeneutics for nearly 250 years, the regulative approach focuses on how the interpretive agent should align his or her intellectual dispositions, motivations, and habitual thinking practices (both voluntary and involuntary) before and throughout the interpretive task. Borrowing from Roberts and Wood's epistemological insights, VH can be defined as a regulative approach to hermeneutics that "describes the personal dispositions of the agent rather than providing direct rules of epistemic action. It focuses on forming the practitioner's character and is strongly education-oriented."[11] All this cannot be taken to mean that there is no place for analysis or definition, but that these elements without primary attention to the underlying motivation and virtuous habits of the mind are too malleable, theory laden, and bias-sensitive to be, on their own, anything but longitudinally impotent in attaining and justifying the deepest forms of textual understanding.

Those who seek a quick fix, a new framework, or the codification of interpretive rules will find no comfort in a virtuous approach. Yet, it is the virtuous agent who remains as the great unifying center that holds the most promising solution to span the distance between the hope for a form of realistic meaning that has driven both confessional and modern hermeneutical approaches. This is accomplished while still acknowledging some of the inescapable critiques offered by Existentialism and Postmodernism's hermeneutical priorities. All legitimate epistemic desiderata, including those that exist in the realm of hermeneutics, can be brought together in one conception—that of the excellent epistemic agent, the person of intellectual virtues.[12] Shaping the interpretive virtues of this type of agent is the formative task of VH.

As a regulative system that is fundamentally concerned with the manner in which the discipline of hermeneutics is pursued, it is clear that being virtuous, while necessary for properly justified textual understanding, is not sufficient for the acquisition of interpretive goods. Since all hermeneutical systems prioritize specific skill sets that correspond to

10. Roberts and Wood, *Intellectual Virtues*, 21.
11. Roberts and Wood, *Intellectual Virtues*, 22.
12. Roberts and Wood, *Intellectual Virtues*, 42.

the desired end of the particular analytical model, it is important to understand the relationship between skills and virtue within the regulative expression of VH. The end of VH is a justified understanding of the text which expresses itself in its explanatory and integrative depth. Possessing a consistent and habituated intellectual motivation to be open-minded, generous, just, and courageous with the intent of acquiring the reliable satisfaction of these qualities in the various practical domains of cognitive endeavors is praiseworthy and possesses justificatory powers, but understanding, as defined in VH, is dependent on discipline-relevant skills regulated by virtue. Zagzebski gives the most succinct and helpful definition of skills: "Intellectual skills are sets of truth-conducive procedures that are acquired through habitual practice and have application to a certain area of truth acquisition.[13]

As virtue theory has continued to gain hearing in both the ethical and epistemological contexts, the question of the relationship between skills and virtues has become an increasingly more debated topic. The importance of this debate to hermeneutics is central to the VH approach. While virtues are often debatably connected to other matters (e.g., faculties, processes, capacities, or temperaments), Zagzebski explains the particular persistence of the debate concerning skills by acknowledging the foundational similarity that, "Skills, like virtues, are acquired excellences."[14] Aristotle, Roberts, Wood, James Wallace,[15] and Sarah Broadie[16] join Zagzebski in separating skills from virtues. Julia Annas[17] and William Hasselberger[18] argue that the virtues are themselves skills, and Matt Stichter goes even further to claim that "Virtues can be understood as *specifically moral skills*."[19] In *Virtues of the Mind*, Zagzebski offers the most complete and persuasive cataloging of arguments that have been offered across the spectrum of virtue theorists to maintain a separation between skills and virtues.[20] The most compelling of the arguments

13. Zagzebski, "Recovering Understanding," 177.

14. Zagzebski, *Virtues of the Mind*, 106.

15. Wallace, *Virtues and Vices*.

16. Broadie, *Ethics with Aristotle*.

17. Annas, *Intelligent Virtue*.

18. Hasselberger, "Knowing More," 775–803.

19. Stichter, "Practical Skills and Practical Wisdom, 436.

20. Zagzebski, *Virtues of the Mind*, 106–15.

offered involve the matters of volitional usage or non-usage of a skill, motivations, and the location of value.

Skills, unlike virtues, can be intentionally left unused. Take as an example professional tennis player Nick Kyrgios, who has reached multiple quarterfinals in Grand Slam tennis tournaments and peaked as the thirteenth-highest-ranked player in the world.[21] These feats are only attainable if one has a highly-developed skill at playing tennis. During the fourth game of the second set of his match against Richard Gasquet at the 2015 Wimbledon Championships, he appeared to choose not to employ his skills in returning the ball during multiple consecutive volleys.[22] This choice to not use his skills is a difference between virtues and skills. One cannot possess a virtue and simultaneously not employ it; this is by definition a failure to possess the virtue since, as Aristotle has pointed out, a virtue is, "a firm and unchangeable character."[23] To possess the ethical virtue of kindness prohibits the willful choice to act unkindly. "To go awry in any of the parts of a virtue is to fall short of the virtue."[24] By "parts of a virtue," theorists mean that virtuous agents must (1) do what is virtuous and (2) possess certain dispositions related the virtuous action. These dispositions are (a) knowledge of what they are doing (not accidental action), (b) intention to do what they are doing (motivation), (c) certainty and firmness in their action (habituation), and (d) the experience of joy in acting inline with the virtues and achieving their desired end.

Virtues, like skills, have a productive ability, but skills need not possess the consistent motivational component that is inherent within a virtue. Two surgeons may perform with equal skill and success the same surgery, the successful removal of an appendix. In observing only the outward measure and presentation of their skill, there is no differentiation between them. They are acquired and habituated excellencies. If one surgeon preforms the surgery out of a motivation to restore the health of an individual plagued by an acutely inflamed appendix from an ingrained character trained to compassion and mercy, that surgeon employed the skill regulated by a deeper and psychically prior level of virtue. Whereas, a surgeon who skillfully performed the same surgery on an individual

21. "Nick Kyrgios | Rankings History | ATP Tour | Tennis," www.atptour.com/en/players/nick-kyrgios/ke17/overview.

22. Chammas, "Wimbledon 2015."

23. Aristotle, *Nicomachean Ethics*, loc. 726.

24. Wood, *Epistemology*, 44.

who had no need of the surgery simply to bill the patient to finance the surgeon's trip to Barbados still possesses the surgical skill but not out of a virtuous motivation. The skill and result of the surgeries were identical, but the second surgery was not justified because of the viciously selfish character of the surgeon. In explaining how RVE differs from a skills virtue approach, Abrol Fairweather explains, "To have an excellence of character requires a normative commitment to the end one reliably attains, whereas to have a skill simply requires that the end attained is due to a competence involving training, understanding and discipline."[25] Virtues necessarily, unlike skills, "involve something besides actions—something that reveals our motives, commitments, values, and conceptions of the good."[26]

Finally, skills and virtues differ in the manner and location of their value. Skills have value dependent upon the situation in which the skill is manifested. One may possess the skill to repair the compressor of a ten-ton air conditioning unit, but the measure of the value of that skill is dependent on external factors. The skill is exceedingly valuable in August in Phoenix, Arizona, but dramatically void of value in January at Point Barrow, Alaska. The virtues are generically and intrinsically valuable regardless of the situation. The skill of identifying complex syntactical relationships in textual constructions is not intrinsically valuable since it would possess little value in a situation that was attempting to find subterranean aquafers. This particular skill accrues its value in being utilized within the proper domain of hermeneutical inquiry. The intellectual virtue of attentiveness is intrinsically good, both in what it produces and, even more, in how it makes the agent in a global sense a better thinking agent and a generally better person. As Aristotle points out, production is not the only measure of the value of virtue. "Every virtue we choose indeed for themselves (for if nothing resulted from them, we should still choose each of them)."[27]

The difference between skills and virtues is summarized by Zagzebski's conclusion,

> Virtues and skills have numerous connections, but virtues are psychically prior to skills. I propose that this is because the motivational component of a virtue defines it more than external effectiveness does, whereas it is the reverse in the case of skills.

25. Fairweather, "Duhem-Quine Virtue Epistemology," 678.

26. Battaly, *Virtue*, 64.

27. Aristotle, *Nicomachean Ethics*, loc. 447.

Virtues have a broader range of application than do skills, at least typically, whereas skills tend to be more subject specific, context specific, and role specific.[28]

By identifying VH as a regulative rather than an analytical program, the psychically prior nature of the virtues demands that the program give deliberate and sustained attention to the formation and ongoing nurturing of the interpretive virtues rather than choosing expediency by giving pride of place, or worse, exclusive attention to skills, rules, or frameworks. The abiding virtuous commitments of the interpreter are essential to align the frameworks, priorities, skills, and actions that pursue the goal of justified understanding.

Since there remains a close connection between the virtues and the requisite skills of interpretation, VH as a regulative model is especially tuned to the governing of the pertinent and domain relevant skills. Four ways in which the virtues serve to guide the skills stand out. (1) While the skills are more observably effective in gaining and expressing information and accruing deeper understanding by virtue of their pragmatic nature, they are also more malleable and subject to misuse and abuse than the virtues. "To attribute an action or belief to the workings of an intellectual virtue is to identify its ground with an attribute of the agent that is still more stable and less fleeting than is a skill."[29] The pragmatic nature of skills affords more immediate rewards, externally observable production, and relatively easier attainment than the virtues, which makes it unsurprising that skills tend to be the focus in specific domains' training manuals. Even though the skills are more immediately pragmatic, it is the enduring nature of the virtues that allows for the long-term effective utilization of the skills. "Skills serve virtues by allowing a person who is virtuously motivated to be effective in action."[30] The severing of the subservient role of skills to virtues makes them far more likely to be illegitimately totalized and misused in practice. (2) The generic nature of the virtues allows them to balance and attune the full-range of corresponding skills that are connected to the broad domains of the virtues so as to maintain the direction toward the reliable attainment of the motivational goal encapsulated in the virtuous agent. "Virtues can also be skills, or involve skills, though not all skills are virtues, since many

28. Zagzebski, *Virtues of the Mind*, 114.

29. Axtell, "Introduction," xvi.

30. Zagzebski, *Virtues of the Mind*, 112.

skills fit us for functioning excellently, not in generic human contexts, but in specialized ones. Again, all virtues bear some relation or other to skills by which we negotiate generically human activities or situations for activities."[31] Skills, in themselves, possess neither the sufficient motivational energy nor overseeing capacity that the virtues, as the more generic and psychically prior elements, possess. (3) Discerning between the array of available skills falls to the motivational and governing component of the virtues. Various skills are more adept at performing necessary actions than other skills within particular domains of knowledge. A hammer may be able to drive both a nail and also a screw, but the nature of the task to be accomplished and the underlying virtue of attention to detail will guide the carpenter to which skill and tool (e.g., a hammer or a screwdriver) is better suited to the moment. Since a primary element of the virtues is not only the motivation to attain a certain end but also the reliable attainment of that end, the virtues serve to draw the attention and energy of the agent to those skills most effective at accomplishing the domain-relevant task. Speaking specifically in relation to textual interpretation, "A concern for truth and justice, a concern both to know and transmit truth, and a concern both to receive and to give justice, and whatever epistemic skills will promote the satisfaction of these concerns," lies at the heart of VH.[32] In this expression, Roberts and Wood expose the necessity of the motivational concern of the virtues to compel the attainment of the specific skills to achieve its goals. (4) The practical wisdom (phronesis) of the virtuous agent maintains the proper and timely implementation of all the skills to guide the interpretive agent not just to attain justified understanding but also the general conduct of life and inquiry as a whole toward the best life. "Virtues require being practically wise about what is good and bad for people, and about how various practices fit into an overall conception of the good life. In contrast, skills do not require making these kinds of value judgments."[33] Wood contends even further that, "Skills can be cultivated and deployed in ways relatively disconnected from human flourishing. (Think of the Unabomber, for example.) A mature intellectual virtue, by contrast arises out of a concern for human wholeness."[34]

---

31. Roberts and Wood, *Intellectual Virtues*, 59.

32. Roberts and Wood, *Intellectual Virtues*, 136.

33. Stichter, "Practical Skills and Practical Wisdom in Virtue," 436.

34. Wood, *Epistemology*, 52.

If the VH model is correct that the most important thing that is brought to the textual encounter (apart from the text that is at the root of the encounter, without which there is no need for hermeneutics in the first place) is the underlying dispositional and noetic character of the interpreter prior to the crafting of models, rules, and methods, one would expect to see some reflection of this in textbooks on the subject. A survey of twenty-five of the most significant hermeneutical texts from the last fifty-five years from diverse theological and academic backgrounds reveals the nearly complete paucity in discussing the topic. Almost every book unsurprisingly begins with a discussion of the desired outcome of their hermeneutical model (e.g., authorial intent, objectified historicism, existential melding of horizons, ideological deconstructing of the text, or reader-generated meaning) with no comment on how the *telos* of their work is at all dependent and shaped by underlying epistemological commitments and agent-centered intellectual virtues. Then the balance of the treatment focuses on lengthy discussions of skill sets necessary to engage with genre, language, history, theology, or oppressive cultural structures. The most that is addressed that implies some responsibility for the intellectual approach of the interpreter revolves around pre-understandings and biases, but even this is somewhat removed from the truest regulative impact of VH. To acknowledge biases and pre-understandings is like proudly proclaiming that water is wet as though something revolutionary has been revealed. This silence on the topic could mean that a virtue approach is ultimately irrelevant to the discussion of interpretation, or perhaps, it is an indication that the two dominant metaphysical conceptions of interpretation (realism and irrealism) have equally missed the central regulative matter of how to engage in the dialectic of text and reader: shared virtue between author, text, reader, and receiving community (original and contemporary). VH presents a regulative model that shapes the conduct of inquiry in the midst of all the challenges to gaining a justified understanding of a text.[35] The emphasis on virtuous manners

---

35. Five hermeneutically-focused books stand out as incipient contributors to important elements addressed by VH, while still focusing on their own unique emphases. Vanhoozer introduces the topic of interpretive virtues in a brief section near the conclusion of his work, but leaves much to be done to implement a comprehensive plan (Vanhoozer, *Is There a Meaning in This Text?*). Following Vanhoozer, three other books develop important components of VH without comprehensively uniting their distinct themes. (Briggs, *Virtuous Reader*; Starling, *Hermeneutics as Apprenticeship*; and de Waal Dryden, *Hermeneutic of Wisdom.* A final book worthy of mentioning in this context is Mickelsen, *Interpreting the Bible*, which comes very near the discussion

of intellectual inquiry is not to be appended to hermeneutical systems, either as a paragraph in the prologue or in the epilogue, but they are fundamentally integral to every aspect of the task from assigning the *telos,* pursuing proper skills, engaging in the work, acquiring understanding, justifying the interpretation, integrating the whole experience in the noetic structure of the interpreter, and communicating the acquired understanding in a cogent manner to others. In short, VH is a regulative epistemological approach to attaining interpretive goods.

The Virtuous Agent Rather Than the Virtues of an Agent

It is easy to see how an emphasis on the intellectual character of the interpreter as defined by a class of motivational and reliably productive virtues could be reduced to something far less than intended by the concept of a *virtuous interpreter.* The focus becomes the individual virtues as they are defined and categorized. Inherent in this possibility is the isolating of the virtues into discrete packets of excellences that are viewed separately from each other and seen as niceties on an aretaic buffet selected at the whims, tastes, and proclivities of an individual. In centering the justifying capacity of an interpretation within the domain of the virtuosity of active agents who inquire into textual meaning, something more than an isolated virtue, or several virtues, even when properly defined and possessed, is necessary.

When the individual characteristics are the focus rather than the totality of the agent's virtuous character, the possibility exists that VH descends into an approach that can be summed up in trite beatitude-like phrases of, "be open-minded," "be diligent," "be fair." James Montmarquet sees danger in reducing the virtues to simply trying harder at certain beatitude-like efforts, "reducing the quite rich and interesting array of epistemically desirable qualities to a single, rather attenuated (if pure) notion of making a suitable effort in regard to truth (or, again, other epistemically desirable ends). If that mere exertion of effort is all there is to epistemic virtue, one might well doubt its importance or centrality to epistemology."[36] Although these are good and virtuous beatitudes, this is a standard far below what a virtuous interpreter whose hermeneutical inquiries rise to the

---

of specific intellectual virtues prior to the emergence of virtue epistemology in the final chapter entitled, "Balance through Care and Practice."

36. Montmarquet, "'Internalist' Conception of Epistemic Virtue," 136.

level of contributing justification to an understanding must possess. Virtuous people, either ethically or intellectually, "are excellent as people in general, rather than merely excellent in some specific occupation or role."[37] Therefore, a virtuous interpreter possesses a highly-tuned excellence of intellectual character that can be described as a necessary constellation of domain-relevant virtues, but not purely individualized and isolated traits apart from the whole of the person's character.

A virtuous character elevates the hermeneut to a level of motivational and reliable success, which is the precise element that projects justification from the agent's intellectual character to textual understanding. This perspective inculcates the nature of the virtues beyond platitudes and allows the focus to properly be centered in a virtuous agent rather than an agent possessing this or that discrete virtue. While even a virtuous character can never fully transcend the human limitations of perspective and bias, it is the truly virtuous individual that has the greatest potential to reach the highest possible attainment of this elusive goal. This agent seeks to understand rather than merely use others (including texts) and seeks to integrate new knowledge into an increasingly morally and noetically good persona. Other systems often seek to master and control for the benefit of oneself or one's exclusive community. Virtue ultimately gives a platform from which to hope for more than ideology and self-obsessed interpretive ends.

As an example of the inadequacy of the isolating individual virtues, Brutus does not become a virtuous interpreter simply by working on being more open-minded. Even though being open-minded is consistently counted among the intellectual virtues, and its inclusion into Brutus's noetic framework would be positive and necessary for him, this isolated characteristic is not sufficient for him to be considered virtuous. Consequently, the trait conventionally called open-mindedness cannot convey justification; only the virtuous intellectual agent can accomplish that end. Let's assume that Brutus decides to be better and chooses to embrace a more open-minded approach. He would be open-minded to the possibilities of understanding within the text as well as to others' interpretations without the holistically attuned virtuous character that would enable him to discern between the merits of the other interpretations. Potentially, other more vicious interpretations could be adopted if Brutus only adds open-mindedness. He could listen to others who might understand the

37. Battaly, *Virtue*, 6.

passage to authorize a general program of gynocide for all women who do not show complete deference to all men in every setting. Or he could change his mind to embrace a less violent understanding but equally vicious interpretation of the passage that perceives the text to be about patriarchal gender roles in twenty-first-century American agriculture, which is unrelated to the meaning of the text. Being open is certainly necessary for a healthy intellectual inquiry, but it is not sufficient for an intellectually virtuous character. Brutus requires a transformation of his whole intellectual character, not just one trait, in order to transform his hermeneutical endeavors. Other character defects in his noetic habits continue to plague his work. While it may be true that if he has been less than open-minded when encountering the text or the input of other interpreters and he would be better to nurture a more open frame of mind when reading, he has also demonstrated his failure to do justice to the author, be humble in ascribing meaning, be attentive to important details, and, potentially most important, persistently love truth. Brutus reminds us that VH must be about more than individual and isolated traits; it must take a holistic approach to intellectual character and its impact on the task of hermeneutics.

Zagzebski admits the possibility that the addition of a discrete virtue may even potentially make an agent worse without the habituation of a more holistic virtuous character. Her example of a courageous Nazi soldier who may actually perpetrate more harm and vicious effect than a cowardly Nazi illustrates this possibility. In her approach, the individual virtue is still worth nurturing, since by its acquisition, the vicious agent is closer to achieving a virtuous character, leaving less "work to do to attain a high level of moral worth."[38] Even with this caveat, the need to develop more than an individual trait is paramount in the hope of using VH as a manner to justify textual interpretations.

The order of operation must be kept clear in the consideration of this program. Driver helps to define this proper order in her definition of VE: "One could picture a form of virtue epistemology in which justified beliefs are those beliefs an epistemically virtuous person would have. This raises the question of what an epistemic virtue is."[39] In her definition, she begins with the "virtuous person" and then moves to the question of what epistemic virtues are. The central point is the agent; the enumeration and

---

38. Zagzebski, "Recovering Understanding," 93.
39. Driver, "Moral and Epistemic Virtue," 123.

explication of various virtues serves only to place descriptive expression to who a virtuous interpretive agent is and how that impacts what she reliably does. The goal is the development of intellectually virtuous interpretive agents who engage in the task of textual interpretation from a holistic, deeply ingrained, and thoroughly habituated disposition that is properly motivated to gain understanding and is generally reliable in doing so. William Hasselberger captures this emphasis well: "The fundamental moral epistemological standard is instead a certain kind of person: a virtuous, experienced, and practically wise person, who constitutes a living 'norm' in 'the activity of thought and choice in regard to the various departments of life.'"[40] If the priority in emphasis is given to individual virtues without the proper understanding that those virtues are ultimately helpfully reductive and descriptive explanations of the components of a virtuous interpreter's overall character, then the likelihood of viewing the "buffet" style approach to the virtues is greatly increased to the detriment of the entire program. John McDowell, in addressing virtue ethics, agrees with the emphasis on the specific virtues as being the secondary matter to the recognition of right action. In this way, "the nature of virtue is explained, as it were, from the outside in."[41]

The idea of using a collection of descriptive terms to express the varied facets of a unified and singular concept or individual is attested in a well-known virtue text from the NT. Paul's expression in Gal 5:22–23, generally referred to as his teaching on the fruit of the Spirit, is a fitting example of concentrating on the unified nature of a concept while still employing individual descriptors. In many ways, this is a Pauline expression of Christian virtue. The noun, fruit (καρπός), is a singular noun and not the often erroneously assumed and taught plural, fruits (καρποί). He then employs the appropriate third person singular verb, ἐστιν, further emphasizing the singular nature of the fruit that he is detailing. Paul is not detailing the *fruits* of the Spirit as though they, as a multiplicity, exist independently of each other, but the singular concept of the *fruit* of the Spirit. To be virtuous in the Pauline sense is not to possess one, two, or several of these descriptors (love, joy, peace, patience, kindness, goodness, faithfulness, gentleness, and self-control), as though they can be picked depending on an individual's preferences, talents, or desires. Rather, his focus is on the fruit of the Spirit in the lives of Christians,

40. Hasselberger, "Knowing More," 775.
41. McDowell, "Virtue and Reason," 331.

which encompasses all the descriptors he enumerates. The same is true when considering the virtuous interpreter. The focus is on the holistic sense of the excellent interpretive agent and not on individualized virtues. The breakdown of the agent's intellectual character into individual virtues is only a useful method to analyze what makes her excellent but cannot be construed as discrete packets of excellencies that exist independently.

If the concept of a holistically virtuous interpreter is to be admitted as the exemplar to which all interpreters who seek a justified understanding of a text can seek to be conformed, then the opposite would be the corollary concept of a vicious interpreter. It is unlikely, although conceptually not impossible, to envision an interpreter who is motivated, and knowingly aware of the defect in his motivation, to believe falsehood or to misunderstand a text, which seems to be the appropriate obverse of a virtuous interpreter. In this example, to be vicious is to have a vicious motivation that reliably acts in ways to accomplish the internally motivated vicious end. If hermeneutical vice is defined in this way, it would require, for example, that an intellectual agent who possesses the vice of gullibility to be volitionally conditioned to "try to believe things one takes to be beyond the bounds of proper standards of credibility."[42] An example would be the interpreter who willfully and habitually believes that which she does not believe to be possible about a text (e.g., interpreting Rom 12:21 to be about white rhinoceroses). Few of the developments of even the most broken hermeneutical models and erroneous hermeneia fit this definition of vice within the interpretive tradition. If this is the only model of interpreting in a vicious manner, then little could be expected to be gained from a virtue approach, but Aristotle is quick to point out that although success "is possible only in one way," it is possible to "fail in many ways."[43] The vices of interpretation are expressed in motivations and outcomes that thwart understanding a text and are discernable in a great range of expressions that need not be as obvious as the willfully gullible interpreter.

Brutus, as presented, is a vicious interpreter of the Eph 5 text not because he is willfully, blamably, and knowingly motivated to discover a false understanding of the text, but because his underlying intellectual character reliably produces false understandings. His blameworthiness is in the deficiency of his intellectual character which keeps him from

---

42. Montmarquet, "'Internalist' Conception of Epistemic Virtue," 138.

43. Aristotle, *Nicomachean Ethics*, loc. 779.

discovering a justifiable understanding of the text under consideration. This tendency to produce false understandings is what is most indicative of a vicious interpreter. By examining those characteristics that tend to impede justifiable understandings of a text, the case for virtue-based approaches becomes even clearer.

If one considers open-mindedness a virtue, in an Aristotelian framework which sees virtues as the mean between vices of deficiency and excess, then the deficient vice would be dogmatism. Every ideological starting point can be guilty of closed-minded dogmatism. In hermeneutics, this dogmatic perspective can be guilty of closed-mindedness in many ways. One prevalent form of hermeneutic dogmatism is seen in forcing a particular traditioned theological/philosophical framework to limit the impact and freedom of the text to fulfill the illocutions of the author or to silence the interpretive contributions of those who interpret from a position outside of the prevailing interpretive community in which an interpreter is situated. The virtuous agent possesses an integrity of character that has a stability that allows for open interaction with foreign and disparate perspectives. This openness does not necessarily equate with ultimate acceptance of every framework, interpretation, or agenda, but it is able to engage and seek to understand the outside perspective as it is in itself before accepting or dismissing it illegitimately on the basis of dogmatic adherence to one's own biases and ideology. As Battaly defines the virtue, "To be open-minded, one must consider alternative perspectives *appropriately* [emphasis added]."[44] Appropriately is not the same as unreservedly. This is true for engagement with the biblical text or subsequent hermeneia resulting from various subsequent interpreters of the original text. William Klein, Craig Blomberg, and Robert Hubbard address these same two loci when speaking of verifying a biblical interpretation: "To verify an interpretation requires weighing two types of evidence: evidence pertaining to the text itself and evidence involving the interpreters."[45] Specifically addressing the ability to engage with outside interpretations, they "recommend that interpreters make it a practice always to consult others with whom they may *disagree* in order to test the validity of their conclusions."[46] Their use of the term *verify* corresponds to the VH concept of justifying understanding. The ability to draw justificatory contribution

---

44. Battaly, "Acquiring Epistemic Virtue," 1.

45. Klein et al., *Introduction to Biblical Interpretation*, 201.

46. Klein et al., *Introduction to Biblical Interpretation*, 203.

from the interpretations of others requires a virtuous treatment of the others, or it becomes only an exercise of proof-texting (when interpreters agree) or creating a straw man (when they disagree), neither of which has the capacity to offer any meaningful justification. Only fully engaging with the other (text or interpreter) from a holistically virtuous position that can be seen in the traits of open-mindedness, generosity, justice, love, and courage overcomes the vice of dogmatism and allows for a deepening justification of an understanding of a text.

Becoming a Virtuous Interpreter

In approaching the idea of virtuous interpretive agents, one is quickly confronted by the challenging and somewhat nebulous nature of the task. Having already established that skills, rules, and methodologies are to be differentiated from, and ultimately, dependent on the virtues present within the agent, it is not surprising that the rigid and predictable nature of memorizing Greek paradigms of noun endings, diagramming sentences, exploring literary structures, considering communal responses to the text, and consulting archeological findings from the ancient originating society of the text are more concretely experienced assignments than nurturing a virtuous stance to interpreting a text. It is also true that as a virtuous approach places skills and methods as necessary, but, ultimately, second-level matters, both conceptually and often temporally, below the attainment of increasing measures of a virtuous interpretive character, contemporary Western culture, which prizes tolerance[47] and multivalence in interpretation, further minimizes many of the traditional concrete methods and skills that tended to accompany the agenda of Modernity with its misguided pursuit of certain and objective understanding. As a result, the more concrete skills like archeology and historical reconstruction are rejected in approaches like New Criticism's Formalism, as well as postmodern expressions of deconstruction and Reader-Response frameworks,

---

47. While tolerance is the cornerstone of contemporary liberal society, it is a specific concept of tolerance. D. A. Carson identifies an important shift in understanding tolerance. Traditionally, tolerance was practiced as a robust tolerance of the people who espoused differing ideas while rigorously evaluating the ideas themselves. Now, tolerance is expressed in the inability to critique ideas while civility toward those who adhere to the ideas is continually disregarded (*Gagging of God,* 31). In this way, society seems to adhere to one remaining virtue when it comes to worldviews, beliefs, and ideas: "It is forbidden to forbid," but this does not offer a strong foundation to support virtuous activity.

but they are not replaced with anything that can anchor the interpretive tasks. VH, like more contemporary approaches, realigns the focus from exclusive methodological and skillset obsessions, yet in distinction to the cutting away of all moorings that embrace an albeit humbled form of determinate meaning within a text, VH looks to a new anchor point, the development of a stable virtuous character.

If Zagzebski and, more distantly, Aristotle are accurate that the motivational component is central to a virtuous approach to epistemology and includes emotions, desires, motives, and attitudes, then it is not surprising that attaining this key justifying center of interpretation within the properly attuned character of the interpreter is not as simple and straightforward as acquiring functional skill sets.[48] The development of the motivational element of the virtuous agent is the most obscure component of the task. In virtue theory, it is not enough to do the right thing or attain the right outcome, but it must be done intentionally and even with a joy that follows from doing what aligns with one's underlying virtuous nature. Simply put, a virtuous agent does the right thing, for the right reasons, and reliably achieves the right outcome. In all of this, the array of factors that influence the motivational piece exists as the greatest complication for those concerned with its inculcation. How does one attain or develop a motivational desire? How does one change an attitude? Especially when, as Annas, while acknowledging that intellectual virtues often interact with emotions, correctly points out that, "moral virtues essentially involve emotions and feelings in a way not true of the intellectual virtues."[49] The affective dimension of the moral virtues has an admittedly more immediate, concrete, and practical engagement within the agent than is most often the case in the more ethereal world of belief formation and justification. One feels more acutely the immediacy of the emotions that attend to courageous action in the face of imminent danger to life and limb than the attending emotions of courageous intellectual formulation, at least in their nascent moments. So, it is more than just developing the attitudinal and affective character of the agent in an immediately practical way; it is doing it in the realm of the more detached and delicate world of noetic functions.

Motivations are deeply connected to the affective functions of humanity, and their impact has immense power in shaping or limiting

48. Zagzebski, *Virtues of the Mind*, 15.

49. Annas, "Structure of Virtue," 21.

intellectual endeavors. In a helpful shorthand definition, Sruthi Rothen-fluch defines motivation as "nothing more than an action-directing emotion."[50] Battaly traces this view of the place of emotions back to Aristotle, which stands in contrast to the antecedent philosophy of Socrates. According to Aristotle, "emotions and desires can causally overpower knowledge, preventing us from performing acts we know to be virtuous."[51] This is his definition of intellectual *akrasia*.

In the realm of the interpretive task, this emotion-enabled *akrasia* can be observed when an agent shapes or distorts interpretive insights out of a fear of dogmatic, denominational, or cultural repercussions rather than offering a courageous expression of an accurate textual understanding regardless of potential personal or vocational ramifications. Any programmatic or regulative approach to VH has to involve a process that trains more than the inadequate concept of the disembodied mind of modernism as the seat of objective reasoning but also rejects the uninhibited proliferation of polyvalent interpretation and perspectivalism of postmodernism. The full nature of the human agent as a thinking/feeling/willing being created in the image of God and set within a social and particularized historical setting must be habituated to express the shared, stable, and most broadly attested understanding of virtuous character when approaching the text.

Pentecostal scholar Amos Yong further applies this affective development to the task of biblical interpretation: "If homo sapiens are not only thinking but feeling animals, and even more so, are thinking creatures precisely because they are sensing and perceiving—loving, desiring, hoping—creatures, then there is no right thinking (orthodoxy) about biblical or theological interpretation without also right feeling (orthopathos)."[52] Traditional virtue models have addressed this comprehensive transforming of the human agent by means of "assimilation, largely by imitation and under direction and control. The result is a growing understanding of what is done, a choice of it for its own sake, a fixity and steadiness of purpose."[53] The importance of apprenticeship to fitting virtuous interpretive exemplars is central to this process of direction and growth. Habituation through repetition and guided practice is reinforced

---

50. Rothenfluch, "Virtue Epistemology and Tacit Cognitive Processes," 398.

51. Battaly, "Acquiring Epistemic Virtue," 3.

52. Yong, *Hermeneutical Spirit*, loc. 991.

53. Smith, "Introduction," loc. 154.

through the stages of virtue development: naivety, enkratic inconsistency, self-discipline, and finally, virtuous interpretive character.

The viability of VH depends on several key conditions, not the least of which is the possibility of the existence of virtuous interpreters who can serve as suitable exemplars. In the preceding section, the emphasis on the holistic nature of a virtuous agent's character as the source of justification for textual understanding is hope-filled (in that the possibility of a justifying center that embodies the best of human capacities is largely free of the subject/object dialectic that has plagued Modern and Postmodern formulations, and admits social, spiritual, and affective contributions), but it is also daunting. If a thoroughly integrated and holistic virtuous character is the requirement, rather than simply acting in certain ways in certain circumstances, can anyone truly attain the lofty status of a virtuous interpreter? Furthermore, if apprenticeship to a fitting exemplar is a foundational piece of the attainment of a virtuous character, the answer to that question becomes a hinge to the entire approach.

A sustained criticism of virtue approaches to both ethics and epistemology has come from the view known as Situationalism, which challenges the plausibility of genuine virtuous agents, and has been espoused by leading critics like John Doris and Mark Alfano.[54] Doris bases his rejection of the usefulness of a virtue approach on the rejection of a holistically integrated system of character within an agent, which he refers to as a globalist view. He argues that empirical evidence suggests that character is not as prevalent, ingrained, or stable as virtue responsibilists contend, and he uses individuals like situationally-influenced Nazi doctor Josef Mengele, who could be both charming and cruel as an archetypal example.[55] Using the virtue of compassion as the test, he concludes that "empirical evidence indicates that compassion-relevant behavior is far more situationally variable than the globalist theses of consistency and

---

54. Alfano's approach in *Character as Moral Fiction* (2013) is a form of reinterpreted situationalism which embraces the idea that virtues are situationally conditioned and not as concrete and stable as responsibilists advocate, but still possess value as "factitious" aids in developing proper behavior (ethics) and thought processes (epistemology) by creating self-fulfilling prophecies. Tell someone they are generous, and they will likely act more generous. Though appropriately considered situational, this thesis does little to impact the effectiveness of a VH approach since it assumes that advocating for virtues within an agent can compel them to demonstrate the characteristics of the virtues. Though philosophically significant, the functional expression of this view does little to diminish the effectiveness of a virtuous approach to textual interpretation.

55. Doris, *Lack of Character*, 58.

evaluation would have us believe."[56] Essentially this argument assumes that the rarity, or general absence, of true virtue in practice argues against both the possibility or usefulness of a virtue approach to epistemology. As the following discussion of how an interpretive agent can develop a virtuous stance to knowing and interpreting demonstrates, this critique that precludes the ability to identify fitting virtuous exemplars is a potentially destructive critique to the model.

Two responses to the situationist's challenge are helpful in building the case for the viability of VH. Nathan King argues that even if the situationist is correct in saying that a truly virtuous agent is exceedingly rare, this need not deconstruct the idea of a virtuous approach to knowing, and by extension in this research, interpreting. "The rarity of the virtues might show that responsibilism does not explain the epistemic behavior of typical epistemic agents. Responsibilism might nevertheless perform useful empirical and regulative functions. For instance, it might predict and explain the epistemic conduct of the most successful epistemic agents—the cognitively privileged '1%.'"[57] The mere fact that one cannot find an unlimited, or even abundant, source of truly virtuous exemplars need not disallow the usefulness of the concept. Rather than damaging the approach, it may support it. In a discipline as rich, textured, complicated, and disputed as hermeneutics, it would seem to be more likely that the most virtuous interpreters whose ingrained and habituated virtuous stance should be relatively difficult to attain, and consequently, at the highest degrees, relatively rare rather than commonplace. The second response comes from Christine Swanton, who argues that virtues need not be perfectionistic to be considered virtues (a recurrent theme in most situational critiques). She argues that virtues exist as a threshold concept, enough of which present in an individual, constitutes being virtuous. A virtue then becomes, "Something to be praised, or as something which is very useful for well-functioning of the agent and/or the wider community. On that conception, in a world characterized by considerable evil, neediness, and frequent catastrophe, less than ideal states may count as virtuous."[58] In Swanton's approach, the idealized concept of a virtuous agent which attains near perfection is not necessary to consider someone genuinely virtuous. In a postlapsarian frame of reference, the concept of a

---

56. Doris, *Lack of Character*, 60.

57. King, "Responsibilist Virtue Epistemology," 250.

58. Swanton, *Virtue Ethics*, 25.

threshold view of virtues seems more tenable and helpful than the overly idealized image that some critics seem to pillory as a straw man. Mc-Dowell's description of virtues as "reliably right judgments" is similar to Swanton's threshold perspective and equally admits far more potentially virtuous interpreters in practice and as exemplars.[59] Rosalind Hursthouse makes a similar case by the examination of poor behaviors, blind spots, or limitations from nearly inescapable social contexts of otherwise ideal moral agents. In her example, the fact that one's forebears may have been generally virtuous but failed in one particular, and historically located matter, need not dismiss the concept that a virtuous agent can still be posited against which a contemporary agent may evaluate his or her actions.[60] If a would-be interpreter is looking for a suitable exemplar and the idea that an idealized and essentially perfectly virtuous individual is the only possible solution, there is little hope for satisfying this condition, but using Swanton, McDowell, and Hursthouses's frameworks allows for a much larger array of potentially virtuous masters for the hermeneutical disciples, thus overcoming the criticisms of situationists.

Apprenticing in the Interpretive Virtues

The development of interpretive virtues, with particular attention to the necessary and fully-integrated motivational component, requires more than the acquisition of justifiable propositions. It seems readily apparent that one can know that, "It is good to be courageous" without being able to summon up actual courage in the face of real danger. Even more fundamentally, one can assent to the idea that courage is good without possessing any desire for courage regardless of any immanent external circumstance. In the realm of interpretation, it is one thing to know that the contemporary extension of the illocutionary impact of an author's text requires carefulness, attention to detail, a love of truth, creativity, and courage while not being gripped by the motivation or practiced habits to carry any of these to completion.[61] The development of proper motivations is tied closely to the experience of emotions. As Amy Coplan

---

59. McDowell, "Virtue and Reason," 342.

60. Hursthouse, *On Virtue Ethics*, 148–50.

61. The concepts of locution (what is said), illocution (what is accomplished by the words), and perlocution (the response elicited from a reader) are borrowed from J. L. Austin's speech-act theories expressed in his work, *How to Do Things with Words* (1962).

concludes, "Moral education must include more than learning what is right and wrong. It must include the training and habituation of our emotions so that they can be conditioned, through practice and experience, to track the appropriate things. Our education, including the stories we are told and the music we listen to, our environment, and the company we keep all matter greatly."[62]

The presence of morality stories—mythical, fictional, and historical—emerging from oral, literary, and artistic sources, involving heroes, saints, and sages all point to the necessity of some form of embodiment of the virtues in suitable exemplars to affectively capture thinking and acting agents with enough force to inspire persistent motivational transformation. [63] These narratively and relationally expressed exemplars become archetypes who inspire descendants who prize their example and add to the influence of their lineage through continued exemplification of their virtuous character. This is another potential overlap between virtue epistemology and Smith's emphasis on testimony as epistemology among pneumatologically-attuned Pentecostals where he sees Pentecostal testimony pointing, "to the irreducibility (and perhaps primacy) of 'narrative knowledge.'"[64] By virtue of testimony, those from any tradition that values the place of retelling one's story create an ongoing traditioned collection of suitable epistemological exemplars and corresponding exemplary qualities. David Brooks observes that, "Moral improvement occurs most reliably when the heart is warmed, when we come into contact with people we admire and love and we consciously and unconsciously bend our lives to mimic theirs."[65] This warming of the heart can be experienced through embodied narrative expression, direct relationship with a living mentor, and, as will be argued in subsequent chapters, spiritual encounters, and it exists as a striking contrast to the purposefully cold and detached ideal of Modernity. J. de Waal Dryden picks up on the same theme that embraces the emotive, or passion, level of seeing the task of hermeneutics by speaking of them as "ordered loves." These ordered loves are observable in a "rubric of right actions, right reasons, and right motivations."[66]

62. Coplan, "Feeling Without Thinking," 147.

63. These are the three classes of moral exemplars that Zagzebski identifies (Zagzebski, *Exemplarist Moral Theory*, 96.)

64. Smith, *Thinking in Tongues*, 62.

65. Brooks, *Road to Character*, xv.

66. de Waal Dryden, *Hermeneutic of Wisdom*, xxii.

A properly attuned sense of interpretive virtue is profoundly influenced by the highly social context of the tutelage of exemplars. Virtue theory is a socially attuned and communicated expression of abiding and stable meta-values, which refuses to descend into the purely relative world of the most radical forms of perspectivalism that characterizes many contemporary frameworks. While different times and cultures may order the virtues differently and include some diversity on their individual periphery, these meta-virtues are nevertheless, "those qualities that have appeared on the greatest number of lists of the virtues in different places and at different times in history."[67] The most influential, epistemological, and interpretive exemplars not only demonstrate these meta-virtues but do so in a way that inspires imitation and, in an Aristotelian frame, emulation.[68]

This need for an embodied and relational context is one of the taproots of the current revival of virtue theory. Kristján Kristjánsson's evaluation of the parallel discipline of ethics is accurate and applicable to virtue epistemology when he argues that, "declining trust in the ability of pure reasoning principles—untethered from experiential association with real people in real situations—to enact lasting changes in the moral make-up of young people," has been the reason for the renewed prominence of virtue theory.[69] This same loss of trust in detached reason and its resultant inability to motivate any lasting stability in the developments of hermeneutics also led to a profound decline in confidence in Modern interpretive sciences. Rudolf Bultmann gives clear expression to this crisis in interpretation in his influential 1925 essay which voiced his form of existential hermeneutics, *"Das Problem einer theologischen Exegese des Neuen Testaments"*: "In all the cases mentioned, the text is viewed at a distance, in the desire to see 'what is there,' with the presupposition that what can be perceived is perceived *only* without reference to one's own position and that it is possible to interpret the text without, at the same time, interpreting its subject matter."[70] Without embracing Bultmann's subsequent demythologizing hermeneutical program, his

---

67. Zagzebski, *Virtues of the Mind*, 89.

68. Kristjánsson defines Aristotle's use of emulation to be "characterized by pain at the moral superiority of a moral exemplar and by a desire to reduce the moral distance to her/him without diminishing the latter's standing in any way ("What Can Moralogy Teach Us," 29).

69. Kristjánsson, "What Can Moralogy Teach Us," 26.

70. Bultmann, "Problem of a Theological Exegesis," loc. 1828.

diagnosis of the problem within Modern hermeneutics is insightful. There is a need, even further, an inescapability, for an embodied experience of the interpretation of the text. While he identified an adaptation of Martin Heidegger's Existentialism as the necessary embodiment, which ultimately proved too individualistic and unnecessarily ahistorical, VH looks to exemplars of intellectual and interpretive virtue, both near and far, to address this need to embody the task of hermeneutics in order to avoid the untenable detachment of Modern hermeneutics.

Many works have already been published that offer glimpses into the fertile field of identifying suitable virtuous interpretive exemplars as it pertains to the biblical domain of the discipline. Briggs offers one of the most detailed treatments of the place of the biblical canon, specifically the OT, as, among many things, an exemplar for virtuous interpretation: "The scriptural texts will have their own particular contribution to make toward one's reflection on the question of what sort of reader one should be. There has to be some kind of hermeneutical give-and-take between text and reader, allowing the reader to work on the text at the same time as the text works on the reader."[71] In the case of a canonical context of hermeneutics, which is the realm of the scriptural task, some understanding of virtues and virtuous interpreters is inherently established by the nature of the canon itself.[72] The corpus of materials within a canon already offers both implicit and explicit commendations of interpretive virtues as the canon expresses approval of particular habits and characteristics of interpreters within the literature,[73] as well as, demonstrating how chronologically later writers within the canon approached the task of interpreting preceding texts.[74] The intent of this section is less focused

71. Briggs, *Virtuous Reader*, 9.

72. In speaking of a "canonical" context in this paragraph, something different and more general than the traditional and theologically loaded meaning is intended. By canonical, the idea of an established and authoritative collection of literature is what is being considered. This definition would include the Bible but could also include collections that are not viewed with the same religious implications (e.g., the Shakesperean canon, the Aristotelian canon, etc.).

73. Stephen Fowl and L. Gregory Jones use the story of Ruth, Boaz, and Naomi as an example of an implicitly narratively expressed exemplification of interpretive virtues in their book, *Reading in Communion*.

74. Using the biblical canon as an example, contemporary students of interpretation can potentially identify and be motivated through emulation and encouragement by the virtuous interpreters and virtuous interpretations woven throughout the biblical canon, (e.g., the speeches of Moses in Deuteronomy as an exemplar of interpretation in the handling of preceding materials from Exodus and Leviticus, the

on the vivisection of the various potential exemplars to identify the particular virtues that they embody and more concerned with the need and impact that such exemplars have in developing the regulative approach to VH. The embodiment of virtues deemed desirable by the canon of literature being interpreted is a very helpful resource in shaping the motivational and actionable interpretive habits of potential interpreters. This is the tightest circle in the virtuous context in seeking for interpretive exemplars. As Stephen Fowl and L. Gregory Jones point out, "While there certainly is a temporal distance between the settings of Scripture and our own, the most important complexities are not historical but moral and theological."[75] If this is true, then the moral values expressed by the text (intellectual and ethical) become central in shaping, through exemplification, the capacity of a reader to transcend the most important forms of distance that exist between text and interpreter. The acknowledgement of a generally recognizable and stable shared core of intellectual virtues between the writer, canon, readers, and reading community serves as a critical common ground that allows understanding to pass between all the interpretive interlocutors.

The use of canonical resources as exemplars for subsequent readers raises the previously addressed issues of frameworks, methodologies, and skills. As has already been established, the categories of frameworks, methodologies, and skills are secondary to the underlying issue of interpretive virtue in seeking to justify a reading of a text. This will neither disallow nor absolutize any of these three categories for contemporary interpreters. The primary issue is the intellectual and interpretive character of the biblical exemplar. By acknowledging the cultural, temporal, and technological differences between the era of the text and the interpreter, VH allows for any individual skill or method used by an ancient canonical interpreter to be acknowledged within the historical particularities of the canon without demanding that they be universally required, or even admitted, in all subsequent interpretive settings. It is the virtuous agent that is more stable and archetypal than the methodology, even when it is methodology that is present within the biblical text. It is the governing

---

various Psalmists' interpretive values as applied to the text of the Torah, the Gospel of Matthew's many interpretively rich usages of OT texts, Paul's interpretive virtues applied to OT and pagan (Acts 17:28) texts, and most influentially within a Christian interpretive context would be the interpretive virtues exemplified in the Gospels in the teaching of Jesus.)

75. Fowl and Jones, *Reading in Communion*, 1.

principle of phronesis that is seen in the virtuous character of the interpretive agent that guides the contemporary hermeneut to deliberate well in the use of pertinent available interpretive resources while not being strictly limited by the Ancient Near Eastern, rabbinical, or Greco-Roman era's techniques. One can observe this in the use of allegory,[76] *pesher*,[77] *midrash*,[78] numerology,[79] and rhetorical schemes.[80] The fact that a canonical interpreter of previous biblical literature virtuously employs the frameworks, methods, and skills common in his era need not *sanctify* their methods for all places and times (of course it should be acknowledged that it does not preclude their use in proper yet distant settings as well). Conversely, the accumulation of further tools and resources available to contemporary interpreters is not incompatible with virtuous interpretation and should not be dismissed simply because they were not available or in vogue during the time of a particular canonical interpreter.

In order to read a text virtuously, in this case the biblical text, one is most attuned to a proper reading when the text is read according to the virtues embedded within it. The hope of this context as a meaningful exemplar is explained by Starling: "An increase in our attentiveness to the interpretive practices of the biblical writers and a readiness to educate our interpretive faculties in light of these practices should work as a healthy corrective to the worst excesses of interpretive arbitrariness and foster a healthier and more faithful interpretive conversation."[81] While acknowledging the potential value of the canonical setting, this emphasis is also susceptible to an immediate critique of circularity. How can one be imprinted upon by the exemplar of interpretive virtues of a text without first interpreting the text from which they are sourced? What is prior? The interpretive virtues of the text or the interpretation of the text? How can one know that one is being moved by the proper virtues exemplified within the text without coming to the text with some pre-understood

---

76. Gal 4:21–31.

77. Matt 3:3.

78. John 6:26–59.

79. Rev 13:18.

80. The manner in which Luke expresses the many speeches of Acts demonstrated the interpretive use of rhetoric in canonical writing. Ben Witherington observes that, "There was thus room for Luke to make his speech source material his own, and to seek to make each summary rhetorically appropriate to the speaker, the occasion, and the subject matter." Witherington, *New Testament Rhetoric*, 46.

81. Starling, *Hermeneutics as Apprenticeship*, 20.

body of interpretive virtues, especially as these virtues are being posited as the proper and necessary ground to justify an interpretation in the first place? Is there an expectation that an interpreter approaches a text as a *tabula rasa* from a virtue perspective until imprinted upon by the text? While the canonical context has been designated in this research as the tightest circle of context in searching for suitable exemplars embodying the virtues in order to interpret that particular canon, this does not mean that it is the only context of virtues that are brought to bear in the reading.

The fundamental problem of circularity as it relates to the interpretive task of a canonical setting is addressed by widening the potential pool of possible exemplars. Beyond the innermost circle of the virtuous interpretive context within a canonical setting, at least two other circles of interpretively virtuous exemplars can be identified. The nearly universal acknowledgement that no interpreter approaches the text from the place of an intellectual vacuum shapes the next circle of exemplars. Anyone who approaches a text to seek to understand it brings with her embedded traditions which also include the tradition's approved intellectual virtues. A "social context is intrinsic to the nature of a virtue as traditionally understood."[82] Roberts and Wood illustrate this reality in the context of what is perceived to be the most Modern, and, presumably, least socially-traditioned setting, the physical sciences. "Even solo epistemic practices have a social dimension: the laboratory scientist will belong to a tradition of experimentation."[83]

At this level's most restrictive perspective, there exists a social circle that embodies the interpretive tradition of the most immediate Christian tradition that a would-be hermeneut would encounter. This circle of virtuous context admits an array of potential exemplars that have been shaped in the long tradition of biblical interpretation. While the biblical text predates most of the interpreters who would be considered potential interpreters from within the tradition, these exemplars from the Christian context often form a functionally prior cohort of virtue communication for most readers. Before reading with the intention of understanding and applying the biblical text, most contemporary interpreters are influenced by the virtuous tradition, and by exemplars within the tradition, that are present within the particular dogmatic or experiential tradition within which they are most closely associated (e.g., Liberal, Reformed,

82. Zagzebski, *Virtues of the Mind*, 43.
83. Roberts and Wood, *Intellectual Virtues*, 114.

Lutheran, Evangelical, Pentecostal, Anabaptist, Eastern Orthodox, Roman Catholic, etc.). The loci for these virtuous exemplars to exert influence on interpretive protégés is multiple, diverse, and powerful. With the rise of postmodern thought, "Scholars have started to recognize the central role communities play in the formation of character."[84] The selection of texts used, manner of application, and often-told stories of a tradition embody the taxonomy of interpretive virtues that a community, and its interpretive exemplars, prize in approaching the text.

As an example, any interpreter who is influenced by traditional Protestant virtues will be shaped by the value of intellectual courage as it pertains to hermeneutics. While each subset of Protestantism would be capable of offering a suitable exemplar, one need only look as far as the father of the movement to find an archetypal figure and moment. In the late afternoon of Monday, April 18, 1521, at a trial convened in the town of Worms in modern-day Germany, one of the great embodiments of intellectual and interpretive virtues was played out in vivid expression. Having been pressed by Johann Eck, acting as the spokesman of the Holy Roman Emperor, Charles V, to self-identify his works as heretical, Martin Luther refused to recant his writings that gave rise to and nurtured the nascent Reformation. In his famous response, he declared,

> Unless I am convinced by the testimony of the Scriptures or by clear reason (for I do not trust either in the pope or in councils alone, since it is well known that they have often erred and contradicted themselves), I am bound by the Scriptures I have quoted and my conscience is captive to the Word of God. I cannot and will not recount anything, since it is neither safe nor right to go against conscience. May God help me. Amen.

Or more succinctly, and possibly apocryphally, "Here I stand, I can do no other, so help me God, amen." The whole of Protestantism, including the most extreme poles of the community (e.g., liberalism and fundamentalism), have embraced this celebration of the courageous interpreter who will not be swayed by political pressure, theological dogma, or any form of coercion once convinced of the intent of the text.

It is this elevation of the virtue of intellectual courage that has been disseminated through the tradition in this story's multiplied retellings. While a valued virtue within the tradition, it serves as a fitting caution against isolating any individual virtue from the holistic concept of the

84. Fowl and Jones, *Reading in Communion*, 9.

virtuous agent. In isolation from the other virtues and the general application of phronesis, this appeal to intellectual courage has also been the source of the fragmentation and radical individualization that has plagued the Protestant tradition since Luther. Out of this tradition, philosophers could prod individuals "To think for oneself,"[85] theologians were free to open a perilous ditch between uncertain historical contingencies and potential eternal truths,[86] or seminaries were established upon the foundation that "the Christian religion should be proclaimed without fear or favor and in clear opposition to whatever opposes it, whether from within or without the church, as the only way of salvation for lost mankind."[87] What seems to be most significant is that the courage to hold to one's interpretation even at great personal, professional, and physical cost is deeply embedded into the virtuous structure of Protestant interpretive virtues. This is not to comment on the greatly varied methodologies, skills, and frameworks that have grown up within discrete segments of the broadest tradition (as is evidenced by the diverse collection of voices alluded to earlier in this paragraph), but simply to acknowledge that the intrepid interpreters who bravely stand for the truth that they believe they have discovered are highly revered figures in the history of Protestant thought.

Still within this circle of the traditioned context is a further expanded view to include those who exist beyond the strict confines of one's own narrowest stream of Christian tradition (e.g., Protestantism). Biblical interpretation has a long tradition that transcends any singular denomination or theological framework. Within this broadest tradition, contemporary interpreters can identify the outlines of the ideal of a virtuous interpreter. In this frame, the challenges of circularity that attend to the canonical level of context can be overcome as the broader social and theological traditions prepare interpreters to engage the text from a place of acknowledged pre-interpretive virtuous values that have been modeled, prized, and passed on through generations of readings of the text. Yong addresses how a theological interpretive approach attempts to accomplish this form of traditioned reading. Even to the level of terminology, his explanation demonstrates significant affinity for a virtuous model of traditioned exemplars. He says the process should

---

85. Kant, *Critique of Judgement*, loc. 2630.

86. Lessing, "On the Proof of the Spirit and of Power," 87.

87. Machen, "Westminster Theological Seminary," 8–9.

emphasize that sacred texts ought to be read in accordance with the ecclesial practices that generated these canonical writings to begin with, and that therefore contemporary readers were best advised to adopt these traditioned postures and their related interpretive habits. Doing so would not just nurture sensibilities and instincts required for faithful interpretation but also enable the reparative practices for Christian life and witness attested to in the Scripture.[88]

The final circle to be explored includes the broadest possible context of human thinking and interpretive activity. As reflected in the primary thesis of this research, the idea that the general context of epistemology is the proper starting point for repairing the current confusion within the field of hermeneutics emerges naturally because it is often the most pronounced source of the interpretive science's most persistent problems. Textual interpretation and the general pursuit of knowledge are not limited specifically to the biblical context or biblically shaped community. It is reasonable to expect that interpreters may bring with them a collection of innate excellencies of thinking and interpreting honed by practice that would be applicable to the various discrete domains of knowing. These domains include general literary and specifically biblical textual interpretation without a pre-existing commitment to the canonically-expressed intellectual virtues. If true, this circle of context helps to mitigate against the claims of a self-destroying circularity within a VH approach.

Is it possible for exemplars to exist in virtuous interpretive practices that can be applied within the biblical context that are embodied in individuals entirely separate from the community shaped by the canonical text? Is it possible to observe virtuous tendencies and behaviors in those who are removed from the confessional or regenerate community? Briggs addresses this issue:

> Scripture is not a closed book to those not yet virtuous enough to behold in it what is written. Such a critique is often aimed at virtue-oriented approaches to biblical interpretation. It is suggested that they seem to require the work of moral formation to take place in the interpreter as a self-contained project, now conceived of as a kind of entrance requirement to the task of reading the Bible in the first place. Clearly this is not right.[89]

88. Yong, *Hermeneutical Spirit*, loc. 175.
89. Briggs, *Virtuous Reader*, 99.

The Apostle Paul leaves open this possibility in his discussion of the universal guilt of humanity in light of the demands of divine righteousness. He admits that, "When Gentiles, who do not have the law, do by nature things required by the law, they are a law for themselves, even though they do not have the law. They show that the requirements of the law are written on their hearts, their consciences also bearing witness, and their thoughts sometimes accusing them and at other times even defending them."[90] The biblical framework acknowledges that though potentially diminished, the fallen human mind and heart still possess a meaningful residual echo of the moral witness of its Creator. Just as human beings are capable, even in a fallen state, of nurturing elements of virtue that correspond to the divine *telos* of humanity,[91] so also, it remains possible that humans still possess a noetic capacity for intellectually virtuous activity apart from the regenerative context.[92]

Roberts and Wood admit this possibility in the formulation of their responsibilist epistemology: "These powers are innate, given with our nature as human beings," even though innate does not necessarily "imply possession by every individual human being; it implies possession by every normal individual."[93] This present, even if darkened and limited, possession of virtuous capacities opens the possibility of outsiders possessing some form of justifiable understanding of reality, including that of texts. Plantinga does not use the specific terminology of virtues, but his discussion of the broad and narrow elements of the image of God within humanity fits in this discussion. Although the narrow sense of the image of God, which afforded humanity extensive and intimate knowledge of God, and the right affections, has been "nearly destroyed"

90. Rom 2:14–15.

91. Paul admits this reality as well when he declares in his unregenerate state he was "blameless" concerning the righteousness contained in the Law of God (Phil 3:6).

92. It is important to note that it is a different matter to acknowledge the residual thinking and acting capacities of human beings in line with divine righteousness without extending this discussion into soteriological contexts. Humanity's ability to, on occasions, still pursue knowledge and even potentially act in morally right ways does not erase the ultimate need for salvation as the free gift of God in Christ. The focus of this research at this point is to demonstrate that interpreters have the possibility of possessing some rudimentary and innate interpretive virtues that can be nurtured through the observation of cultural exemplars when approaching the reading of a text which is not strictly dependent on the embedded virtues within the examined text. No argument of the human capacity to earn or attain regeneration by human means is implied by this argument.

93. Roberts and Wood, *Intellectual Virtues*, 85.

by sin, the broad sense which "involves our resembling God in being persons—that is, beings with intellect and will remains more intact. Like God, we have intellect. There is also will, however: we also resemble God in having affection (loves and hates), in forming aims and intentions, and in being able to act to accomplish these aims and intentions."[94] This broad image "was damaged, distorted" but not eradicated.[95] On account of this, it is apparent that all divine image bearers, albeit deeply affected by sin, still have the capacity to rightly pursue and attain epistemological products, properly deemed to be knowledge. To deny this possibility is to deny any and all intellectual achievements except by those who are within regenerate community. While some, including Cornelius Van Til, have subscribed to this form of extreme view in his Reformed Christian Epistemology, "Any theory of knowledge based upon principles acceptable per se to the 'mind of the flesh,' . . . is doomed to utter failure; not only failure as an avenue to Christian faith, but as an avenue to any form of knowledge whatsoever,"[96] this view seems unwarranted, unhelpful, and pragmatically unsustainable in a world filled with properly ascribed knowledge by all sorts of knowing agents (regenerate and unregenerate). VH acknowledges that some level of virtuous intellectual and interpretive character may be present and active in readers outside of one's own theological or metaphysical community.

In examining the three circles of context in which exemplars may be identified, several important matters can be acknowledged. First, the criticism that VH begs the question by locating interpretive virtues within the body of canonical literature, like Briggs does in *The Virtuous Reader*, is addressed by expanding the horizon of potential virtuous exemplars to the interpretive community subsequently developed beyond the canon, as well as, to the broadest and best examples of the human intellectual community and its activity. Second, the pool of exemplars, while not limitless, is more accessible than many critiques seem to allow. Ultimately, Battaly is correct in observing that, "Even if there are relatively few exemplars around who fully possess the nearly global virtues, there are likely to be some agents around who are closer to fully possessing the nearly global virtues than we are."[97] For the naïve or develop-

---

94. Plantinga, *Knowledge and Christian Belief*, 47.

95. Plantinga, *Knowledge and Christian Belief*, 47.

96. Van Til, *Defense of Christianity and My Credo*.

97. Battaly, *Virtue*, 158.

ing interpreter, there will be more than enough relatively more virtuous interpreters from whom to draw formative and impactful influence. The further one advances in the process of attaining and habituating the virtues, the fewer exemplars there will be to observe, but even in this place, there will be those who have advanced further in virtue attainment to look to as the embodiment of desirable intellectual character. Finally, it is right to observe that the entire system of identifying and being shaped through inspiration and emulation at the feet of virtuous exemplars confronts a primary deficiency of many modern literate cultures. The idea of the individual scholar who reads and studies in isolation and silence a fixed printed text does not fit within the VH approach. A virtue approach is more attuned to the social and communal setting of reading; it is more sensitive to the concepts of wisdom often embodied in an oral context than in the more individualized literate settings of the modern Western academy. Walter Ong's groundbreaking research on orality and literacy exposes this reality,

> Human beings in primary oral cultures, those untouched by writing in any form, learn a great deal and possess and practice great wisdom, but they do not 'study'. They learn by apprenticeship—hunting with experienced hunters, for example—by discipleship, which is a kind of apprenticeship, by listening, by repeating what they hear, by mastering proverbs and ways of combining and recombining them, by assimilating other formulary materials, by participation in a kind of corporate retrospection—not by study in the strictest sense.[98]

The exemplars are not simply scholars; they are wise and experienced models who are relationally encountered rather than coldly examined. This type of apprenticeship is the prescribed model of virtue attainment. Ong's words serve as useful concepts to capture the manner by which an exemplar can transmit a virtuous interpretive framework to a willing and desirous learner: hunting with (which would be *interpreting with* in this setting), discipling, listening, repeating, mastering proverbs, assimilating, participating in corporate retrospection.

Having acknowledged that three circles of context exist where potential virtuous exemplars can be identified that can both shape future interpreters as well as rescue VH from falling into a trap of destructive circularity, it is necessary to recognize one further characteristic of these

98. Ong, *Orality and Literacy*, 8.

contexts. The interpretive virtues do not stand in contrast to each other between the various contexts. Acknowledging that the innermost circle is drawn from the canonical context should not be taken as a statement that what exists in this circle is fundamentally different than what exists within in the outermost circle. At most, the differences in the various contexts are matters of emphasis and, potentially, priority between the various circles. The choice of the image of concentric circles is intentional. All the virtues contained in the two inner circles are also contained in the more general epistemological circle. They are elucidated more clearly and illustrated more sharply as it pertains to the interpretive text being examined as one moves toward the canonical center, but it is the recognition that the virtues are stable, broad, and recognizable in settings that may be dramatically diverse in many other respects (e.g., language, culture, worldview, and temporal location) that helps to identify the traits as being virtues in the first place. Zagzebski's definition deserves repeating that virtues are, "those qualities that have appeared on the greatest number of lists of the virtues in different places and at different times in history."[99] It is entirely unsurprising, and very supportive of this research, that the virtues in the epistemological context are also identifiable in the traditioned and canonical contexts as well. This reality also allows interlocutors from confessional, academic, and even antagonistic frameworks to contribute some forms of useful understanding in interpreting a text, since the best and most justifiable interpreters are drawing from a common pool of interpretive virtues.

One final explanation is necessary before concluding the discussion of the place of exemplars in the development of virtuous interpreters. The natural tendency in a discussion like the preceding material is to desire the listing of suitable exemplars by name. Are Karl Barth, Rudolf Bultmann, Friedrich Schleiermacher, D. A. Carson, Kevin Vanhoozer, or Gordon Fee virtuous or vicious? It is neither bold nor controversial to proclaim, in a Christian context, the exemplary status of Jesus, Moses, or Paul as virtuous interpreters, so the following discussion only explores the reasoning for avoiding naming either widely known or generally obscure extra-canonical interpreters. This choice to avoid naming names is not novel. Aristotle remained silent in naming possible virtuous agents in the *Nicomachean Ethics* who could be embodiments of his philosophy. While the exact reasons for Aristotle's silence in this matter are beyond

---

99. Zagzebski, *Virtues of the Mind*, 89.

easy identification from his text, there are at least seven important reasons why this desire for specific names, while unsurprising, is not entirely helpful in the light of this research.

(1) To name any particular virtuous exemplar by name, it would be expected to seek to name a globally virtuous individual. While this research leaves open the possibility of this agent existing, at best, it should be admitted that they would be very rare and, likely, on account of their virtues, eschew their identification as the globally virtuous model for all would-be hermeneuts. (2) While a careful reading of the VH model acknowledges the inability to universalize methods, skills, or frameworks, and also admits to the inability of reaching what may be determined to be the final, ultimate, and certain interpretation of a text, the inevitable tendency would be to attempt to ascribe some level of these attainments to the hermeneutical produce of someone labelled as the ideal virtuous interpreter. Even the most virtuous interpreter may occasionally fall short in her task of a justified understanding of a text either by virtue of noetic limitations or bad interpretive luck. A virtuous interpreter is more likely to attain, in the longitudinal frame, the most justified understanding of a text, but this is no guarantee, nor does it need to be. (3) Being virtuous does not necessarily equate to being notable or marketable in contemporary settings. Success in interpretive endeavors is required for one to be a virtuous interpreter, but success does not always equate with fame or notoriety. In a global society, recognition may be as dependent upon one's ability to generate a social media buzz as it is related to the virtuous nature of one's intellectual character or the explanatory excellence of one's interpretive understandings. It may also be related to timing, luck, novelty, geographic location, or capitalistic concerns like revenue-generating capacity. All these preceding matters may contribute to success by certain measures but have little to no connection to the quality of the interpretation or virtue of the agent. It is entirely possible that truly virtuous, even globally virtuous interpreters, may be little known outside the immediate context of their influence due to a variety of factors. For the naming of a potential exemplar to be of value in a research project as a means to represent an ideal, there would need to be some level of recognition and acquaintance with both the character and the production of the individual, at least within the community of serious interpreters. Further research beyond this specific work could highlight a potentially virtuous exemplar, but that would almost certainly need to be a stand-alone volume rather than the dropping of a name within a broader work.

(4) Another reason to resist naming individuals (especially beyond the canonical context) is the great value of relationship in framing the exemplar's influence with a protégé. As the author of this research, I have been shaped by the intellectual character of many important individuals. In my journey as an interpreter, I have been privileged to read the writings of, hear, sit in classrooms with, collaborate with, and be corrected by many that stand out as exemplars in my maturation. Most of these names would do little to inspire the development of virtue in others regardless of the virtuosity of their interpretive character since the experience of guided practice requires a close connection and can accomplish more than a list of names with a brief synopsis could ever accomplish. (5) While virtue as deeply-ingrained character traits offers the hope of something more stable across time, culture, language, and geography than rules or skills, it is still susceptible to the potential frailty of human agents. If a person were inscribed in a text as being an exemplar, only to have a previously hidden intellectual character flaw exposed, the temptation to use this singular example as a means to discredit the value of the entire program is too high. More would be gained by simply focusing on the worthy traits of virtuous agents while leaving the identification of specific exemplars to the emerging protégés. (6) By concretizing the exemplar by name, the emphasis too easily becomes enmeshed in a singular personality rather than the transcendent body of virtuous character traits that the individual possesses. The goal of virtue exemplification is inspiration and emulation to a type of intellectual character, not the precursor to an unattainable hagiography. Finally, (7) In citing a potentially renowned and sufficiently notable individual who exists in the minds of many as some form of exemplar, or even, interpretive genius, there is the risk of extending the possibility of emulation beyond a motivating factor into a demotivator. Not everyone can or will achieve the fame, market share, and depth of insight that specific and notable interpretive superstars may possess (to borrow King's aforementioned phrase, the privileged interpretive 1 percent). If the protégé is continually comparing herself to unattainable standards, especially considering that many of these factors have little to do with the mentoring of interpretive virtues, the process can be destroyed in discouragement and distance rather than being encouraging and inspiring. For these reasons, it is advisable to focus on the traits and not the potential names of possible exemplars.

Habituation in the Interpretive Virtues

While proper exemplars are necessary to the development of a virtuous interpreter, it is not sufficient in itself. Borrowing from the Aristotelian frame, habituation of the virtues is a process that requires both time and experience along with the presence of exemplars "who explain their actions and motivations."[100] Practice and repetition are necessary to acquire any complex trait or skill and integrate it into one's persona. One cannot expect to virtuously handle a text without having a practiced approach that regularly employs an intellectually virtuous starting point. The necessity of practice and repetition raises the more important consideration in the process of habituation of the stages of the development of a virtuous interpretive character.

Just like the stages of practicing any complex skill or trait, the process is marked by demarcations of development. The experience of learning keyboarding is a helpful example. Any individual with at least one finger, a suitable vocabulary, and the ability to recognize the characters of the alphabet can use a traditional QWERTY keyboard to communicate thoughts.[101] The rudimentary "hunt and peck" method works, albeit slowly and disjointedly. If one sets oneself to the task of learning a more efficient manner of keyboarding, the process begins as a laborious task that has embedded within it the hope of a positive potential outcome of increased speed and accuracy. When first learning the proper placement of the fingers, the pressing of each particular key by an appropriate finger, and the ability to string letters into words, each step is consciously and deliberately enacted, often by the force of the will. Early in the process, every step is painfully efforted with fingers that must be individually and consciously compelled to do their assigned tasks. Even after gaining some proficiency in proper technique, there is a tendency to abandon the better method of keyboarding for the temporary comfort of the old "hunt and peck" method, especially under pressure by a concern for time

---

100. Battaly, *Virtue*, 153.

101. After previously discussing the differences between skills and virtues and decidedly affirming their status as distinct matters, the question can be raised whether the following analogy is appropriate or cogent. In comparing the acquisition of a skill like keyboarding to the acquisition of intellectual virtues, the primary overlap between skills and virtues is highlighted, the necessity of practiced habituation. It is this shared practiced acquisition that is often the cause and justification for inappropriately equating virtues and skills. The following analogy is not creating a comprehensive equating of the two categories but using the shared nature of being practiced as a useful illustration.

or desire for ease. This can overpower what one knows to ultimately be the better method. With more practice, the strokes become more natural and less forced, but they still require conscious awareness of the process, and a willful determination to not slip back into the bad habits. Finally, after a lengthy process of guided practice and consistent repetition, each keystroke becomes the nearly automatic expression of the trained mind and hands. The keyboardist need not consciously or willfully consider the process, but simply follow the well-trained and habituated skill. In the end, the speed, accuracy, and ease of keyboarding feel natural. The progression from untrained to weakly trained to self-disciplined, and, ultimately, to mastery is mirrored in the process of developing appropriate interpretive virtues within the knowing agent. True attainment of the virtue is less about mastering rules, but far more about developing the "feel" of the experience through repeatedly practicing the right things, the right ways, for the right reasons.

Hookway extends this even further, suggesting that a properly-tuned virtuous epistemic agent is observed not only in the actions taken, but in the "considerations and questions that emerge as salient in the course of practical deliberation that lead up to action or that monitor it."[102] In this way, the virtuous agent's actions and responses appear almost natural and automatic, but only because the virtues have become so ingrained and habituated that they not only guide the activity but even the admittance of what matters are truly salient to the project at hand. The more deeply habituated the intellectual virtue, the more it appears to be "natural," when in truth, it is the highest expression of truly acquired virtue. Just as an excellent keyboardist appears to automatically and naturally generate text by the well-trained fingers when they are simply demonstrating the highest level of practiced and ingrained skill, so also the truly virtuous interpreter is able to produce wise, understanding, and justified interpretations almost naturally because the ingrained virtues direct not only the act of interpretation, but the almost immediate evaluation of what to consider salient in the project. It is important to not confuse the idea of "natural" or "immediate" in reference to the directive force of the properly habituated virtuous interpretive character to mean the actual work of interpreting itself is easy or somehow intuitive. Interpreting, even virtuously (maybe especially virtuously), will call for diligence, and at times hard work and time-consuming effort, in dealing with the specific

---

102. Hookway, "Epistemic Norms and Theoretical Deliberation," 395.

questions of a text, but the willingness to consider the right things in the right ways will be the natural tendency of a virtuous agent. An interpretive agent who possesses a highly tuned level of the virtue of phronesis, the practiced ability to recognize matters of saliency in the interpretive acts, deliberates effectively what considerations in a particular text bear the greatest importance to gaining understanding and then applies the proper attention, skill, and effort to produce effective hermeneutical products. This stage of attainment is not gained immediately or without significant effort and practice.

Zagzebski summarizes the Aristotelian stages as naïve imitation (mimesis), inconsistent application of the virtues in a phase described as akrasia, self-control (which is characterized by doing the right things but only with concerted effort, sometimes against one's own immediate desires), and the final stage of possessing the virtues as an individual who exhibits genuine phronesis and attains Aristotle's ideal of consistently acting from a "firm and unchangeable character."[103] This staged development of the virtues is first expressed in the context of moral virtues, is extended to the intellectual virtues by epistemologists like Zagzebski, Battaly, Hookway, and others, and is applied into the realm of interpretive endeavors in this research. This entire process is the expression of how the virtues become habituated in an agent's life. From this vantage point, the process is compatible with theistic or naturalistic models of development. But as will be demonstrated in the final chapter, theological interpretation not only admits, but properly exposes, the limitedness of this process apart from a pneumatological contribution that overcomes the inescapable noetic effects of humanity's fall into sin.

The aforementioned stages are readily recognizable in a VH model of education. In the earliest stage of naïve mimesis, an interpreter may attain an accurate understanding of a text by following the technique, and even more importantly, the virtuous approach of a more advanced exemplar. The learner still exists as a naïve interpreter because she engages in the task not from an embedded sense of virtue, but only in imitation of one who does. This naturally diminishes the justifiability of the interpretation even if it does not change its explanatory scope. As previously expressed, justification flows from the interpretive agent to the interpretation. When the practices are engaged out of a secondary imitation of a virtuous agent

---

103. Zagzebski, *Virtues of the Mind,* 150; Aristotle, *Nicomachean Ethics,* loc. 718.

rather than a first-level virtuous approach, the interpretation may still possess a form of justification, but one that is diminished.

In reading a text, a naïve learner may employ many virtuous qualities like attentiveness, open-mindedness, courage, justice, perseverance, and creativity, after observing a virtuous and effective interpreter in practice. The differences between the two are not always recognizable on the surface, but they are important in the development of a virtuous hermeneut. Motivation, stability, and habituation may either be wholly lacking or selectively lacking in an act of pure mimesis. It is possible for a person who does not possess a virtue to act in a way fully characteristic of that virtue (e.g., a cowardly man may act in a courageous way like he has observed a truly courageous individual do, but only to impress onlookers and not out of courage like the genuinely courageous exemplar).[104] It is the deficiency in abiding motivation or stability in acting from the properly motivated virtue that limits the ongoing justification of the naïve interpreter's work product. The limiting of his or her action to mimesis affords no confidence that the current or any future interpretation will reflect a consistent implementation of the virtuous frame, unlike the truly virtuous agent who reliably functions from the proper motivational and generally successful center of interpretive virtue.

At the *enkratic* stage, the interpreter may recognize the worthiness of the practices and motivations that characterize a truly virtuous hermeneut and even desire to attain the same level of interpretive maturity, but he does not yet possess the fixity of character that marks true virtue. Influences, desires, emotions, and circumstances can overpower what may be a genuine desire to consistently engage a text from a virtuous frame. This stage is characterized by the weakness of the virtue's presence in an interpreter, not its absence. By possessing the virtue in a weakened sense, this interpreter is still more advanced than the one who simply imitates someone else who possesses the virtue. The *enkratic* interpreter potentially falls prey to multiple weaknesses. It is *enkratic* to accept evidence that one knows to be insufficient or inaccurate in interpreting a text simply because the evidence supports a desired interpretive outcome or preserves an otherwise inadequate paradigm. This is the situation described by Yehezkel Kaufmann in his monumental work, *The Religion of Israel, from Its Beginnings to the Babylonian Exile*, as it pertained to the

---

104. Wallace, *Virtues and Vices*, 53.

willingness to accept the conclusions of the Graf-Wellhausen Documentary Hypothesis long after the evidence ceased to support it:

> Wellhausen's arguments complemented each other nicely, and offered what seemed to be a solid foundation upon which to build the house of biblical criticism. Since then, however, both the evidence and the arguments supporting the structure have been called into question and, to some extent, even rejected. Yet biblical scholarship, while admitting that the grounds have crumbled away, nevertheless continues to adhere to the conclusions.[105]

Even when the foundations of an interpretive framework were undermined by evidence, both historical and linguistic, some interpreters persisted in adhering to it. The failure to be open-minded to evidence, humble to admit a need for realignment, and courageous enough to break with dominant but outdated academic hegemony are all examples of interpretive *akrasia*. Other examples of *akrasia* could include the willingness to overstate evidence, failure to investigate a pertinent matter for interpretation out of laziness or boredom, a rejection of an interpretation based on bias or prejudice, or shaping interpretation on the basis of perceived popularity or unpopularity rather than on sound explanatory foundations of understanding.

The final stage before attaining the threshold of virtuous interpretation is self-discipline. Unlike the *enkratic* stage, this interpreter does not fall prey to the weaknesses as often or as easily. What differentiates this individual from a truly virtuous interpreter? Zagzebski offers this explanation:

> At this stage a person has to stop herself from accepting inadequate or poor testimony or lapsing into ways of speaking or reasoning of which she disapproves. But, unlike the previous stage, she does it successfully. Still, she lacks the virtue because she finds it difficult to weigh evidence properly or judge authority reliably or reason with care and according to the rules. Her behavior may be correct, but it is not grounded in a 'firm and unchangeable character.'[106]

Virtue requires the right actions for the right reasons. This reliably produces right outcomes, but as implied in the preceding quote, one more element may also be embedded that a purely self-disciplined individual fails to attain. The virtuous interpreter delights in the experience of

105. Kaufmann, *Religion of Israel*, 1.
106. Zagzebski, *Virtues of the Mind*, 155.

justified interpretation. This joy, which may correspond to Aristotle's prized *eudaimonia*, contributes to the character of the virtuous agent. The self-disciplined agent has progressed a considerable distance in the work of VH, but the absence of the deeply ingrained and joyous experience of the practice leaves the endeavor just short of the full justifying capacity that emanates from the virtuous interpreter.

Conclusion

The program to develop VH involves both an understanding of the goal to be attained and a prescribed manner to attain it. It begins at a level prior to the actual investigation of the text itself. VH begins with the development of the interpretive agent as the foundational step. VH is intended to be a regulative program that addresses the frameworks or methods of delving into a text as the secondary step that emerges as the agent first develops and matures in the interpretive character. Ultimately, VH serves to identify the kind of interpreting agent who is most likely to engage the text in ways that will tend to the most justifiable understandings. The process of affecting the proper change and development in an interpretive agent's intellectual character is a long journey that is not easily attained. The identification of proper exemplars who inspire is a primary step. They inspire not only by the quality of their interpretive product (both in justifiability and depth of understanding), but most importantly by the nature of their intellectual character. These exemplars perform their work well, for the right reason, and in the right ways. Undoubtedly, a good exemplar will have much to offer in the way of acquisition of skills and adopting of frameworks, but their most difficult and necessary work impacts the motivational core of a virtuous interpreter. By their example, an apprentice experiences the powerful influence to not only value that which is good and leads to the most justifiable interpretive product, but they also instill passion, joy, and the motivational-core of the task as well. Once a would-be hermeneut is apprenticed to appropriate mentors, the ongoing task of moving from imitator, to weakly virtuous, to self-disciplined, and finally to a virtuous interpreter is accomplished by guided practice and ongoing habituation in virtues, motivations, actions, and skills.

Paul Herman presents an interesting application of virtue theory in the development of scholars in the discipline of history (a field that is itself a specific form of interpretation similar in many ways to biblical interpretation). He speaks of the foundational need to develop virtuous intellectual character traits. These traits transcend the domain of professional pursuits, be they history or biblical interpretation. "The attitudes, character traits, and abilities that scholarly personae cultivate accompany scholars when they leave the office."[107] One cannot truly develop intellectual or interpretive virtues in total isolation from the rest of one's thinking and acting life, but the presence of intellectual virtue, absent skills, frameworks, and methods appropriate to the discipline being discussed, is not longitudinally successful (or even virtuous). Scholars "also need qualities of skill in order to be recognizable" as a scholar in a particular field.[108] This is where he delineates between the virtues on one hand and the skills on the other to combine into an overall scholarly persona. This persona comes to maturity in the stages of development through guided practice. As one combines a virtuous character with the properly nurtured skills, defined by Baehr as, "A kind of competence: essential to their possession is an ability to perform a certain task,"[109] they emerge with a persistent and recognizable persona as a virtuous interpreter.

Returning to our case of Brutus, the development of a VH approach informs what could be done to help him become a better interpreter of the biblical text, but it involves the shaping of his entire persona. He must become not only a better thinker and a more skilled reader, but he must also become a better person. The task of developing a virtuous hermeneut who possess a persona that leads to the most likely outcome of justified understanding of a text is a comprehensive program that addresses the holistic nature of the interpretive agent; his work as an interpreter cannot be divorced from his character (intellectual and ethical) and his interpretive practices. If Brutus's fundamental problem exists in his intellectual/interpretive character, then he must begin by finding a more advanced virtuous exemplar to whom he may apprentice himself. He can and should pursue these exemplars in the canonical text, the traditioned and even more generalized context of interpreters who are virtuous in interpretation as well as the pragmatic understanding of thinking and living well in general (phronesis). Before he will read well, he must be motivated to read well. Before he can understand better, he must have an inner transformation of desires, motivations, emotions, and belief-forming

---

107. Herman, "What Is a Scholarly Persona?," 355.

108. Herman, "What Is a Scholarly Persona?," 360.

109. Baehr, *Inquiring Mind*, loc. 407.

processes. These tasks are first mirrored by observing others and then developed in consistent and practiced habituation. Brutus can advance, but it must be a comprehensive approach that looks beyond simply "trying harder" or "being more careful." The interpretive persona demands a more ingrained intellectual character that shapes the practice by the development of proper skills and, ultimately, the engagement of the text. The question for Brutus at this point is the same question that confronts the detailing of VH: what are the virtues that are uniquely suited to the task of interpretation? The need to move Brutus beyond generalized ideas to specific intellectual character traits requires a deeper understanding of what comprises a virtuous interpretive character.

THREE

Interpretive Virtues

Introduction

IN THE LONG AND diverse history of biblical interpretation, the words of the Qoheleth seem particularly relevant: "What has been is what will be, and what has been done is what will be done, and there is nothing new under the sun."[1] There is likely nothing that can be inserted into the field of hermeneutics that cannot find some precedent. As a result, the connection between virtues and interpretation is not an entirely novel concept. Some find an echo of virtuous interpretation in the guiding principle of Augustine's hermeneutics. In his work, *On Christian Teaching,* he establishes a virtue, love, as the deciding influence in interpretive matters. "Therefore in dealing with figurative expressions we will observe a rule of this kind: the passage being read should be studied with careful consideration until its interpretation can be connected with the realm of love. If this point is made literally, then no kind of figurative expression need be considered."[2] Love is considered a virtue in both ethical and epistemological domains. Whether Augustine's use is aligned with the epistemological use, and correspondingly, a VH usage, is a debatable matter. It seems that he uses the ethical concept of love as a pre-understood limitation to admissible potentialities in interpretation. Though a demonstration of a connection to the broadest ideas of virtue theory, Augustine's

1. Eccl 1:9.
2. Augustine, *On Christian Teaching,* 80.

love-condition fails to capture the intent of VH since it does not guide the regulative approach to intellectual and interpretive work.

More recently, Vanhoozer, clearly echoing the epistemologist, Zagzebski, points to a more plausible and helpful intersection between virtue theory and interpretive activities.[3] "When readers display interpretive virtue, their cognitive capacities exemplify not merely proper function but *excellence*."[4] He then lists seven virtues that characterize how an interpreter can handle a text *ethically*. His list of faith, hope, and love, which he acknowledges are taken directly from the biblical text and have been traditionally called the theological virtues,[5] are combined with more epistemologically derived virtues of honesty, openness, attention, and obedience. Whether dealing with the domain of philosophy or hermeneutics, the inevitable trajectory of virtue studies arcs toward some descriptive list of what counts as virtue, just as Vanhoozer does in his work. Nearly every major work of virtue epistemology contains some list of what qualifies as an intellectual virtue. Most of these lists have significant, and occasionally, complete overlap between the diverse collection of authors. Rather than viewing these lists as the ends to be pursued in themselves, it is better to see them as Hasselberger describes them,

> as generic principles of conduct . . . taken to be abstractions or generalizations drawn from the conceptually prior, and far subtler, ethical understanding embodied in a virtuous agent's character, including her characteristic patterns of attention and emotional response, and her sense of what matters, and of how to act well, in a heterogeneous range of particular circumstances.[6]

One does not become virtuous by pursuing a list, but in identifying that which is the most excellent dispositions that characterize the most creditable agents in a particular domain of intellectual pursuit. Roberts and Wood agree: "It seems to us that the motive characteristic of a virtue is in no case, or almost no case, the desire to have the virtue."[7] The lists are helpful in summarizing and propositionalizing that which ultimately

---

3. Vanhoozer defines interpretive virtues as a disposition of the mind and heart that arises from the motivation for understanding, for cognitive contact with the meaning of the text. Zagzebski had previously defined.

4. Vanhoozer, *Is There a Meaning in This Text?*, 377.

5. 1 Cor 13:13.

6. Hasselberger, "Knowing More," 775.

7. Roberts and Wood, *Intellectual Virtues*, 76.

exists, ideally, as an embodied reality. With this understanding, it still seems necessary to give further shape to the idea of VH by identifying pertinent virtues that are exemplified by the virtuous interpreter.

Vanhoozer's list is cited as a starting point for several reasons. Firstly, it is the earliest application of the contemporary iteration of RVE into the discipline of biblical hermeneutics. Secondly, it expresses the hybridity of canonical and epistemological sourcing and expression that generally aligns with this research. Thirdly, it remains representative of other lists that have emerged subsequent to his work in *Is There a Meaning in This Text?* (1996).

While useful as a starting point, his list is not sufficient for the development of VH. His treatment of the virtues as they apply to hermeneutics is groundbreaking but not developed sufficiently to show how the virtuous agent is capable of contributing justification to the understanding gained in interpretation, which is the heart of VH specifically, and virtue epistemology more generally. The how and why of this is central to explaining that lists of virtues are useful beyond simply being a list of nice or ethical ways to interact with a text. It is more than appropriate, courteous, or proper; it is justifying in an epistemological and hermeneutical sense. His utilizing virtues from a biblical and non-biblical frame is useful but can be expressed more cogently. Ontologically, it can be argued that they exist in the world as a result of the Creator, so they are observable in both biblically—and naturally—occurring expressions.[8] Briggs acknowledges the same concept: "Doubtless such a case could be made, that the Aristotelian (and perhaps Thomist) categories are fundamental, with the concomitant perspective that 'general' hermeneutics is rooted in the way God has made the world and therefore offers its resources to the specific 'special' task of interpreting the Bible."[9] The idea of concentric circles of context is more useful in emphasizing the continuity of the virtues without creating any form of unnecessary bifurcation between biblically expressed and non-biblically discerned virtues. A list that separates the two is susceptible to the charges of destructive circularity in the

---

8. The choice of the word *naturally* demands further explanation. *Naturally* is not intended to imply an independent existence or emergence apart from the divine act of creation and the Creator. *Naturally* should not be equated with *naturalism*, which begins with the presupposition of creation's independence from a creator. In this case, *naturally* is the best available term to express that these virtues have a discoverability in ways beyond special revelation.

9. Briggs, *Virtuous Reader*, 29.

argument by demanding that virtues to interpret the text are necessarily understood and ingrained before engaging the text. The pneumatological key addressed in the following chapter ultimately expresses the relationship between the function and scope of the virtues in both spheres. The following list of interpretive virtues is expressible and defendable in both spheres, thus meriting their inclusion in VH.

No virtue list is exhaustive, but the following ten descriptive terms serve as the most salient virtues in VH. As has been previously argued, the focus should be upon a virtuous agent rather than individual virtues, but this does not preclude the necessity of certain virtues or clusters of virtues being especially pertinent and highlighted within specific forms of inquiry. "The underlying idea is that inquiry makes certain fairly generic demands on us as cognitive agents, and that the possession of different clusters or groups of intellectual virtues equips us to meet or overcome these demands."[10] The list proposed here is divided into three clusters. Categories of the intellectual virtues have been offered by various philosophers to help differentiate between clusters of organically related and diverse virtues (e.g., internal/external, self-regarding/others-regarding, act-distinct/act-inherent). While useful in their own right, these descriptions can be grouped in a more explanatory manner as it pertains to VH. The first set of six virtues is classified as being attitudinal (love of understanding, open-mindedness, justice, humility, courage, and perseverance), the second set of three as functional (attentiveness, creativity, and generosity), and the final one as a type of master virtue (phronesis). This categorization is the most helpful organizational approach to understanding how they are mutually supporting. These categories are not rigid silos that separate the virtues, since even the attitudinal ones will, at times, necessarily express themselves in some function or skill. Functional ones, by their nature as virtues, will likewise contain some motivational or attitudinal component. They are categorized in order to demonstrate which element of the virtue is at the forefront of its application to hermeneutics. Rather than isolating the virtues, the image of weblike interconnectedness is expressed in these categories. The production of justified understanding of a text will "typically require the exercise of multiple virtues."[11] This is especially true since textual interpretation cuts across genre-specific issues; and cultural, linguistic, and chronological boundaries. The deliberative

10. Baehr, *Inquiring Mind*, loc. 269.
11. Herman, "Scholarly Persona," 360.

excellence of knowing how to adapt the mutually-supportive structure of the interpretive virtues in the light of these challenges gives rise to the need for the master virtue of phronesis. "This variety suggests that a virtue of practical wisdom [phronesis] governs the practice of excellent reading and determines which of the other virtues come into play at any given moment in the pursuit of that practice."[12]

The need for the presence of all ten virtues in the intellectual character of a virtuous interpreter does not mean they are equally significant in the interpretive task. Certain virtues are more relevant and important, or more contested in the realm of hermeneutics. This is demonstrated in Vanhoozer's use of the designation, "prime interpretive virtue," to describe a specific virtue. Likewise, Baehr's questions concerning specific types of inquiries possibly requiring or emphasizing different virtues more than others admit the possibility of weighting some virtues more than others depending on the unique demands of a particular discipline: "What exactly is the (intellectual character-relevant) structure of this domain? What sorts of demands does success in this domain make on a person's intellectual character? Which intellectual virtues are relevant to meeting these demands? And how exactly are they relevant?"[13] This potential of varying degrees of significance given to individual virtues as they apply to interpretive tasks is reflected in the following treatment of the necessary virtues, with five of them garnering more attention than the remaining five. The first four dispositional virtues (love of understanding, open-mindedness, justice, and humility) and the master virtue of phronesis stand apart in their importance to the work of the hermeneut in the contemporary context and will, consequently, receive more attention in the text.

Interpretive Virtues

Attitudinal Virtues

Love of Understanding

In the introduction to this chapter, phronesis is designated as the master intellectual virtue. In a similar manner, it may be equally fitting to designate the love of understanding as the mother interpretive virtue

12. Roberts and Wood, *Intellectual Virtues*, 134.
13. Baehr, *Inquiring Mind*, loc. 2552.

because it exists as the source from which the other virtues issue and draw continual sustenance. In Zagzebski's construction of virtue epistemology, she designates her approach as being a motivation-based system rather than primarily a *telos*- or ends-based system like the Aristotelian pursuit of *eudaimonia*. With such a high priority placed upon the motivational piece of the virtues, she addresses what "affective state that initiates and directs action" is of such value to compel an agent to pursue knowledge and understanding of the highest value, and her answer is love. "Other things being equal, acts motivated by love of some value are highly valuable."[14] In the footnote to this quote, she explains further, "I also think that acts motivated by love of some value are more valuable than those that aim at the same value but without the motive of love or appreciation for the value."[15] This answers the foundational epistemological question of what makes knowledge (and in the case of interpretation, understanding) more valuable than true belief (or accurate understanding). An abiding and deeply ingrained love of understanding within the active interpretive agent conveys value to the understanding because it is trained to be satisfied with nothing less than understanding, since that is its beloved. Having tasted of the satisfaction of its deepest passion, a virtuous interpreter will settle for no cheap substitute or easily-gained counterfeit in place of genuine understanding. This same passionate devotion to understanding is woven throughout all the other interpretive virtues, not as their singular or sole motivation, but as their originary and prime motivation. To say that someone possesses the virtue of the love of understanding is to say dramatically more by way of order of magnitude than that they simply desire understanding. Roberts and Wood extend the definition to include, "an eagerness for acquaintance, a desire for significant information and the solid support of actual or possible beliefs."[16] Love is both affective and volitional in warming the heart and directing cognitive action.

Richard Burnett points out an often-overlooked emphasis embedded into Karl Barth's hermeneutics. For Barth, "The real problem of hermeneutics is love."[17] As is typical of Barth's theology, the emphasis is on the otherness of God, so it is no surprise that the idea of love is predicated

---

14. Zagzebski, "Search for the Source of Epistemic Good," 17.

15. Zagzebski, "Search for the Source of Epistemic Good," 17.

16. Roberts and Wood, *Intellectual Virtues*, 132.

17. Burnett, *Karl Barth's Theological Exegesis*, 207.

on it being first a gift to a person from God. But equally importantly, love requires an external object. "What we love—if we love at all—is always something else or someone else. Of much apparent loving of another we have to ask whether the other really is another, whether it has in fact a basic object, and therefore whether it is real love at all."[18] Love acknowledges, even demands, the existence of the other. In Barthian theology, the other to be loved is God, and it cannot be love if there is no object to be loved. In his theological hermeneutics, the undeniable other is the self-revelation of God. In the realm of VH, if love of understanding is to be conceived of as a virtue, there must be an object for which this love has acquired a taste. Those systems that say *all* that is available in a hermeneutical inquiry is an understanding of self or a projection of the self fail in this particular virtue. To *love* understanding requires understanding to be something other than the reader, or it is more likely a form of vicious interpretive narcissism. Norman Holland says, "All of us, as we read, use the literary work to symbolize and finally to replicate ourselves."[19] If he is correct, then interpreters are less like the mythological Hermes, the messenger of the gods, from whom hermeneutics gained its name, and more like the mythological Narcissus, who became so absorbed in only seeing his own reflection in a pond that he ultimately withered away. Self-love as an obsessive compressing of everything external to oneself as being only the projection of oneself, including in the form of literary engagement, is not a virtuous love. It is no virtue to love what does not, cannot, or ceases to exist once embraced in love. Love does not eradicate the other, but supremely values it as a desirable other. "Love of knowledge would not be a virtue if truth were in principle inaccessible to human cognitive operations."[20] The fact that a virtuous interpreter pursues, desires, longs for, and finds joy in the attainment of understanding requires that understanding of meaning implanted by the author must have some sense of existence which the virtuous interpreter subjectively encounters. Textual meaning is an other as it exists external to the interpreter.

If one loves understanding, how does the virtue translate into meaningful activity in the realm of interpretation? In the first place, it compels the act of inquiry. Even if love of understanding is only contingently related to the attainment of understanding, it is "constitutive of, and not just

18. Barth, *Doctrine of Reconciliation*.
19. Holland, "Unity Identity Text Self," 816.
20. Roberts and Wood, *Intellectual Virtues*, 81.

instrumentally related to, the project of free and responsible intellectual inquiry."[21] When an interpretive agent loves understanding, it requires the initiation of activity that seeks to complete its desire; it compels a sufficient inquiry. Ralph Waldo Emerson demonstrates this by way of the opposite in his essay, *Intellect*: "He in whom the love of repose predominates will accept the first creed, the first philosophy, the first political party he meets."[22] It is impossible for a virtuous agent to read a text without the corresponding motivation to acquire an increasing level of understanding involving explanatory and integrative power. "It is an enormous aid in driving excellence of understanding. Understanding often emerges only with concerted intellectual activities like exploring, testing, dialectical interchange, probing, comparing, writing, and reflecting. These practices require virtue for the best prosecution."[23] It justifies the understanding not simply by its presence, but because its presence will find no rest until it moves from ignorance to explanatorily rich and emotionally and spiritually satisfying understanding. The fact that the agent loves understanding does not necessarily guarantee the attainment of it, but its passionate drive and consuming affection renders the motivation within the agent an abiding virtue because of this motivation and its compelling force to pursue understanding. When combined with the other virtues and governed by phronesis, the agent who loves understanding will be far more likely to reliably gain it than the one who does not.

A love of understanding expressed in the pursuit of textual understanding is also willing to sacrifice, including the self-sacrificial willingness to set aside previous biases and incorrect beliefs, in the pursuit of what is beloved. When confronted by other matters that human agents often love, the success or failure of a hermeneutical inquiry is dependent upon what is comparatively loved more. Of those competing allegiances that often stand most opposed to the pursuit of understanding, inordinate love of self and comfort stand preeminent.

If the interpreter is motivated by a greater love of self than of gaining understanding, the perpetual temptation to eschew difficult understandings, confronting realities, foreign or inconvenient ideas, and potentially transformational encounters with something outside of herself will overpower the potential opportunity to gain a deeper contact with reality, at

---

21. Montmarquet, "'Internalist' Conception of Epistemic Virtue," 140.

22. Emerson, "Intellect."

23. Roberts and Wood, *Intellectual Virtues*, 50.

least the deeper reality of the text. The reader will be left with only the unsatisfying limitedness of her own self. Blaise Pascal expresses the danger of this self-deluding self-love: "This aversion for truth exists in differing degrees, but it may be said that it exists in everyone to some degree, because it is inseparable from self-love . . . We are treated as we want to be treated; we hate the truth and it is kept from us; we desire to be flattered and we are flattered; we like being deceived and we are deceived."[24] The temptation to be deficient in a love of textual understanding keeps understanding distant and unjustified. In the realm of interpretive understanding, it is necessary to differentiate between the textual understanding that is either facilitated by the virtuous disposition of the love of understanding or impeded by a form of deluding love of self. This exists at a different level than the integration of understanding into the believing system or resultant actions of the reader. It is possible to love understanding, and from this motivation, pursue and attain understanding while rejecting what is ultimately understood of the text. The love addressed here is of textual understanding.

Consider a simple illustration. A sportswriter may compose this text: "Tom Brady is the greatest quarterback to ever play in the NFL." A love of understanding in interpreting this text can motivate a deep explanatory inquiry. What are the criteria used? Passing yards, Super Bowl victories, touchdown completions, indefinable leadership qualities, or rugged good looks? What textual and linguistic matters should be explored? Is there significance to the choice of word *greatest* rather than *best, most accomplished*, or *effective*? What is the genre of the text: news article, satire, or comedy? These matters and many more can be pursued in the inquiry to understand what this text means, but there is a difference between understanding what this text means and the acceptance or affirmation of its meaning. As an interpretive virtue, love of understanding finds sufficient satisfaction in the motivation to love understanding the text, not necessarily affirming or loving the understanding that the text expresses. In this example, a virtuous reader may justifiably understand what the text expresses in saying that "Tom Brady is the greatest quarterback to ever play in the NFL," in part because of the virtuously loving motivation to understand it with all the richly-textured and explanatory fruit of the inquiry, but still think that both Payton Manning and Drew Brees are greater quarterbacks than Brady. The way in which self-love would

24. Pascal, *Pensées and Other Writings*, 179.

impede understanding is not in deeming that Manning or Brees are better on the basis of extra-textual considerations, but in being blinded by one's own love for the Indianapolis Colts or New Orleans Saints; or to generally love one's own opinion to such an extent as to understand the text to mean that Tom Brady is a cheater. The interpreter may believe this on basis of an understanding accrued from a diverse collection of sources, but to be a virtuously-motivated reader, he cannot let his biases, love of his own opinion, or love of his own previously-constructed understandings overpower his desire to understand the expression of the other in the text. Love of understanding in the hermeneutical domain, though conceptually related, is not the same as love of understanding in the broadest epistemological frame.

The interpretive virtue of love of understanding prizes, cherishes, pursues, inquires, is emotionally drawn to, and supremely values the attainment of understanding, and as a result, it contributes to the justifiability of an understanding by how it motivates an agent to acquire the understanding. The opposite is also true, and agents who engage with a text with a deeper love of self, comfort, or ideology will functionally undermine the justification of their understanding by undermining its value and diminishing the motivational energy that it lends to the task of excellent inquiry.

To love self or ideology more than textual understanding expresses itself by using and manipulating a text instead of understanding it. While ideology is a real and powerful motivator in actions, including interpretive actions, it need not be the only motivation, nor is it invincible in its influence. Love as an other-pursuing reality, both intellectually (pursuing understanding) and morally (pursuing goodness), stands against ideologies that only serve the reader's power, community, or dominant culture in which the reader is located. An interpreter may not be able to fully transcend his locatedness, but this cannot mean that they are powerless in the face of ideological agendas. Ideological agendas are a distinct form of self-love. Love of understanding is not love if it is powerless to confront self-deluding ideology. De La Torre, who argues against stable meaning as expressed by an author in a text and emphasizes the thorough locatedness of interpreters, still cannot avoid hedging on his proclamations. "When we read the Bible, we read it from our social location, a reading that *usually* [emphasis added] justifies our lifestyle even if, at times, our lifestyle contradicts the *very essence* [emphasis added] of the gospel message."[25] What is the *very essence* of the gospel if not some sense of universal and stable meaning? What allows a reading that avoids the *usually* self-justifying interpretation? In the frame of VH, there is an uncontested place for an understanding of the text that speaks from a location and to all locations. An agent motivated by a love of that understanding is precisely the one that typifies the readings that are the best exceptions to De La Torre's *usually* self-justifying ideological readings. Again, in his text, he says, "No biblical interpretation is ever developed in a social or cultural vacuum. *Most* [emphasis added] interpretations are autobiographical, where we ascertain the meaning of the text through the telling of our own stories, projecting onto the Bible how we define and interpret the biblical story in light of our own life experiences."[26] His statement concerning the social locatedness of all interpreters is certainly accurate, but that does not mean all understanding is, as a result, purely a projection of the self or one's own ideological commitments. He even intuitively understands this when he hedges again by saying *most* interpretations are autobiographical. Again, a VH that cherishes love of understanding over love of self fits within this niche left open by De La Torre.

A love of textual understanding may ultimately implement, or in a sense, use, the understanding gained from the text (e.g., one may replace a faulty alternator in an automobile after understanding a text explaining how to do this). But this is different from a predetermined ideological manipulation of the text to serve one's own preconceived agenda. Love is a high standard, but that is precisely the purpose of a VH. It is not intended to be easily attained, since virtue should reflect the highest excellencies of human cognitive activity. The worst of interpretation is that which sees only self or pursues only the easiest, most comfortable course; the best of interpretation pursues, through passionate inquiry, the other of textual understanding without regard to effort, time, or blindly-held precommitments.

Open-mindedness

The examination of individual virtues serves to reinforce the weblike nature of a virtuous intellectual character with significant overlapping domains within the various virtues. This is true of open-mindedness as well, but it stands out amongst the other virtues in a significant manner.

25. De La Torre, *From the Margins*, loc. 745.
26. De La Torre, *From the Margins*, loc. 154.

It can be argued that of the nine other virtues considered in this chapter, open-mindedness is the only virtue that can be seen as necessary to gain understanding. While, taken as a whole, the virtues serve to justify and facilitate accurate understanding, one must admit that some level of understanding could be attained without, say, a love of understanding, perseverance, or courage, but this cannot be said about open-mindedness. The only way that new understanding or deepened understanding can be assimilated is the presence of some level of openness to receive it. A mind closed to understanding cannot attain new understanding since it will neither pursue it nor receive it when presented with it. Open-mindedness exists as a necessary virtue to such a degree that Wayne Riggs uses it to demonstrate that whatever criteria one uses to establish a list of intellectual virtues (e.g., motivation, *telos*, culture, or bare intuition), it is a philosophically-attuned intuition that demands for the inclusion of open-mindedness. For Riggs, any theory that fails to count open-mindedness as an intellectual virtue would be implausible.[27]

As is the case with many of the virtues, general and intuitional familiarity with the virtues, in this case, open-mindedness, often breeds a sense of understanding without pausing to consider the manner in which a virtue truly functions as an intellectual excellency. Is being open-minded the equivalent of holding all beliefs in a loose manner, what Roberts and Wood designate as "flaccidity"?[28] Some who extol the virtue of open-mindedness seem to embrace this definition. William Hare and Terry Mclaughlin imply this very thing when answering concerns about open-mindedness. In their defense, they ultimately argue for the differentiation between those few beliefs that can justifiably be "firmly held" and those about which we should be open-minded. By framing this dichotomy, they admit that open-mindedness is only expressible as some form of doxastic doubt about beliefs currently held by the cognitive agent. Is an agent left between the two options of firmly-held beliefs, which are essentially defined as justifiable closed-mindedness, and being open-minded, which means either not believing or significantly doubting one's standing beliefs? If this is the only definition of open-mindedness, it seems likely that few, if any, interpretive agents, or human beings in general, could rightfully and virtuously be called open-minded. Few would embrace a world in which the most excellent intellectual agents

27. Riggs, "Understanding 'Virtue' and the Virtue of Understanding," 206.
28. Roberts and Wood, *Intellectual Virtues*, 188.

are not allowed or simply do not believe what they propose to believe. For open-mindedness to function as an interpretive virtue, it must be able to influence the activity of the interpreter even where the interpreter genuinely, deeply, and firmly holds to his or her beliefs.

Baehr picks up on this tension in understanding open-mindedness. He details three different approaches to open-mindedness. The first, he identifies as the "conflict model." In this approach, the agent is compelled, "to temporarily set aside one's doxastic commitments about a particular matter in order to give a fair and impartial hearing to an opposing belief, argument, or body of evidence."[29] The capacity to genuinely accomplish this is debatable, but even more, it assumes that open-mindedness only functions where agents are confronted with contrary information to what they already hold. Open-mindedness, at the very least, must be more broadly conceived of than a manner of intellectual conflict management. Many moments of intellectual and interpretive open-mindedness do not necessitate a doxastic disagreement between the agent's standing beliefs and new information. The development of richer and fuller explanatory understanding of a text need not take place only on the level of changing one's mind, but can include adding to understanding already embraced.

The second model Baehr describes is the "adjudication model." This is expressed when the agent holds no particular belief, but is weighing the evidence for two possible competing beliefs (e.g., a jurist considering evidence for guilt or innocence in a trial). In this way, open-mindedness is, "essentially a disposition to assess one or more sides of an intellectual dispute in a fair and impartial way."[30] Although attuned to a different form of conflict or dispute, this model still assumes that disparate or conflicting beliefs must be weighed. Where the conflict model is centered on conflicts between standing beliefs of the agent and beliefs foreign to the agent, the adjudication model presupposes conflict between two beliefs, both of which are foreign or, at the least, new to the agent.

While both of the preceding models must be included within the virtue of open-mindedness, they have not yet reached the conceptual core of the disposition. Open-mindedness may also apply to a non-conflictual reality of attempting to *grasp* a "foreign or challenging subject matter."[31] After considering these three frameworks, Baehr synthesizes a

29. Baehr, *Inquiring Mind*, loc. 1823.

30. Baehr, *Inquiring Mind*, loc. 1853.

31. Baehr, *Inquiring Mind*, loc. 1866.

generalized definition: "An open-minded person is characteristically (a) willing and (within limits) able (b) to transcend a default cognitive standpoint (c) in order to take up or take seriously the merits of (d) a distinct cognitive standpoint."[32]

Baehr's evaluation is helpful in understanding insufficient and generalized conceptions of open-mindedness that are prevalent in the realm of virtue discussions. His synthesized definition moves to a more acceptable core understanding of the virtue that admits the possibility of both holding to strong personal intellectual commitments but also being able to transcend these commitments in order to allow for a more robust dialogue with the text or its commentators. In the textual frame, Burnett describes this characteristic in Barth's hermeneutics as entering into a "relationship of faithfulness with every author," even if that relationship may not be permanently maintained in every circumstance upon further consideration.[33] In this way, the naïve flaccidity of the interpreter is rejected as not being virtuous. In its place is the demand for a faithful interacting and consideration of all contributors before evaluating the durability of the relationship. As helpful as Baehr's definition and Barth's explanation are, they still lack a final explanatory element. Riggs offers this final piece that affirms the holding of strong beliefs while remaining open to new understanding, whether pursuing Baehr's goal of transcending one's own beliefs or Barth's relationship of faithfulness toward the author. For Riggs, the necessary condition is the concept of fallibilism, but the important distinction is that the fallibilism is attached to the agent, not the belief. "To be open-minded is primarily an attitude toward oneself as a believer, rather than toward any particular belief."[34] With this understanding established, Rebecca Taylor offers the final condition required to attain a virtuously open mind: an open-minded agent possesses a disposition "to seek self-knowledge about her cognitive strengths and weaknesses and to self-monitor based on this self-knowledge."[35]

A proper understanding of open-mindedness in the frame of an interpretive agent demands both internally—and externally—attuned senses. When encountering a text, the interpreter must faithfully engage new, foreign, conflicting, contradictory, or deepening understandings

---

32. Baehr, *Inquiring Mind*, loc. 1938.
33. Burnett, *Karl Barth's Theological Exegesis*, 197.
34. Riggs, "Open-Mindedness," 180.
35. Taylor, "Open-Mindedness, 200.

from the text or from subsequent commentators on the text. For Yong, this includes the possibility that the encounter with others and their understandings may necessitate, "further researching the matter and to revising their position as appropriate (while being cognizant that the complexity of some disagreements may not yield complementary resolution even in their lifetime."[36] Furthermore, the hermeneut must be continually active, whether in the presence of a text or in the absence of a text, in assessing her own attitudinal disposition. She must be willing to remain open to the possibility that deeply-held beliefs may ultimately need to be reevaluated and adjusted on the basis of the agent's own fallible nature.

An individual who fails in either of these two elements of open-mindedness undermines the justifiability of any subsequent understanding of a text by related hermeneutical vices of commission and omission in regard to open-mindedness. The interpretive vice of commission is actively clinging to false beliefs, biases, or dogmas by rejecting new and potentially conflicting information into one's understanding without a fair hearing. The interpretive vice of omission is the failure to actively pursue new understanding, regardless of whether it confirms or contradicts previously held beliefs and understanding. Textual understanding within a virtuous frame is continually open to deeper and richer levels of understanding, thus lending justification to the interpretation. Failure to be open to this deepening of understanding limits the justification that any interpretation can accumulate by illegitimately assuming a position of the infallibility of the hermeneutic agent.

Klein, Blomberg, and Hubbard advocate for an intentional form of open-mindedness in assessing one's interpretation of a text. In their discussion about how interpreters "validate" (a term that fits within the semantic range of what this research refers to by the designation *justify*) their interpretation, they "recommend that interpreters make it a practice always to consult others with whom they may *disagree* in order to test the validity of their conclusion."[37] While the context of this specific recommendation is focused on those in a broadly-defined faith community, they extend open-mindedness further. "In some instances unbelievers might shed crucial light on the meaning of biblical texts that

36. Yong, *Hermeneutical Spirit*, loc. 6301.

37. Klein, Blomberg, and Hubbard, *Introduction to Biblical Interpretation*, 203.

believers might miss."[38] While the scenarios that Klein, Blomberg, and Hubbard refer to depend on their framework of mutually exclusive and exhaustive domains of believers and unbelievers, it is valuable to further pluralize the potential sources of potential interlocutors. Marginalized peoples from both the believer and unbeliever categories are also important contributors to the expanding hermeneutical discussions. As Randolph Richards and Brandon O'Brien demonstrate, the value of this may confront the dominant Western interpretive community in important ways. With centuries of culturally—and academically—embedded individualism focused on internal concepts of innocence/guilt, the Western interpreter may be properly corrected in his textual understanding of David's interaction with the prophet Nathan or the Apostle Paul's idea of shame[39] by an interpreter from other geographical and cultural perspectives who are trained to the idea of externally experienced honor/shame within collectivist societies.[40] This is a conceptually easy place to insert open-mindedness because it recognizes the relatively closer interpretive location enjoyed by the non-Western interpreters to the world of the text's origin than the Western interpreter, but, even here, other voices can still be engaged.

Post-Colonial interpreters, along with the diverse collection of other interpretive communities, including those from perspectives like Liberation Theology, Black Theology, Gay Theology, Feminist Theology, Womanist Theology, and those broadly defined as interpreters from the margins, present another opportunity to pursue virtuous open-mindedness. Many interpreters engage a text in order to read *against* it rather than to understand it as it is. Even in this setting, a virtuous interpreter is able to engage in the process of both externally being open to the ideas of others so as to be able to potentially better understand a text, but also internally monitor the embedded biases and assumptions that reside in the fallible but virtuous interpretive agent. De La Torre explains why these readers from the margin should be included in an open-minded dialogue.

> When the Bible is read from the social location of those whom society privileges, the risk exists that interpretations designed to protect their power and privilege are subconsciously or consciously constructed. Those who are the authority of society

38. Klein, Blomberg, and Hubbard, *Introduction to Biblical Interpretation*, 205.

39. See also: Krister Stendahl, "Apostle Paul and the Introspective Conscience of the West," 78–96.

40. Richards and O'Brien, *Misreading Scripture with Western Eyes*, loc. 1283.

impose their views upon the text and confuse what they declare the Bible to say with what the text actually states. To counter this, autobiographical interpretations from the margins of society challenge the claim by the dominant culture that its interpretation of the text is objective and thus superior to any other reading.[41]

Open-mindedness to the diverse chorus of voices including the author, the text, the author's community, and the various and oft disparate voices of the globalized and pluralistic contemporary milieu need not disorient a virtuous interpreter. The deeply-ingrained nature of the interpreter's intellectual character including, but not limited to, open-mindedness, provides a more stable point of engagement with others. The virtuous agent is able to engage with increasing self-awareness of one's own limitations and a sincere sensitivity toward others that serves to contribute to the interpretive inquiry.

Open-mindedness is not the equivalent of flaccidity or naiveté but a virtuously guided willingness to transcend and walk in faithfulness with others in order to properly hear their perspective. Some of these perspectives will deepen understanding and be ingrained into the interpreter's understanding, while others will ultimately be dismissed as not contributing to the goal of justified understanding for a variety of reasons (bias, ideology, facticity, shallowness, etc.). Being open-minded does not demand the ultimate embrace of every perspective, but a willingness to hear it and the agent offering it well, with a level of virtuously-attuned excellence that allows each voice, including the interpreter's own voice, to be understood before evaluating the understanding it offers. An ingrained intellectual virtue of open-mindedness is the proper corrective to contemporary deterioration of tolerance as presented by D. A. Carson:

> Under the impact of radical hermeneutics and of deconstruction, the nature of tolerance has changed. In a relatively free and open society, the best forms of tolerance are those that are open to and tolerant of people, even when there are strong disagreements with their ideas. This robust toleration for people, if not always for their ideas, engenders a measure of civility in public discourse while still fostering spirited debate over the relative merits of this or that idea. Today, however, tolerance in many Western societies increasingly focuses on ideas, not on people. The result of adopting this new brand of tolerance is less discussion of the merits of competing ideas—and less civility. There is

41. De La Torre, *From the Margins*, loc. 146.

less discussion because toleration of diverse ideas demands that
we avoid criticizing the opinions of others; in addition, there is
almost no discussion where the ideas at issue are of the religious
sort that claim to be valid for everyone everywhere: that sort of
notion is right outside the modern "plausibility structure" (to
use Peter Berger's term), and has to be trashed. There is less civility because there is no inherent demand, in this new practice
of tolerance, to be tolerant of people, and it is especially difficult
to be tolerant of those people whose views are so far outside the
accepted "plausibility structures" that they think your brand of
tolerance is muddleheaded.[42]

Carson's thoughts are a reminder that being virtuously open-minded is
not the same as in the aphoristic warning to not be so open-minded that
your brains fall out. A virtuously open-minded person is *always* tolerant
of people and open to giving a fair hearing to all ideas before determining
by the implementation of the full range of intellectual virtues as well as
virtuously directed skills, methods, and frameworks their ultimate interpretive worth in adding to the most justifiable forms of understanding.

Justice

Few virtues can boast of a more impressive attestation in ancient thought
than that of justice. Plato and Aristotle both consider justice (δικαιοσύνην),
along with prudence (φρόνησις), self-control, and courage, to be counted
among the cardinal virtues. Aristotle goes so far as to declare, "Justice
is often thought to be the greatest of virtues, and 'neither evening nor
morning star' is so wonderful."[43] Hebrew Scripture and literature equally
elevate justice in both canonical and non-canonical expressions. By the
time of the writing of the apocryphal book, The Wisdom of Solomon,
during the Second Temple Period (likely composed sometime in the first
century BCE), these identical cardinal virtues were thoroughly incul-
cated into the Jewish wisdom tradition (Wis 8:7).[44]

The ubiquity and priority of justice as an ancient virtue did not
equate with unanimity in conceptual understanding as evidenced by

42. Carson, *Gagging of God*, 32.

43. Aristotle, *Nicomachean Ethics*, loc. 1613.

44. Wis 8:7: And if a man loves righteousness, The fruits of wisdom's labor are
virtues, For she teaches *soberness* and *understanding, righteousness* and *courage*; And
there is nothing in life for men more profitable than these.

Socrates's lengthy dialogue across multiple books on the topic in Plato's *The Republic*. For all of the diversity in the discussions concerning the nature and basis of justice, Wayne Pomerleau makes clear the centrality of the virtue in his useful summary statement, "Western philosophers generally regard justice as the most fundamental of all virtues for ordering interpersonal relations and establishing and maintaining a stable political society."[45]

In considering the great diversity in formulations of justice in various ancient and contemporary systems, the search for a suitable definition that unifies the fundamental element of the virtue is complex. At the least, there exists a core idea of rendering to another or another's group what is rightly (i.e., justly) deserved. Added to the complexity of expressing an agreed-upon definition is the increased complication of its application in an epistemological and hermeneutical context. Stewart Clem exposes the apparent struggle in casting justice as an epistemological virtue before proceeding to offer a new line of argumentation to defend its place in the discipline: "Prima facie, it would seem that justice has no immediate place in epistemic evaluation, even on the most robust varieties of virtue epistemology."[46] This seeming irrelevance is related to the inescapable interpersonal or socio-institutional context of justice, especially when addressed as a moral virtue.

Attempting to conceive of the task of knowing in an interpersonal or socio-institutional manner that is analogous to a just action excludes a great amount of the subject matter generally considered central to epistemology, since many forms of knowledge involve no necessary interaction with others.[47] Justice, as a virtue that governs interactions on the basis of desert, demands that it "must be, first and foremost, in us as individual persons, in our attitudes towards each other."[48] Justice, as a virtue, demands more than fairness, which could be erroneously invoked by some as a form of evidentialism that sees the ascribing of weight to evidence in a just (i.e., fair, appropriate, commensurate, proportionate) manner; it requires the desert-based implication toward another agent, not just toward an object or toward evidence. Justice renders to another what their state,

45. Pomerleau, "Western Theories of Justice."

46. Clem, "Epistemic Relevance of the Virtue of Justice," 302.

47. Chief among the forms of knowledge that require no interpersonal or social dimension are those generally considered to be self-knowledge or knowledge seated within one's own self (e.g., sensations, thoughts, and mental states).

48. Kristjánsson, "Justice and Desert-Based Emotions," 55.

function, actions, or being rightly deserves based on their state, function, actions, or being. According to Aristotle, it is "complete virtue, but not absolutely, but in relation to our neighbour."[49] Justice is the epitome of virtue for Aristotle, but it does not exist apart from a neighbor to whom it is granted. Aquinas centers justice in the regulating of human will, "solely in the point of its extending to operations that relate to another."[50] The one category of knowledge that fully engages with this type of interpersonal or social context is that of weighing testimony from another. The connection between the epistemological concern of testimony is paralleled in the hermeneutical task of interpreting a text. Clem persuasively argues that, "It is conceivable that there may be instances when 'what is due to another' is of epistemic relevance. I am thinking here specifically of the function of testimony in belief formation, or, more broadly, when reliance on others is an integral component of belief formation (which turns out to be quite often)."[51] Texts serve as objectively existent artifacts of the testimony of an author. Consequently, the act of interpretation includes the virtue of justice in interacting with the written testimony of another and becomes subject to the same expectations of justice in the epistemic variety. Vanhoozer acknowledges this same connection in arguing for "the rationality of trust in testimony, and for the need for the kind of epistemic conscientiousness that inclines one to attend to the interpretations of others."[52]

Having established the place of the interpretive virtue of justice, since the entire hermeneutical endeavor is an engagement between various testimonial agents, it is necessary to detail which agents are consistently part of the community of contributors to the task. Authors and interpreters are the most obvious, but not the only agents or social groupings that are involved in the task of interpreting a text. Hermeneutics admits several personal agents and collective agents into the dialogue with the text. VH demands that every participant deserves a just reception into the conversation that seeks deeper and more justified forms of understanding. As Aquinas has noted, the proper subject matter for the virtue of justice is in those areas where there is an element of something

---

49. Aristotle, *Nicomachean Ethics*, loc. 1613.

50. Aquinas, *Summa Theologica*, loc. 49555.

51. Clem, "Relevance of Justice," 204.

52. Vanhoozer, *Biblical Authority after Babel*, 233.

due or undue to another,[53] and the dialogue within the community of participants involved in interpretation is just such an operation. Each of the interlocutors in the hermeneutical dialogue should have a reasonable expectation of proper treatment in accordance with their place within the discussion, and the violation of this expectation is not only an act of injustice, but also, an impediment to attaining a justified understanding of the text. At the very least, the agential contributors to any hermeneutical inquiry should include: the author, the reader, both the broader generative and receptive communities in which the authors and interpreters are embedded, and the line of various interpreters/interpretive traditions that have previously interacted with the text.

As evidenced in much of the discussion concerning the virtue of justice (especially in the Platonic frame), it is not to be considered as simply treating all agents exactly the same. Justice acknowledges the variation of desert depending upon certain factors. This acknowledgement of specified deserts due each participant of the discussion commensurate with their nature and function within the interpretive dialogue carries two important qualification to its application to VH. First, all agents deserve an equivalent baseline reception simply due to their inclusion within the interpretive dialogue. Second, beyond this foundational expectation of justice due to each participant, certain deserts are due to each participant that are unique to their standing in the interpretive community. Each of these qualifications demands further explanation.

Whether speaking of the author, reader, or any interested community, it is justice to exert oneself, as much as it is possible, to allow contributors to be heard on their own terms. Any hermeneutical model that totalizes the perspective of one contributor at the expense or silencing of another fails to meet the obligation of justice. This is a fundamental flaw in many postmodern constructions of hermeneutics which vilify the ascribing of any meaningful contribution to the testimony of the author expressed in the text that they wrote. Robert Stein accurately explains the effect of this type of approach: "Texts were interpreted as independent units in total isolation from their authors," and in reference to formalism, "The New Criticism totally disconnects the text from the original author. It is as if text magically appeared on the scene without father or mother."[54] The act of silencing the engagement of the author, the author's willed

---

53. Aquinas, *Summa Theologica*, loc. 29011.

54. Stein, "Author-Oriented Approach to Hermeneutics," 452.

intention (i.e., illocution), and the contribution of the author's surrounding community, is illegitimate, overreaching, and ultimately unjust. This same illegitimate silencing has happened to the reader and the reader's community as seen in some modern approaches like *Religionsgeschichtliche*, which disregarded the reader and any attempt at an applicable or relevant theology with an approach that presupposes an objective certainty within the historical context (ironically, often equally detached from the intentional will of the author). It was this approach that compelled Barth to famously declare, "My complaint is that recent commentators confine themselves to an interpretation of the text which seems to me to be no commentary at all, but merely the first step towards a commentary."[55] For Barth, doing justice to interpreting an author's text demands justice for the contemporary reader's time and community as well. Using John Calvin's approach as an example, he sees the just interpreter moving from "having first established what stands in the text, sets himself to re-think the whole material and to wrestle with it, till the walls which separate the sixteenth century from the first become transparent!"[56]

The temptation to perpetrate unjust silencing is especially prevalent when differences and conflicts may be present between agents in the hermeneutical dialogue. A respectful engagement that does not flatten differences or coerce agreement where it may not exist is a just action. Paul Ricoeur presents this conceptual priority in his treatment of the dispute between the competing hermeneutical system of Hans-Georg Gadamer and Jürgen Habermas's *Hermeneutik und Ideologiekritik* as he asks, "Is it possible to formulate a hermeneutics which would render *justice* [emphasis added] to the critique of ideology, which would show the necessity of the latter at the very heart of its own concerns?"[57] From this starting point, he treats each position with respect and thoroughness, examining how Gadamer and Habermas contribute to the conversation, and only then begins to address how their disparate approaches may engage in meaningful dialogue. It would be injustice to disregard Habermas's critiques and interpretation of Gadamer without first seeking to understand him on his own terms. This same privilege is to be extended to Gadamer as well. Ricoeur provides not only a conceptual framework to pursue, but also an exemplar for what it can look like. As he states concerning his

55. Barth, *Epistle to the Romans*, 6.
56. Barth, *Epistle to the Romans*, 7.
57. Ricœur, *Hermeneutics and the Human Sciences*, 23.

intention, "My aim is not to fuse the hermeneutics of tradition and the critique of ideology in a super-system which would encompass both. As I said at the outset, each speaks from a different place. Nonetheless, each may be asked to recognise the other, not as a position which is foreign and purely hostile, but as one which raises in its own way a legitimate claim."[58] Briggs characterizes Ricoeur's work as, "Doing justice to each competing claim on its own terms, and in particular seeing how each account might succeed in offering a way of understanding the other."[59]

While all agents in the hermeneutical dialogue have due to them the basic justice of being understood as they would like to be understood (a kind of hermeneutical Golden Rule: Treat other agents in the interpretive dialogue as one would want to be treated), there is the persistent truth that the different participants are sufficiently differentiated in their function within the dialogue so that justice demands certain actions commensurate with their standing in the dialogue. Consider the function of the author. While some contemporary constructions have predicated their existence as hermeneutical systems on the destruction of the author as the initiator of meaning in a text, a just engagement with a text cannot adopt this position. Roland Barthes, writing as a post-structuralist, exposes what is behind this unjust reception of an author's text: "By refusing to assign to the text (and to the world-as-text) a 'secret,' i.e., an ultimate meaning, liberates an activity we may call countertheological, **properly revolutionary, for to refuse to halt meaning is finally to refuse** God and his hypostases, reason, science, the law."[60] In his zeal to reaffirm a just and, ultimately, liberated role for the reader, he pursues an agenda to silence not only the authors but the Author (i.e., God). "Classical criticism has never been concerned with the reader; for that criticism, there is no other man in literature than the one who writes. We are no longer so willing to be the dupes of such antiphrasis . . . We know that in order to restore writing to its future, we must reverse the myth: the birth of the reader must be requited by the death of the Author."[61]

It is the thesis of this research that a virtuous agent approaches the entirety of the task of interpretation from a motivation to come to understanding. A virtuous agent is motivated and reliably acts in ways

---

58. Ricœur, *Hermeneutics and the Human Sciences*, 48.

59. Briggs, *Virtuous Reader*, 97.

60. Barthes, *Rustle of Language*, 54.

61. Barthes, *Rustle of Language*, 55.

that reflect the highest ideals of interpretive agents, which are collectively known as interpretive virtues. To do justice is more than a simple act; it is the deeply ingrained and habituated intention of the agent which immediately rules out-of-bounds any approach that posits its existence upon the intentional silencing (i.e., death) of another participant in the dialogue. This is only more egregious when that silenced participant is indispensable and foundational to the occasion that brings the interlocutors together, namely the presence of the text inscribed by an author. Consider the antithesis of Barthes's approach as Roberts and Wood describe Gadamer's hermeneutic: "Gadamer's model of reading as a sort of respectful conversation between equals suggests that respect for authors who are at a distance of culture or time may be an unusual trait, and one that is certainly a virtue for human beings who have a natural tendency toward cultural and historical chauvinism."[62] This respectful conversation cannot be built upon a foundation of dismissiveness.

In many constructions, the primary injustice that is perpetrated is in the rejection of any sense of differentiation that is due in the way that justice is expressed to the various partners in the interpretive process. If interpretation is to be *interpretation*, the author must be given the *just* place of the originator of the text and the intention (i.e., illocution) expressed through it. This privileged place does not disallow the influence of sociocultural and linguistic limitations that may be felt or even imposed upon the author within her context, but it acknowledges the willed intention of an author in bringing the text into existence. Interpretation is a mediating task that engages something and seeks to understand it and extend its understanding into new contexts. Locke describes true reading/interpreting as involving: reflecting, making observations from what is read, digesting, and using understanding to build something from what is understood.[63] This is different than what many contemporary constructions attempt to do. De Waal Dryden describes many postmodern approaches as the critique of the ideological structures of the biblical text, which are then "refashioned into something more palatable."[64] Palatability in this context is determined by the interpreter and the contemporary reading community in which the interpreter is located. In refashioning the meaning of the text to align with the ideology of the interpreter, it is no longer

---

62. Roberts and Wood, *Intellectual Virtues*, 132.

63. Locke, *Of the Conduct of the Understanding*, 20.

64. de Waal Dryden, *Hermeneutic of Wisdom*, 9.

interpreting but creating a new text aligned to the ideological frame of the interpreter who is now turned author. The conflating of interpreting and authoring is an act of injustice that fails to render proper due to the author of the text being interpreted. The interpreter is free to create new texts, but it is injustice to silence the author and her expression within the text and refashion it to fit the interpreter's agenda and still call it interpretation of the original text. This does not mean that interpreter has no freedom or voice. Interpreters are *just* in disagreeing with a text, exposing inconsistencies and biases in the author's expression, extending the original text's illocution into new and diverse settings by exploring its perlocutions, or authoring a new text out of the engagement with the original text. While it is true that an interpreter *can* take a text and choose to use it, manipulate it, or twist it, this is a fundamental failure to render what is just and deserved by the text and its author. The ethical conception of justice demonstrates the same possibility. The ability of one to dominate, silence, abuse, oppress, or even kill another is not commensurate with the demand of justice. Ability is not approval. Just because a text can be twisted, manipulated, silenced, or coerced to mean what it was never intended to mean does not imply that this is acceptable to do. In a VH model, these kinds of actions directed toward any member of the interpretive dialogue are illegitimate and destructive of any endeavor that genuinely seeks understanding.

Humility

The introduction of the concept of interpretive humility is seemingly atypical to the other virtues in this discussion. While not possessing complete unanimity in the metaphysical rooting or practical expression, the other virtues still find strong attestation in both Greek and Judeo-Christian formulations with significant overlap in understanding. Humility appears to stand in a different place. Alasdair McIntyre observes that, "The only place in Aristotle's account of the virtues where anything resembling humility is mentioned, it is as a vice."[65] [66] In contrast, Vanhoozer

---

65. MacIntyre, *After Virtue*, 177.

66. The passage that MacIntyre is referencing from Aristotle is found in his discourse on virtues as being the golden mean between two vicious extremes, specifically as relating to honor and dishonor, in Book II, Part 7: "περὶ δὲ τιμὴν καὶ ἀτιμίαν μεσότης μὲν μεγαλοψυχία, ὑπερβολὴ δὲ χαυνότης τις λεγομένη, ἔλλειψις δὲ μικροψυχία."

describes humility as "the most important virtue,"[67] and in another place, "the prime interpretive virtue."[68] The solution to this disparity and the potential usefulness of humility as an interpretive virtue is resolved in proper definition.

Precision in the definition demonstrates that there is far less of a conflict between what is defined as interpretive humility by both VH and Vanhoozer than seems apparent in an English translation of Aristotle's *Nicomachean Ethics*. The word that Macintyre references concerning the only usage of humility, as a vice, in Aristotle is not related to the biblical or epistemological concept of humility. In no biblical text, including the more contemporaneous with Aristotle, Septuagint, is the word which Aristotle used in his discussion of the vices and virtue of honor used. In all cases, the biblical virtue of humility is constructed upon entirely different semantic domains.[69] Aristotle contrasts vanity (χαυνότης), which emphasizes a sense of inward emptiness in comparison to outward presentation, with μικροψυχία. In this contrast, he emphasizes not an inordinate puffed-upness of appearance as seen in vanity with a chronic smallness of the soul. Smallness of the soul, while somewhat related to some possible definitions of humility in relation to ideas concerning honor and dishonor, is far from the concept of humility as it pertains to epistemological or interpretive endeavors. A specific form of proper evaluation of self rather than a chronic and destructive smallness of soul is a much more pertinent rendering of the interpretive virtue of humility.

Roberts and Wood attempt to sketch a comprehensive picture of humility. The primary method of their definition is to define humility as the opposite of a broad range of related concepts (e.g., arrogance, vanity, conceit, egotism, grandiosity, pretentiousness, snobbishness, impertinence, haughtiness, self-righteousness, domination, selfish-ambition, and self-complacency), with a specific emphasis on vanity and arrogance.[70] The ethical dimension of their discussion is uncontested, but the breadth of their definition is so expansive that it lessens its effectiveness in application to epistemic concerns. In reference to vanity, they seek a form of humility that is characterized by a "lack of concern with status."[71] Lack

---

67. Vanhoozer, "Imprisoned or Free?," 92.

68. Vanhoozer, *Is There a Meaning in This Text?*, 463.

69. The Hebrew word used in the OT is עֲנָו, which is related to being bowed down. The Greek word in the LXX is ταπεινος. In the NT, the root word is ταπεινοφροσύνη.

70. Roberts and Wood, "Humility and Epistemic Goods," 258.

71. Roberts and Wood, "Humility and Epistemic Goods," 263.

of concern need not be ignorance of status, but a general lack of concern about it. A person who demonstrates an awareness of and even a concern regarding status in their field of epistemic pursuits may, but not necessarily, be boorish in work or relational context, but it does not seem to follow that concern for status would inevitably lead to vicious intellectual habits. One can easily envision a scientist who pursues good intellectual ends (e.g., curing a deadly disease) by equally virtuous motivations and methods who also rightfully appreciates the recognition of his success by his peers. This awareness of and desire for proper status would be disallowed by Roberts and Wood's definition. The fact that "concern for status *often* [emphasis added] weakens and confuses more important concerns, with bad behavioural and epistemic consequence" does not necessarily equate it with being vicious.

As an epistemological and interpretive virtue, humility must mean something more than a lack of concern for status if it is going to aid in reliably gaining justifiable understanding of a text. It also must be more than holding to a radically-attuned postmodern sense that sees humility as requiring a "weakened attitude toward a specific belief."[72] This belief-centric view of humility creates an odd sense of intellectual schizophrenia that supposes the simultaneous position of belief and not-belief as the only appropriately humble way to approach knowledge. Humility as doubting one's beliefs is an unreasonable demand on the interpreter. Dennis Whitcomb, Battaly, Baehr, and Daniel Howard-Snyder (WBBH) give a far more plausible solution to the dilemma posed by humility by focusing not on the holding of a specific belief but upon the fallibility of the believing agent. Humility is a "proper attentiveness to, and owning, one's intellectual limitations."[73] By shifting to an agent-centered focus on the virtue of humility, agents are able to strongly hold to and vigorously defend their beliefs and interpretations while acknowledging their own fallibility in the attainment of this understanding. In this way, humility shares a strong connection with the working of the virtue of open-mindedness. While a justified understanding attained by the careful work of the agent is genuinely believed, a deeply ingrained sense of one's own intellectual limitations will not permit the final and certain closing of the interpretive process. WBBH ascribe four characteristic dispositions to agents who own their own limitations: (1) a belief that

72. Taylor, "Open-Mindedness," 200.
73. Whitcomb et al., "Intellectual Humility," 516.

they have limitations and that negative intellectual outcomes can often be attributed to them, (2) a willingness to admit them to others, (3) a genuine care and seriousness about these limitations, and (4) regret but not hostility toward the presence of these limitations.[74]

Applying WBBH's view of humility to interpretation produces a boundless multiplication of limiting personas that are as diverse as the number of interpretive agents since each agent possesses an entirely unique composite of limitations, but there are some fundamental limitations that can be ascribed to every interpretive agent as a core demand for interpretive humility. In regard to interpreting the biblical text, consider these basic limitations present for every contemporary interpreter. Interpreters are limited by their point of view, which necessarily stands at some distance to the biblical text and author. There are no contemporary interpreters who can suppose themselves to possess the exact cultural, linguistic, historical, or psychological vantage point as the author, since those contextual realities no longer exist anywhere in the world today. They were the unique combination of factors present in a place and time far removed from the contemporary world. Schleiermacher and Dilthey supposed a form of spiritual or psychological union to transcend this distance into a universal certainty of authorial intent, but empirical evidence, philosophical critique, and the multiplication of mutually exclusive interpretive results from their system have demonstrated the ultimate futility of the approach. Interpretive humility rejects the hubris that emerged from the Schleiermacher-Dilthey system that believed that the interpreter could understand the text better than the author. Interpretive humility acknowledges, with some sense of disappointment, that no tool, resource, or technique can fully overcome agents' limitations to put themselves fully into the mind or spirit of the author. Beyond the limitation of distance, interpreters bring with them a series of biases when approaching a text. These biases emerge from sociological settings, the locatedness of the interpreter on a continuum of power-relationships in the world (either as the privileged or the marginalized), religious frameworks, and the perennial problem of egotism (both personal and corporate). The owning of one's limitations, rather than seeing the inescapable reality of biases as a reason to reject a discoverable meaning in a text, instead, reaffirms the necessity to remain vigilant against the intrusion of bias into hermeneutical endeavors and admits this tendency to others, even when virtuous interpreters may not

74. Whitcomb et al., "Intellectual Humility," 519.

be consciously aware of their influence at any specific moment. Ironically, the owning of the inescapable presence of bias provides the greatest resource against its distorting influence.

By ingraining the virtue of humility that admits limitations, an agent answers the extremes of both Modernity and Post-Modernity and produces what Vanhoozer calls a hermeneutic of humility and conviction.[75] The hubris of certainty is dismissed, not because there is no stable meaning embedded within the text, but because the agent engaging it is ultimately a limited being not possessing a perfected god-like point of view. On the other hand, the skepticism of Post-Modernity is not allowed to preclude an agent from deeply believing and gaining a justifiable understanding gained through virtuous inquiry. At the least, a humble agent owns an openness to continued refinement or correction to an understanding of a text since it can only be a justifiable approximation of the embedded meaning. All interpretation is pursued by limited and flawed interpreters and interpretive communities. Jeannine Brown effectively captures the sense of humility's influence in interpretation:

> The goal of understanding the author's communicative intention is a worthy and responsible goal. That we will not fully or perfectly reach it is no reason to give up trying. In fact, we should work diligently to hear as best as we are able the voice of Scripture that often contravenes our own. The truth of our locatedness in interpretation should, however, encourage humility as we come to the biblical text. Such a humble stance is a good thing, for it keeps us aware that our reading might be a mistaken reading, our interpretation a misinterpretation.[76]

Interpretive humility as a necessary contributor to the virtuous intellectual character of a biblical hermeneut also possesses an aspect that anticipates the final chapter of this research. Jens Zimmerman acknowledges the theological dimension of humility and its historical attestation within the confessional interpretive community: "The reliance on the Holy Spirit in interpretation effects interpretive humility . . . The Puritan John] Owen insists on the interpretive humility that should come with the Christian's belief in the power of God's word."[77] An awareness of the limitations of the interpreter is the inescapable consequence of the view

75. Vanhoozer, *Is There a Meaning in This Text?*, 455–56.

76. Brown, *Scripture as Communication*, 126.

77. Zimmermann, *Recovering Theological Hermeneutics*, 115.

that acknowledges the existence and necessity of spiritual assistance in attaining and applying the meaning of the biblical text. One cannot simultaneously hold to dependence and hubris. Dependence on the Holy Spirit is only available to interpreters who begin with a deep sense of their own limitations, in other words, a sense of virtuous humility.

Paul Moser approaches the theological need for humility from a different perspective. He claims that any ability of humanity to gain certainty in apprehending revelation would thwart the ultimate redemptive nature of God's plan directed to humanity. Certainty would be inevitably twisted into human pride at the ability of one to attain perfect understanding, and ultimately obstruct the intent of the curative redemption of the human condition.[78] The redemptive nature of the biblical text presupposes an epistemic and interpretive humility in order to understand it in line with divine intent.

Courage

In examining interpretive virtues, some of the named virtues are solely intellectual in nature (e.g., love of truth and open-mindedness), while others share both a moral and intellectual applicability (e.g., justice and courage). The status of courage, as a virtue, is widely attested in nearly all treatments of the moral virtues, but questions are rightly raised as to the significance of courage in an epistemic context. Is intellectual courage directly truth conducive (or in the case of interpretation, understanding)? Courage seems to be an intellectual virtue that is only indirectly truth conducive, in contrast with the way that attentiveness, perseverance, or most other virtues considered in the chapter may be. While not necessarily truth conducive in specific acquisitional moments, it is required to be globally intellectually virtuous, and therefore, necessary for the greatest possible attainment of knowledge and understanding. It functions most importantly in the anterior and posterior moments that bookend the interpretive experience. Furthermore, the necessity of anterior courage has a primarily internal focus while the posterior application possesses a more externally attuned sensibility. Intellectual courage also illustrates the need for something more than a rule or duty based interpretive epistemology. As Vrinda Dalmiya explains, "To the extent that virtues like creativity and intellectual courage are constitutive of a worthy cognitive

78. Moser, "God and Epistemic Authority," 415.

character, rule following cannot be definitive of epistemic responsibility. Of course, it is important that virtuous persons acquire and follow certain rules, but the point is that her epistemic worth is not determined exclusively by them."[79] Courage often demands the careful and measured willingness to subvert communally accepted, but detrimental rules (just as creativity often does), in pursuit of the goal of greater understanding. Exemplars abound and are often considered amongst the greatest intellectual heroes of history as they courageously broke rules to pursue knowledge and understanding (e.g., Galileo and Copernicus).

The importance of courage as an intellectual virtue is demonstrated by Baehr in his selecting it to be one of only two intellectual virtues that receive a chapter length treatment in his work *The Inquiring Mind*. His definition within the chapter is foundationally useful for any concept of intellectual virtue: "Intellectual courage is a disposition to persist in or with a state or course of action aimed at an epistemically good end despite the fact that doing so involves an apparent threat to one's own well-being."[80] Battaly refines this definition even further: "The courageous person fears all and only what he should. In contrast, those who lack courage are persuaded by pleasure or pain to ignore some of the dictates of reason."[81] Roberts and Wood are even more explicit in expressing its application to interpretive pursuits: "When texts are from a period other than our own, so that a cultural divide yawns between us and the writers, a *courageous* [emphasis added], empathetic, and charitable imaginativeness may be required really to get into what the texts are saying, a humble willingness to learn from people we might be inclined to think of as naïve or primitive."[82] All of these definitions demand explanation as to what the "epistemic good" would be and what potential hindrances, either by pain or pleasure, interpretive courage helps a hermeneut overcome. The epistemic good is obvious—a justified understanding of a text—but the dangers require greater elucidation.

In the anterior position, the threats to effective interpretive inquiry are collectively viewed through the lens of a demotivational form of intellectual angst. Rather than undermining specific interpretive goods, it robs the hermeneut of the will to pursue textually embedded meaning

79. Dalmiya, "Knowing People," 229.

80. Baehr, *Inquiring Mind*, loc. 2258.

81. Battaly, *Virtue*, 38.

82. Roberts and Wood, *Intellectual Virtues*, 49.

before it begins. The parallel to the more broadly observed skepticism that has plagued the post-Cartesian world is readily observable. Genia Schönbaumsfeld addresses how human fallibility and the unavoidably subjective limitedness of perspective have often propelled cognitive agents to experience a debilitating intellectual angst that in its worst forms has resulted in an unwarranted epistemic nihilism.[83] As has been acknowledged in this research, certainty cannot be the goal of hermeneutics nor is the methodologically defined approaches that conceived of a perspectiveless objectivity that envisioned a god-like view from nowhere. The admission of these limitations does not require the abandonment of the pursuit of textually embedded meaning out of an anxiety produced by skepticism. The admission of fallibility is insufficient to attain the conclusion that "everyone could be wrong about everything all of the time."[84] Schönbaumsfeld prescribes the willfully attuned virtue of courage, specifically as expressed by Søren Kierkegaard, as the solution to the intellectual malaise produced by this form of angst. The fact that finitude and fallibility are inescapable elements of the human experience "does not cut us off from having an objective, 'external' world in view . . . It does not seal us off from the real world altogether . . . Consequently, we need to find the courage to accept our finitude without allowing ourselves the indulgence of falling into epistemic nihilism."[85] These epistemically focused descriptions are parallel to the same developments in hermeneutics since Descartes, which have compelled many interpreters to abandon the mere possibility or ability to gain justifiable understanding from the authorially-expressed intent of a text.

The posterior view of courage is externally focused on the potential ramifications of presenting a specific interpretation. Having overcome the angst and fear of fallibility and limitedness to pursue a textually-expressed meaning with ongoing applicational significance, the hermeneut is now subject to a range of external factors that may compel silence or coerce unwarranted reformulation of the attained understanding. With the starting point that all interpretation is, at best, a justified understanding of approximate meaning within the text as willed by the author, the interpreter can fear the unavoidable scrutiny and conflicting views that may be surfaced by the expression of their interpretation. The fear of

83. Schönbaumsfeld, "Epistemic Angst," 7.

84. Schönbaumsfeld, "Epistemic Angst," 5.

85. Schönbaumsfeld, "Epistemic Angst," 14–15.

conflict, failure, or unwanted attention, especially when the interpretation may depart from communally-accepted norms, can silence or lead to the illegitimate adjustment of an interpretation prior to its expression not based on appropriate grounds. This preemptive fear of external pressure is sufficient to effect potential interpretations, but the experience of various reactions subsequent to its expression can become reality and also impact ongoing expression and adherence to the interpretation. The potential loss of status, vocational attainments, or relational community are powerful incentives to submit to fear, which is the reason that the virtuous interpreter must also possess a deeply-embedded sense of courage. This sense of fear can be observed in all cognitive disciplines, but it is especially relevant in religious dialogue because of the ancient and deeply-ingrained nature of the traditions as well as the oft-perceived ramifications of error (e.g., heaven and hell). An interpretation that is perceived as being outside of a particular community's acceptable understanding, whether the view is within a confessional, societal, or academic environment, can elicit swift and devastating punishment both relationally and, at times, even physically. An appropriate fear of being in error, which rightly compels reexamination in the light of more information or the exposure of bias, is different than a cowardly acquiescence to external intimidation. As Zagzebski points out, the more deeply the virtue of courage is integrated into an agent's epistemic/interpretive character, the more likely that, "He may not even have to face contrary temptations at all and will eventually find courageous activity pleasant."[86]

Perseverance

In addressing the disposition of perseverance, King correctly observes that, "Far from being just one among a number of virtues, perseverance is a requirement of the other virtues."[87] It is impossible to conceive of a virtue, moral or intellectual, that would be virtuous without some sense of persistence and determination attached to it. By definition, virtues are necessary only because their *teloi* are difficult to attain, which encompasses some sense of the core definition of perseverance. Surprisingly, perseverance, as a necessary component of other virtues, and as a free-standing virtue in its own right, has garnered minimal treatment

86. Zagzebski, *Virtues of the Mind*, 150.
87. King, "Perseverance as an Intellectual Virtue," 3522.

in the discussion of VE. Many authors list it among their collection of virtues, including names as important to the discipline as Zagzebski[88] and Baehr,[89] but it is not until King (2014) and Battaly (2017) published separate journal articles exclusively devoted to the topic that any significant discussion entered the literature.

Perseverance is often connected to ideas of temporal concerns. To persevere is to see a task to its completion regardless of the time required to accomplish it. When placed within the realm of interpretive concerns, the idea of a time-bound pursuit of completion is inadequate for multiple reasons. The chief reason for this conception's inadequacy is seen in the nature of the goal of VH, a justified understanding of a text. Understanding is a continually-expanding and never-finally-attained reality, since it is always adding explanatory richness and points of connection to other standing justified true beliefs, as well as expanding its significance into new contexts of application as diverse as every receiving reading context. For perseverance to be applicable to interpretive endeavors, it must be attuned to something more than simply expending the full amount of time and effort necessary to complete the inquiry. King and Battaly are both helpful in this regard.

While their arguments are similar, Battaly's definition is slightly more comprehensive because of the inclusion of an affective element. She describes perseverance as involving "dispositions: (1) to make good judgments about one's intellectual goals; (2) to reliably perceive obstacles to one's intellectual goals; (3) to respond to obstacles with the appropriate degree of confidence and calmness; (4) to overcome obstacles, or otherwise act as the context demands; and (5) to do so because one cares appropriately about epistemic goods."[90] In both treatments, the primary concern for perseverance is the overcoming of obstacles to the attainment of the epistemic goal, which in this case would be a justified understanding of a text. The similarity to courage is readily apparent, but the difference would be that courage is a subset of perseverance attuned specifically to pain, pleasure, threat, and danger, and it often involves opposition that requires some form of agency. The obstacles that the virtue of perseverance encounters and reliably acts to overcome are rarely agential and do not generally entail any type of threat or danger. Specific

---

88. Zagzebski, *Virtues of the Mind*, 155.

89. Baehr, *Inquiring Mind*, loc. 179.

90. Battaly, "Intellectual Perseverance," 688.

obstacles that regularly attend to the task of interpretation are obstacles that are intrinsic to the task and those that are both internal and external to the interpreter.

It is not possible to generate a full catalogue of potential obstacles that may be encountered in hermeneutical inquiry. The impossibility of this task is due partly to the obvious fact that the number of obstacles is more than legion, but, more than this, what may be an obstacle to one agent may not be an obstacle to another. When considering the same agent, what may be an object to an agent in one moment or context may not be in another. Obstacles and the intellectual character that perseveres through their presence are extraordinarily context sensitive. The best that can be offered is a basic definition of obstacles and a small sampling of both the internal and external forms of obstacles that could be present in a typical interpretive encounter.

In its most basic formulation, "An obstacle is something that makes it difficult for one to achieve one's intellectual aims."[91] In interpretive tasks, some obstacles are intrinsic to the discipline. While not as indeterminate as some who have extended Derrida's idea of *différance* to mean that *any* and *all* sense of meaning is *forever* deferred in perpetuity, the referential nature of language, nevertheless, is intrinsically complex and a potential obstacle in interpretive tasks. Attempting to approximate the intended purpose in the language of an author is an obstacle, but the nature and general efficacy of human communication has demonstrated that with perseverance and a host of other virtues and skills, it can be attained with some sense of reliability. The extension of significance is also an intrinsic obstacle to the full hermeneutical task. The contingencies of each historical moment do not allow for unhindered extension of significance, but it cannot be then assumed that it is fruitless to carefully consider the relevant application of a historically conditioned text in a disparate historical setting. If one accepts this obstacle as insurmountable, then the reading of any text to gain any form of transformational understanding is an exercise in futility, since even texts generated in immediately preceding moments are situated in a now lost, and never to be repeated, historical moment. Obstacles that arise within the agent through which they must persevere to attain justified understanding include weariness, boredom, distraction (e.g., the mind wandering to other matters not related to understanding the text), emotional frame of mind

91. King, "Perseverance as an Intellectual Virtue," 3512.

potentially unrelated to the inquiry (e.g., the impact of distraction resulting from being angry about a conflict with a friend that preceded the
hermeneutical inquiry), and the perennial problem of biases. Obstacles
that exist externally to the task or the agent but must be overcome include
environmental factors (e.g., temperature, noise, lighting, etc.), criticism,
conflict, or pressure.

Just as much as perseverance compels the agent to press on in the
face of all forms of obstacles, the properly virtuous form of perseverance
also understands the mean between the extremes of giving up too easily and becoming intransigent or obsessive at the expense of other more
worthy interpretive goods. While the former tends to be the more likely
vice for many interpreters, the latter is also observable, and it must be accounted for in a virtue approach. One example of virtuous perseverance
is knowing when to cease or pause inquiry until more information is discovered. This type of obstacle can be seen in a select number of NT textual variants. Some textual mysteries may not be resolvable for a variety
of reasons. In some cases, insufficient textual evidence on certain variant
readings in the light of a lacuna in currently extant texts, especially when
no variant reading is sufficiently different to hinder a general sense of
the broader textual setting, is a situation where virtuous perseverance
will not sidetrack the broader goal of understanding for an unresolvable
point of textual minutia. Virtuous interpretation not only knows when to
keep working through an obstacle toward deeper understanding but also
when to move on because the understanding is sufficient, unattainable,
or unimportant.

Functional Virtues

Attentiveness

The movement from the more dispositionally-attuned virtues to the
more functionally-associated virtues is exemplified in the concept of attentiveness. It is nearly impossible to envision the virtue of attentiveness
apart from the act or skill of paying attention. This close association of
the virtue and the correlated skill leads to some discussion as to whether
attentiveness is simply a skill rather than a virtue. Roberts and Wood emphasize the "skill" nature of attentiveness rather than its status as a virtue
as it pertains to reading: "Our ability to get knowledge from our reading
depends on aptitudes, skills, and accomplishments other than virtues.

Clearly, a decent quick intelligence is important. The ability to pay close attention to what one is reading is one such skill."[92] Baehr argues for its status with other virtues in the realm of textual inquiry, "This might involve having to attend . . . To the semantic subtleties of a text, or to the exact logical structure of an argument. Thus it might require intellectual virtues like attentiveness, sensitivity to detail, careful observation, scrutiny, or perceptiveness."[93] The treatment of the differences between virtues and skills in chapter 2 seems to support the view that attentiveness, as applied to hermeneutical inquiry, is more likely a virtue that is primarily expressed by the skills associated with paying close attention to relevant details. As a virtue, it also includes the motivational component of attaining intellectual goods as well as the inclusion of several other related qualities not exhausted by the skill of simply paying attention (e.g., focus, carefulness, perceptiveness, and scrutiny). Even more importantly, an interpreting agent who possesses the virtue of attentiveness does not just turn on or turn off the ability to read closely and appropriately notice the subtleties of text, context (intertextually and externally to the text), and the potential points of connection with contemporary circumstances. As Gadamer points out, the symbiotic experience of attentiveness is occasioned by the genius of works and the genius of interpreters. The great work invites observers, "to pleasure and contemplation an inexhaustible object of lingering attention and interpretation," which is matched by the interpreter's equal genius in appreciating it.[94]

While many models of biblical interpretation (e.g., historical-grammatical, form-critical, redaction-critical, or many forms of literary analysis) could be highlighted as to how an ingrained and habitual practice of careful attention in interpreting a text is necessary to attain reliably justified understandings, the field of rhetorical criticism is especially useful as an example. George Kennedy's work in this field helps to demonstrate how a person who is motivated, habituated, and joyful in the virtue of attentiveness and the resultant skills of paying attention, perceiving details, and careful scrutiny of primary communicative patterns will be well-suited to gain deeper understanding of a text. Consider his detailing of the central elements of a rhetorical analysis and how the words highlighted in this quotation (italics have been added) fall under

92. Roberts and Wood, *Intellectual Virtues*, 120.

93. Baehr, *Inquiring Mind*, loc. 284.

94. Gadamer, *Truth and Method*, 85.

the broad umbrella of actions, motivations, or abilities of a virtuously attentive interpreter.

> If rhetorical criticism is to be valid, it must be practiced with some *awareness* of the traditions of Jewish speech, of which chiasmus is one, and if it is to be useful it must *embrace* more than style. If fundamental and universal features of rhetoric are *kept in mind* and if we *seek* to use them in *describing the logical and structural features of the text before us*, rather than simply quarrying a text for examples of classical figures, we can significantly enhance our *appreciation* of its meaning without violence to the author's intent. The ultimate goal of the rhetorical analysis, briefly put, is the discovery of the author's intent and of how that is transmitted through a text to an audience.[95]

Phyllis Trible, herself a scholar of rhetorically-focused hermeneutics, offers a description of the process that could nearly be considered a formal approbation of the virtue of attentiveness. She continually speaks of a "close reading" of the text throughout her work, *Rhetorical Criticism*. The idea of "close reading" is a call to not just a skilled form of reading, but an exaltation of the power to focus deeply, read carefully, and pay attention to finely-grained details in function and the resultant form within a text. Any rudimentarily trained reader could occasionally attain the fruits of this type of reading, but only those who have nurtured the deeper sense of the virtue have the capacity to transmit justification in the frame of VH.

Just like the discussion concerning courage, the virtue of attentiveness is practiced in internal and external manners. Internally interpreters are attentive to their own feelings, worldview, biases, gaps in knowledge, and connecting points between the text and already-held beliefs. The external emphasis of the virtuously attentive reader is focused on the full range of textual matters (e.g., history, context, semantics, argumentation, literary devices, genre, affective considerations, etc.).

Creativity

There is no more contested virtue in VE or VH than the status of creativity. Its recognition as a virtue is challenged in multiple approaches or constructed by way of exception to typical virtuous definitions. The most serious challenge to the concept of creativity as an intellectual virtue is

---

95. Kennedy, *Rhetorical Criticism*, 12.

related to the perceived central tenet of VE: virtues are those things that are truth conducive. Bernardo Caslib, disputing Annas's view of virtue epistemology, argues that it is not required that a virtue be directly truth conducive to be considered a virtue. He offers the possibility of additional epistemological goods short of truth that are worthy products of intellectual virtue (e.g., the ability to draw clear ideas that can eventually transform one's predicament into a better one").[96] In this way, he admits creativity as a virtue while acknowledging that it often does not lead to truth.[97] Zagzebski argues similarly that creativity should be counted among the virtues, even while conceding that its "truth conduciveness in the sense of producing a high proportion of true beliefs is much lower than that of the ordinary virtues of careful and sober inquiry."[98] Going beyond Caslib, she also argues that, "The existence of the virtue of creativity is a problem for the thesis that virtue must be acquired by habituation, but I will go further and offer the conjecture that the ability to resist habit in general may actually be a distinguishing mark of creative people."[99] She resolves her assessment of these discrepancies between creativity and her previously established definition by simply declaring them to be an "interesting exception,"[100] which "are necessary for the advancement of human knowledge."[101] For the sake of accuracy and thoroughness, it would seem that simply assigning creativity to a unique and exceptional type of virtue is insufficient for the inclusion in VH unless it can be shown by further investigation to align more closely with the canons of VE.

Matthew Kieran resets the conversation by offering important definitional details. "A creative person is someone disposed to seek out and preform creative acts. An exemplary (or fully virtuous) creative person is someone who is disposed to do so for the right kinds of reasons." From this foundation he summarizes creative acts as involving "abilities, skill, and judgment in a way that tends toward producing something new and valuable."[102] While a helpful starting point, it does not resolve all of the issues. In particular, how does the creation of something new and useful

---

96. Caslib, "Why Intellectual Virtues Matter," 98.
97. Caslib, "Why Intellectual Virtues Matter," 98.
98. Zagzebski, *Virtues of the Mind*, 182.
99. Zagzebski, *Virtues of the Mind*, 124.
100. Zagzebski, *Virtues of the Mind*, 126.
101. Zagzebski, *Virtues of the Mind*, 182.
102. Kieran, "Creativity," 168.

apply to VH? One solution could be the creation of a new text fashioned from the melding of the authorial horizon and the interpreter's horizon as advocated by Gadamer, but that carries the concept further than necessary. The production of an interpretation is inherently something new and valuable (valuable, if the interpretation is done well), since interpretation is not a mimesis or photocopying of the original text. Even without requiring the *melding of horizons* concept, the most rigid and traditional idea of interpretation is acknowledged as the creation of something new while still being directly tied to the intents and purposes of the original text's author. Furthermore, creativity is a fitting description of the best forms of interpretation which fashion new application and significance from the original setting into new and diverse settings. Creativity, in this sense, need not be viewed as necessarily *ex nihilo*; it can be occasioned by creatively encountering a text and creatively re-expressing it in richer and more applicable ways as fresh extensions of understanding.

Margaret Boden exposes the broader possibilities of creative acts by identifying three primary ways that creativity can function: making unfamiliar combinations, exploring conceptual spaces, and transforming the space.[103] While all three forms that she defines can be observed in VH, the third is more rare and would be akin to the great paradigmatic shifts in hermeneutical inquiry. These creative moments would likely not be the typical expression that one would expect when considering a virtuous interpreter. The first two forms of creativity are especially pertinent to the effective interpretation.

The recombining of elements into something new and even surprising is an indispensable task of interpretation. Many elements are part of the textual context including genre, words, historical setting, and worldview, but these can be increasingly more understood and then creatively reapplied into new and diverse contexts. This creative work is not absolutely free, but is the refashioning of what is already present in a germinal form. Even an interpretive skeptic of textual meaning as important as Derrida admits that for him, while metaphysical referents remain beyond plausibility, interpretation is still more than pure reproduction and even the most creative interpretations are still bound by some important considerations. "Without recognizing and respecting all its [the texts] classical exigencies, which is not easy and requires all the instruments of traditional criticism, critical production would risk developing in any

103. Boden, *Creative Mind*, 3–6.

direction at all and would authorize itself to say almost anything. But this indispensable guardrail has always only *protected*, it has never *opened*, a reading."[104] Creativity is needed to open the reading after having used the tools of traditional criticism. To avoid this by seeing each interpretation as a purely new production unhindered by the text's intention falls under Gadamer condemnation as, "An untenable hermeneutic nihilism."[105] The creativity of a virtuous interpreter helps to produce a justified understanding of the text's meaning expressed in relevant ways into continually new settings.

If the first form of creativity expressed by Boden is attuned to the creation of new interpretation in contemporary environs, the second allows more emphasis on the originating context. She defines conceptual spaces as, "structured styles of thought."[106] These structured styles of thought are inevitably different when examining the space of the text and the space of the reader. It is a creative act of imaginativeness to explore these distinct environments. While never perfectly attained, the more virtuously creative interpreter will be able to explore and be open to new insights from a disparate space than the one they inhabit. (This ability to explore spaces for new understanding can also be done within one's own space, since it is not possible that all thoughts that are possible within a space have already been thought.) Creativity is required to be open to a range of possibilities that exists within any particular space. When considering textual spaces, things like genre, worldview, and socio-cultural boundaries appear to be particularly important.

If the preceding two concepts of creativity are considered to be relevant to interpretation, then the fact that creativity can be both acquired and habituated seems more likely in VH than some VE proponents have advocated. There is no reason to believe that the skills of imaginativeness and recombination are beyond the capacity to be observed in an exemplar, practiced, and then ingrained into one's own interpretive character. When the possibility of the theological dimension is admitted, the potential is expanded even further. Wolfgang Vondey describes the current state of Christianity as being in crisis, partly due to a "crisis of the imagination." Drawing from the resources of Pentecostalism's connection of imagination with the Christian life as being ultimately "the story of the

104. Derrida, *Of Grammatology*, 172.

105. Gadamer, *Truth and Method*, 86.

106. Boden, *Creative Mind*, 4.

Holy Spirit," he offers a pneumatological framework for a rebirth of creativity.[107] This pneumatological dimension is central to a VH approach.

Generosity (Charity)

Generosity, like all virtues, is tuned to be effective in settings where effectiveness is difficult and demands something praiseworthy in the exhibiting of the virtue. Borrowing the OT concept of *hesed*, Kartharine Doob Sakenfeld explains that charity, or in this case, generosity, is

> An action performed for the weak party by the powerful one, for the situationally inferior party by the situationally superior one. Because of his powerful status, the superior party is always free not to perform the act of *hesed*; the weak party will have no future opportunity to 'get even' and no outside recrimination or interference (as from legal authorities) is to be feared.[108]

While it can be argued that the authors are in a place of power because they originate the text, its formal structures, and its meaning, they are greatly disadvantaged in many ways within the interpretive dialogue. Authors are most often not present to contest or further explain themselves in light of the manner in which they are treated, understood, or used. There is no recrimination or possibility of retribution when an interpreter abuses a text, wrenches it out of context, and projects external meaning into it when its author is irretrievably absent, often by virtue of death. In this way, the author is literally at the mercy of the interpreter.

A virtuous interpreter refuses to use her freedom to abuse the authorial agent in light of the author's inability to protest poor treatment or further explain oneself but freely chooses to extend the highest levels of grace, charity, and kindness. Roberts and Wood demonstrate this virtue well.

> Consider an act of intellectual charity. I am discussing someone's philosophical book, and I disagree pretty fundamentally with what I take the author to be saying. If I am reading a certain passage charitably, I interpret it so as to attribute as much validity and intelligence to the passage as I can, compatibly with a careful and therefore critical reading. The act of charity in this case is the interpretation. The motive distinctive of intellectual charity (as contrasted with other intellectual virtues) is here my

107. Vondey, *Beyond Pentecostalism*, loc. 527.
108. Sakenfeld, *The Meaning of Hesed*, 234.

concern to treat the author as I would like to be treated were I the author. It is goodwill towards him, a valuing of him as a person and as an author . . . The fact that I interpret the passage so as to attribute as much validity and intelligence to it as I can does not by itself make the act an act of intellectual charity, because as charity, the act has this motivational condition: I must act out of goodwill towards the author. If I make a "charitable" interpretation of the passage, because doing so will enable me better to crush the author in the noetic dust under my feet, then I have not acted charitably, even if I have acted "charitably". But even if I "use" charity in the interest of knowledge and understanding, rather than of crushing my opponent, I do not act from the virtue of charity, since the characteristic aim of charity is the well-being of a person.[109]

By this definition, generosity, like creativity, may not be strictly or directly truth conducive. Generosity is more properly focused on the treatment of the other agent in the dialogue than the dogged pursuit of understanding. If this is true, should generosity be considered an epistemological or interpretive virtue? Apart from it being a right thing to do and generally making the interpreter a better person, it is indirectly more likely to foster the accumulation of more justified understandings than those who function without it. By treating the disadvantaged author with respect, interpreters are more likely to be open to new insights and be more attentive to richer forms of understanding since their disposition and actions are intentionally generous and open. Generous interpretation is not a victimizing of the other in a conflictual or disrespectful approach, but "a sort of respectful conversation between equals,"[110] where even seeming simple or naïve texts are ultimately allowed to possess potential for profound insight, "so the generous-spirited reader, the reader disposed to lavish 'credit' on texts and authors for having something to say, may have an advantage in the harvest of epistemic goods."[111]

While textual study is certainly affected by the traditional subject-object debate that is particularly relevant in many epistemological conversations, there is, at another level, the sense that the text is a medium that occasions the interaction of two agents (author and reader), or more if one properly includes each's formative community. This sense of the

---

109. Roberts and Wood, *Intellectual Virtues*, 74.

110. Roberts and Wood, *Intellectual Virtues*, 132.

111. Roberts and Wood, *Intellectual Virtues*, 132.

subject-engaging-with-a-subject element of hermeneutics has been the source of some of the most significant attempts to anchor the search for the text's meaning in the author's intent. Schleiermacher's approach is one of the most widely-known methods, which is focused on divining the intention of the author through a supposed connection based upon a shared and universal *Gefühl*. It is entirely possible in this approach that the universal *Gefühl* can be experienced with no goodwill directed toward the author, thus making it separate from a generous approach. Although an epoch-making concept, it is not the only way to attempt the task of text-centric agent-to-agent understanding, and generosity becomes especially relevant in forging a new virtuous model.

Schleiermacher's approach to understanding the other can be compared to Alvin Goldman's simulation theory, which is not surprising since Goldman himself labels this as a form of a *Verstehen* approach advocated by Schleiermacher's intellectual descendant, Dilthey.[112] In this approach, we come to know things, ourselves, and others by the process of simulation. The skill of empathy becomes the central capacity of understanding others by seeking to affectively put oneself in the other's shoes. Goldman argues that the success of simulation requires that the inquiring agent possess the ability to "*isolate* or *quarantine* any beliefs or desires of his own that are not shared by the target agent."[113] Unfortunately, in both epistemology and hermeneutics, this attempt to simulate is fatally flawed by often being incapable of rendering much more than the projection of one's own feelings upon the other person or the author in the case of textual interpretation, a distinctly ungenerous approach. Dalmiya dismisses simulation as, "dangerously close to 'remaking' the other according to our own lights rather than 'encountering' her."[114] In the place of simulation, she offers a different approach that she labels as a "method of care." Her method serves as a valuable contribution to the concept developed in this research as generosity, and it stands as a counter to the beleaguered approaches instituted by Schleiermacher and his intellectual heirs. Generosity, as an interpretive virtue, does not pretend to fully "quarantine" one's own beliefs, feelings, or biases. Instead, it seeks to approach the other with a generous and care-filled sense that fosters a potentially transformational encounter with the text and its author. It

---

112. Goldman, "Empathy, Mind, and Morals," 20.

113. Goldman, "Empathy, Mind, and Morals," 22.

114. Dalmiya, "Knowing People," 225.

does this by lavishing upon the other the deepest sense that they matter as agents capable of expressing meaning.

As Montmarquet argues, generosity is in a unique category of virtues that are sufficiently exemplified by the act of trying to be generous. "For instance, not only is trying to be generous, as noted earlier, sufficient for being so on a given occasion; trying to be ungenerous (selfish) will be sufficient for being that."[115] It becomes a virtue when this desire and willful attempt to be generous is habituated and joyfully ingrained into the interpretive character of the agent. By this standard, generosity epitomizes the functional form of interpretive virtue. The disposition cannot be exemplified without the intentional actions of willfully motivated acts of generosity toward another. This is where Dalmiya's method of care becomes helpful. She outlines the basis for justified claims about other minds in five steps, all of which fit within the rubric of generosity. Step one is recognizing the other mind (in interpretive endeavors, the author) in all their particularities as important, which is called "caring about." Step two attempts to shift to the other's point of view in "caring for" the author. "The deeper the initial acknowledgement of worth, the stronger is our involvement with the other."[116] This step proceeds beyond simulation by involving a stronger volitional condition in "caring for" the author. Step three is "taking care," where the interpreter gleans from the "caring for" choice an understanding that is more personal and applicable, where the other's works are cared for as though they are one's own. Step four involves "caring about caring." This reflexive act understands that all the generous actions of caring must themselves be cared about if the virtue is to be an entrenched and ongoing trait of the interpreter. Finally, the truly generous interpreter will seek to convey to the other that all that has been undertaken in the method of care was because they, the author, were considered important and every action of engagement with them through their work was afforded the most willfully purposed sense of generosity and respect.[117] In the case of a deceased author, much of this process will be engaged in as a "virtual, or as-if, goal."[118] The value of Dalmiya's approach is the careful and detailed generosity that engages the entire process, beginning with placing a high value on others and

115. Montmarquet, "'Internalist' Conception of Epistemic Virtue," 145.
116. Dalmiya, "Knowing People," 225.
117. Dalmiya, "Knowing People," 225.
118. Roberts and Wood, *Intellectual Virtues*, 74.

their production with a carefully attuned sense of self-transforming re-
flexivity in the experience. It is important to acknowledge that all of these
steps, including "taking care" (the ability to own the ideas of another in
a highly-valued sense), can take place even when the interpreter may
fundamentally disagree with what the author proposes. Generosity as a
virtue cannot be limited to only those cases where there is agreement
between author and interpreter, but it is most needed in times where disagreement is most acute.

Master Virtue

Phronesis

In the complicated reality of hermeneutics set within a postmodern
context, there is a nearly universal sense that old rules and paradigms
cannot sustain textual inquiry. There is no singular rule-based approach
that can be sufficient to engage all of the particular settings in which a
text may have originated or be contemporaneously read or used. Jean
Francois Lyotard's description of the current situation as "incredulity
toward metanarratives"[119] eliminates an appeal to broader and universal
paradigms to assist in the task offering anything more solid than "dan-
gling prescriptives." What then can be left to navigate any form of hermeneutical discussion, or is the entire enterprise doomed to solipsism? Even
the most radical proponents of the indeterminacy of meaning and approaches like Deconstructionism and playful or game-based approaches
still recognize the need for something that can manage, at the least, the
dialogue in a fair way, even if dialogue is all that remains as the final
possibility for hermeneutics in their view. Ironically, the appeal of more
recent theoreticians like Lyotard and John Caputo appeal to a term heavily utilized by the likes of Gadamer and Heidegger, as well as those who
extend as far back as the NT and Aristotle. Though defined differently by
its various proponents, phronesis seems to be a leading candidate to fill
this complicated space in the history of interpretation, and it is equally
important in the formulation of VH.

Although it is appropriate and well-attested in virtue literature to include phronesis in the consideration of intellectual virtues, it is a virtue that
resides in a unique place in comparison to other virtues. Since Aristotle

---

119. Lyotard and Thebaud, *Just Gaming*, 59.

has served as a significant source of contemporary virtue thought, his understanding of phronesis is important to any further discussion. Rather than detailing the individually habituated character traits (e.g., love of truth, open-mindedness, justice, etc.) as most responsibilists do, Aristotle expressed the intellectual virtues in more broadly-defined categories. "We say that some of the virtues are intellectual and others moral, philosophic wisdom [σοφίαν] and understanding [σύνεσιν] and practical wisdom [φρόνησιν] being intellectual."[120] In this taxonomy of intellectual virtues, the phrase "practical wisdom" is the English translator's attempt to capture the meaning of the concept expressed in the word phronesis.

In his comprehensive approach to ethics, each virtue lies in the mean between two excessive vices, the one being a defect of lack and the other of excess. The ability to determine where the virtuous mean lies in particular cases falls to the work of phronesis. "Virtue, then, is a state of character concerned with choice, lying in a mean, i.e., the mean relative to us, this being determined by a rational principle, and by that principle by which the man of *practical wisdom* [emphasis added] would determine it."[121] In this way, virtue theory is inescapably subjective-centered while resisting relativism. The person of practical wisdom has an experienced, reliably successful, and finely tuned sense of wisdom that guides its possessor toward the properly virtuous balance in deliberative action in each unique situation which is encountered.

For those engaged in the task of hermeneutics, phronesis serves as the master virtue that balances and integrates the expectations of the various interpretive virtues into a coherent and functioning whole. Virtues are by their nature uncodifiable. "Wisdom is a value that is at least difficult, probably impossible, to understand impersonally on the model of rationality. It is likely that wisdom, like friendship, takes a different form in each individual case."[122] They resist all attempts to reduce them to general rules of conduct and demand the practical wisdom of phronesis to direct their expression as embodied, experience-based, and situationally-sensitive excellencies that guide the interpreter to increasingly justifiable understandings of the text.[123] Each interpretive virtue, by definition and function, is an inherently good intellectual disposition which increases

---

120. Aristotle, *Nicomachean Ethics*, loc. 644.

121. Aristotle, *Nicomachean Ethics*, loc. 783.

122. Zagzebski, *Virtues of the Mind*, 20.

123. Hasselberger, "Knowing More," 776.

the personal worth of its possessor and reliably attains the goods of the desired intellectual fruit (i.e., knowledge or understanding). Even when this definition is fully accepted, it is possible to envision scenarios in hermeneutical inquiries that require some form of governing virtue that guides the process, at times giving appropriate weight to a certain virtue over another based on the particular demands of the text, context, or contemporary setting, or in guiding to the virtuous mean a specific virtue demands in a context specific situation. In this way, phronesis fits well in the model of understanding and enacting a text that Vanhoozer proposes in *The Drama of Doctrine*. Phronesis becomes a wise director in the embodiment of understanding the text, drawing from the script (i.e., the text) that which is necessary to properly embody and enact it in performative settings. Scenarios requiring this type of directorial oversight can be easily conceived in at least two differing varieties. The first set of challenges arises within the continuum of a specific virtue and its polar vices. In the second scenario, phronesis is called to adjudicate between the competing interests of different virtues within an interpretive agent when confronting a challenging hermeneutical conundrum.

In the first case, consider the virtue of perseverance. As has been previously defined, the virtue of perseverance is especially important in cases where the interpreter faces obstacles in pursuit of understanding a text. These obstacles may be either internal or external to the agent. Perseverance is the deeply-ingrained character of the reader that presses on in order to understand a text regardless of the source or magnitude of the obstacle. Perseverance as a virtue becomes proportionately more important and praiseworthy as the obstacles become more challenging to the task. It takes little to no sense of virtuous perseverance when the obstacles are easily surmounted. For example, an interpreter who is attempting to read a text is confronted by the obstacle that since the sun has set, the window-filled room in which he is reading has become too dark to accurately discern the differences between the letters "u" and "v". The reader is fully aware of the working light switch that will illuminate the room. It is not an admirable or virtuous form of perseverance to overcome the obstacle of the darkness, in this case to turn on the light switch. On the other hand, there are obstacles that are genuine, complicated, difficult, and potentially impossible to resolve in the light of current circumstances.

Since the birth of the Renaissance movement in Europe during the fifteenth century, the call *ad fontes* has given rise to a dramatic accumulation of ancient NT manuscripts. Some of the most dramatic advancements of the Modern period, as they pertain to biblical studies, involve the accumulation, critical evaluation, and publication of NT Greek manuscripts. From the nearly six thousand ancient manuscripts and fragments which contain portions of the NT, the goal of establishing what is likely the original text of the no-longer-extant autographs has continued to be the pursuit of textual criticism. It is reasonable to assume that any justifiable understanding of a text must begin with a consideration of what is likely to be the authentic text in light of extant textual variants in the manuscript record. The field of textual criticism is important, and to an extraordinary degree, it is generally agreed that it has been successful in coming to consensus about nearly all textual variants, but general consensus does not equate with absolute certainty. An example from John 2:11 can illustrate where the laudable disposition to persevere can impede hermeneutical inquiry and need the master virtue of phronesis to properly apply and restrain it in light of the ultimate goal of a justified understanding.

Both NA27 and UBS4 record the second word of the verse as ἐποίησεν, which would be translated as "he did." The ancient lectionary 1963 from the tenth or eleventh century currently housed at the University of Chicago records this same word without the addition of the Greek letter *nu* (ν) at the end of the word, also known as a moveable *nu*. This word in the original document could not have a *nu* and not have a *nu* at the same time. In other words, one of these variants is what was originally written, and one is a later corruption of the text. A virtuous interpreter wants to work from the original, not a corrupted text. Attempting to garner manuscript evidence and textual family tree details, and to evaluate the dating and general reliability of the various textual traditions in reference to the presence or absence of the *nu* requires vast amounts of time and energy. It would be an extraordinary expression of perseverance to muster all the evidence with the best possible critical evaluations and still not be fully certain as to the original word. Phronesis evaluates the significance of this uncertainty as to its importance in gaining a justifiable understanding of the text and reins in the normally useful disposition to pursue accuracy in the face of all obstacles. The presence or absence of this moveable *nu* has no impact whatsoever on the parsing or defining of this word. With or without it, it is still a third person singular aorist indicative of the word ποιέω. In reference to textual understanding, this variant has no impact on the meaning of the text. (The conversation about the importance of persistence in this matter may be different if the discussion of this research were virtuous textual criticism and not VH.) Phronesis determines to guide the interpreter beyond the tendency to persist in pursuing this part of the inquiry because it recognizes that it is not worth the effort necessary as to its impact on gaining understanding and could actually hinder the more excellent goal of gaining understanding if its pursuit continues to consume the focus of the interpreter. Perseverance is not an absolute concept but is attuned to the circumstances. Only through something like phronesis can determination be made as to when the virtuous expression of perseverance has been attained. Rules, time frames, or ultimate success all fail in being sufficient rules to quantify when perseverance is rightly pursued in any given textual inquiry.

In the second case, the possible competing interests of the virtues of creativity and justice serve as a fitting example. In previous segments of this chapter, each of these virtues has been explained in a manner that justifies its inclusion in a VH approach. Even within the boundaries of the carefully-articulated definitions, it is plausible to see the interests of these distinct virtues in tension with each other in certain interpretive contexts. Creativity often reaches its highest contributions by extending the reach of the creative individual beyond previously-established boundaries. Justice, on the other hand, is often very concerned about maintaining previously settled boundaries of *oughtness*. While one virtue is inherently open to the new and extraordinary, and often destabilizes entrenched structures and paradigms, the other is often the maintainer of the previously-accepted structures, carefully watching that all lines of appropriateness are maintained. Where is an agent to turn when deeply-ingrained virtues exist in tension with each other in the task of interpreting a specific text? "Phronesis seems to act as a manager of possible conflicts between intellectual and moral virtues."[124]

Catechism 1806 of the Roman Catholic Church expresses this unique role of phronesis in vivid language, calling it the "charioteer of the virtues." Roberts and Wood accurately describe the necessity of phronesis in the complex world of reading. "The canons of reading vary enormously with the nature of the text, the reader's purposes in reading, and the status of the text in the practices of the reader's community. This variety suggests that a virtue of practical wisdom governs the practice of

---

124. Caslib, "Why Intellectual Virtues Matter," 100.

excellent reading and determines which of the other virtues come into play at any given moment in the pursuit of that practice."[125]

While the interpretation of all texts in the scriptural record demands the virtues of justice and creativity to be employed to gain an increasingly fuller sense of understanding, these texts potentially find themselves in tension on some of the most volatile social issues where the text and predominant culture (both ecclesial and societal) interact. The creative impulse to explore freedom, reconstruct, and re-vision is confronted by justice's call to maintain proper order in interaction between author, text, reader, and broader originating and receiving communities. Creativity is often the mantle of the revolutionary, while justice wears the robes of judicial keeper of law and order. The ability to navigate these challenges in a way that satisfies the demands of both virtues with an increasingly deeper understanding of a text, which includes not only original setting but the extension into contemporary settings, is the domain of the wise and discerning hermeneut, the phronetic interpreter.

Few today would argue that Christianity advocates for the preservation of the unjust structures of slavery based upon Levitical law[126] or Pauline instructions to Philemon. It has been the creative extension of the gospel's message expressed in Jesus's first recorded synagogue sermon that proclaims the fullest expression of freedom in the Jubilee Year's emancipation proclamation through Christ's work.[127] The wise reader is able to carefully trace the trajectory of the biblical message to extend its transformative call, which sets captives free without doing injustice to the Levitical text. Phronesis gained through years of practice and discernment is necessary and sufficient to balance the sometimes-competing influences of disparate virtues.

Just as *eudaimonia* is not the easy possession of the young and inexperienced, phronesis comes only with maturity and experience.[128] "Practical wisdom, phronesis, requires a lifetime of practice in order to be truly present in a person."[129] Wisdom recognizes the need to allow both creativity and justice to engage in all interpretive tasks while potentially favoring creativity and newness in some contexts and the firmness

---

125. Roberts and Wood, *Intellectual Virtues*, 134.

126. Lev 25:44–46.

127. Isa 61 and Luke 4:17–21.

128. Aristotle, *Nicomachean Ethics*, loc. 2090.

129. Caslib, "Why Intellectual Virtues Matter," 100.

and restrictions of justice in others. The great theological and cultural battles of the next century will be informed by the careful hand of wisdom that "deliberates well about what, among various options, is truly good for human beings, or what constitutes excellent action, here and now."[130] Within the context of biblically-based Christianity, issues like women in ministry leadership and LGBTQ+ matters will demand not only textual expertise but also virtuous interpreters who have a highly-developed sense of practical wisdom to bring the meaning of the biblical text to bear upon contemporary culture.

A virtue that occupies such a prominent place in the overall working of VH demands some further explanation as to how it is acquired and ingrained, especially as it serves the domain of biblical hermeneutics. While not different than the previous discussion of becoming a virtuous interpreter in chapter 2 of this dissertation, the significance of phronesis as a master interpretive virtue is combined with the expressly biblical priority placed on acquiring and acting with wisdom, including the practical wisdom of phronesis, to require further explanation. This explanation serves the dual purpose of providing further clarity on a pivotal component of the overall system but also bridges the discussion of previous chapters which present VH as essentially a general and nearly naturalistic hermeneutic to the final chapter's distinctly theological formulation.

De Waal Dryden builds a convincing case to reorient biblical studies away from an exclusive view of the text as nothing more than a historically analyzed text to a view that embraces it as also being a formative expression of divine revelation in his work, *A Hermeneutic of Wisdom: Recovering the Formative Agency of Scripture*. It is important to note that this reorientation is not the rejection of the historical and sociological situatedness of the text or of the traditional methods used while working with the text, but a call to recognize the necessity of seeing it as revelation that offers a "compelling theological counternarrative," which sees the Bible "as both historical witness and the creative self-revelation of God."[131] The Scripture then "fosters virtue in the believing community."[132] The biblical text not only records the historical development of the nature and faith of Israel and the Church with its necessary doctrinal commitments but also shapes the temporally distant reading community as it

130. Hasselberger, "Knowing More," 778.
131. de Waal Dryden, *Hermeneutic of Wisdom*, xvi.
132. de Waal Dryden, *Hermeneutic of Wisdom*, xv.

pertains to right actions, right reasons, and right motivations. This triad is the heart of virtue theories, including VH. Not only is the text a document to be examined by the hermeneut, it is also an instrument that is continually active in shaping the hermeneut according to its specific expression of practically wise intellectual and moral character. Phronesis is a necessary virtue for interpreting the text but is also the fruit of the text's work within the agent. This cyclical nature of the text requiring phronesis while also producing it in the reader is mirrored in the virtues themselves. Phronesis cannot develop in the absence of other virtues within the agent, but the other virtues are only able to be implemented and guided toward virtuous ends under the tutelage of phronesis. This interdependency of phronesis and the text being studied, the Bible, as well as the same phenomenon being observable with the full array of the virtuous dispositions, presents a substantial challenge to the usefulness of the entire system, unless another component is added to break this potentially destructive circularity.

Phronesis, or practical wisdom, as a means to understand the unfolding plan of God is clearly articulated in Paul's opening words in the Ephesian correspondence, specifically in Eph 1:7–10, "In him we have redemption though his blood, the forgiveness of our trespasses, according to the riches of his grace, which he lavished upon us, in all wisdom [σοφίᾳ] and insight [φρονήσει] making known [γνωρίσας] to us the mystery of his will, according to his purpose, which he set forth in Christ as a plan for the fullness of time, to unite all things in him, things in heaven and things on earth." In Pauline theology, the triune God is the source,[133] means,[134] and assurance[135] of the full measure of grace's work within those who are adopted into the family of God. The theological importance to VH in this, and further passages, is of paradigmatic significance. While phronesis is derived from and directed to the text and necessary for virtue development but also predicated upon some level of previously practiced virtue habituation, its status as a divinely bestowed spiritual blessing gifted by the Lord Jesus Christ breaks the potentially closed circularity of phronesis by opening the possibility of its presence in virtuous interpreters as being a form of *charismata*. This foundational piece of VH prepares the discussion for the pneumatological cornerstone

133. Eph 1:3.
134. Eph 1:6.
135. Eph 1:13–14.

which carries into completion what Starling hoped to accomplish in his work, *Hermeneutics as Apprenticeship*: "This book will focus principally, then, not on the advancement of exegetical science (worthy as that goal is) but on the getting of hermeneutical wisdom—on what it means to receive the biblical writings as holy Scripture and how we are to appropriate their words in our own situation."[136]

Conclusion

If we are to return to the challenge introduced in previous chapters by the case of Brutus, the detailing of the virtues listed in this chapter take on an embodied perspective. Brutus fails to attain any level of justifiable understanding of the biblical text because his approach is tragically flawed on a dispositional level. His desires, motivations, and actions in interpreting a passage like Eph 5 are flawed because he is tragically flawed as an interpreter. Arguments can and must be made concerning the grammatical, historical, and cultural shortcoming of his explanatory understanding of the text, but these will never be sufficiently corrected without a deeper transformation of his interpretive character. Rather than focusing on one or two interpretive virtues, Brutus needs an interpretive conversion experience. It is inadequate to presume that a tweaking of his reading skills or surface-level dispositions will in themselves generate anything resembling the justification of textual understanding that VH hopes to attain.

The virtues detailed within this chapter do possess justifying capacity, but only as they are embodied on the deepest motivational, intellectual, and affective levels of the hermeneut. It is the movement toward becoming a genuinely virtuous interpretive agent more than simply doing actions that reflect some of the listed virtues that matters in the epistemological or interpretive sense. Individual virtues are only visible and integral facets of the broader holistic and ethereal sense of a virtuous interpreter. Only in combining all the detailed virtues into an integrated interpretive character does an agent progress to a virtuous status, which is where the justifying capacity of the system resides. Isolating the individual virtues as though they exist independently of the whole of virtuous character is a self-defeating way to build the system. This self-defeating possibility combined with the critiques of VE from the situationalists, which rightly asks where the "genuinely virtuous interpretive agents" can

136. Starling, *Hermeneutics as Apprenticeship*, 20.

exist in the real world, in a place beyond theory, puts the entire system at risk of collapsing before it offers any hermeneutical fruit. The final piece to solidify the entire edifice is the pneumatological contribution which offers no fanciful escape from the critics but presents a theologically viable alternative. Brutus can be better by finding good exemplars and habituating the dispositions of a virtuous interpreter, but he needs something more to complete his interpretive journey, and this is best addressed by the addition of the theological cornerstone.

FOUR

Pneumatologically-Attuned Intellectual Virtues as a Necessary Characteristic of the Special Case of Biblical Understanding

Introduction

IN THE PRECEDING DISCUSSION, VH is presented as a programmatic approach to textual interpretation that acknowledges that the intellectual character of the hermeneut is a central concern in the task of a meaningful encounter between author, text, reader, and reading community. In the history of interpretive discussions, a perpetual question has been raised concerning the nature of biblical interpretation: is biblical interpretation inherently different than the interpretation of any other text, especially as considered from a confessional perspective, on the basis of its inspired character and authoritative place in the community? As a text with a historical origin and sense, linguistic character, and literary structure, it must be approached in a way that honors its textual identity, but there is more involved in an inspired canonical text. The message of the text itself indicates that it has distinctives in its formation and importance for life because of its message and divine sense. In the light of these additional concerns, a strictly naturalized VH approach is helpful but insufficient to complete the full task of hermeneutics which includes meaning discernment, internal and external transformation, and the embodiment of its truth. By adding a compatible theological distinctive, the limitations of VH can be overcome and aligned with important historical theological distinctives which characterize biblical hermeneutics. Each limitation within the previously presented formulation of VH is resolved for biblical interpretation by the inclusion of a pneumatological perspective. The most persistent challenges to VH, including circularity and theologically defined noetic conditions, are resolved when the interpretive virtues are pneumatologically anchored in a way consistent with New Covenant moral virtues as they are ultimately applied to the concept of illumination.

The Pneumatological Key

In the preceding chapters, an underlying perspective has guided the research: an approach to textual interpretation that employs a responsibilist form of virtue epistemology is possible. Even more, it is a cogent and necessary solution to the contemporary instability of the discipline of hermeneutics in the aftermath of the imposition of Modernity and Post-Modernity's competing priorities. The confidence afforded to this conclusion is undiminished by the initial and anticipated critiques from skeptics embedded in both epistemological and hermeneutical quarters. VH, as presented, answers many of the most pressing questions, and it has thus far offered these answers from a perspective that could be considered general hermeneutics. In other words, the framework of an agent-centered approach that justifies textual understanding by the virtuously attuned intellectual character of the interpreter reliably works in gaining, explaining, and extending into diverse contexts textual meaning regardless of the location, culture, or faith commitments of the interpreter. For example, an open-minded interpreter is better prepared to engage and gain understanding from any text, including the biblical record, than a closed-minded interpreter.

The frame of a general hermeneutic is useful, but it is also limited if VH is to engage the biblical text on its own terms. Every canonical passage is simultaneously a socio-historically conditioned text read from an equally socio-historically conditioned context, but it is also a document filled with theological intention and expression. In the words of de Waal Dryden, "We need a compelling theological counternarrative, and I believe that counternarrative is found in the Bible when it is embraced as both historical witness and the creative self-revelation of God."[1] The application of VH to a text like the Bible that is received and examined with attention to theological intention is subject to and must answer the same critiques that are applied to the discipline of VE, but it has the added resources of theology to address these concerns.

De Waal Dryden identifies his theological counternarrative as being the self-revelation of God which approaches the Bible, in totality, as wisdom, which "presupposes that the redemption of human agency is constitutive of both the message of salvation and the teleology of the biblical text."[2] In this way, the text is not simply read to be analyzed, but encountered in its ability to shape the actions, reasons, and motivations of the reader. This approach aligns with the canonical context of virtue development set forward in chapter 2. Briggs specifically employs the concept of virtues as embedded and expressed within the text as the key to how to best interpret the text.[3] Both of these approaches fail to address the critique of circularity that is often directed at VE. Fowl and Jones express a similar concept with a slightly different emphasis when they advocate for a theological reading that supposes that "Christians need to develop the moral and theological judgement which enables faithful discernment of Scripture's claims on contemporary life. We contend that the development of such judgement requires the formation and transformation of the character appropriate to disciples of Jesus."[4] While compatible with the agent-centered approach of VH, their centering of the interpretive process simply in community, even "communities guided by the Spirit," is most aligned with the *traditioned* community of virtuous interpretive action from chapter 2, but it fails to resolve the most persistent critiques of circularity as well as the problem of the noetic effects of sin.[5] These approaches are vast improvements on rationalistic and presumed "objective" approaches that fail to meet their own unattainable goals of certain identification of textual meaning whether by anthropological projection as in Schleiermacher and Dilthey or through rationalism and historical criticism in the line of Richard Simon, Spinoza, F. C. Baur, and Wellhausen.

1. de Waal Dryden, *Hermeneutic of Wisdom*, xvi.
2. de Waal Dryden, *Hermeneutic of Wisdom*, xx.
3. Briggs, *Virtuous Reader*.
4. Fowl and Jones, *Reading in Communion*, 1.
5. Fowl and Jones, *Reading in Communion*, 31.

The missing component in a generalized VH, as well as the theo-logically attuned approaches represented by de Waal Dryden, Briggs, and Fowl and Jones, is a robustly pneumatological key that directs the entire process of virtue development and its subsequent interpretive acts. Whether circularity or the postlapsarian condition is the source of the critique of a theological VH, the most plausible resolution to all of these concerns is best answered by an appeal to the work of the Holy Spirit in the task of biblical interpretation as expressed through the virtuous interpreters and virtuous interpretive community.

Breaking Circularity Through the Spirit's Work

Baehr, himself an advocate of a moderated and internally focused form of RVE, addresses skeptical concerns that have the potential to derail strong conservative VE models like Zagzebski's approach. The general approach of VH advocated in this research borrows heavily from her model, so this concern must be addressed. He refers to the "worries about vicious circularity" that remain largely unaddressed.[6] Zagzebski's formulation of VE defines knowledge in a way that makes it susceptible to the oft-employed criticism of other epistemological systems like process reliabilism or evidentialism, that of bootstrapping or circularity.[7] In defining this circularity as it pertains to VE, the application of a pneumatological element serves to break its potentially vicious circularity in textual understanding of the biblical record but also in its general epistemological sense.

Zagzebski's definition of knowledge as "a state of belief arising out of acts of intellectual virtue" sets the stage for this circularity.[8] The virtues are those things which lead to and motivate the pursuit of knowledge, and further, the virtues are most clearly those things that reliably produce knowledge. This definition is useful in articulating what the virtues are more than simply cataloguing classical lists of intellectual virtues, but it also brings the circularity to a potentially destructive conclusion. The virtues are virtues, in at least one important way, because they produce knowledge, but knowledge is only knowledge by its inclusion of the virtues.

6. Baehr, *Inquiring Mind*, loc. 3083.
7. Becker, "Reliabilism."
8. Zagzebski, *Virtues of the Mind*, 271.

In constructing the system this way, VR runs the risk of creating a circularity that makes knowledge too easy to obtain[9] and attempts to insulate itself against criticism by being able to answer critical questions by appealing to one part of the circular argument variously shifting between the hemispheres of the circularity depending on the critique. It is knowledge because of its attainment by virtuous motivation and activity, and the virtues are virtues because they produced the knowledge. This is accentuated in its problematic nature when the scaffolding of VE is still dependent on a more classically-defined understanding of knowledge (what Baehr classifies as a conservative approach).[10] Placing the virtues in the condition of what makes something knowledge and then defining the virtues as being virtues because they are present in knowledge creates a scenario in which the conditions beg the definition, and the definition requires the conditions.

Zagzebski acknowledges the potential of circularity—"Since I wish to define knowledge in terms of intellectual virtue, intellectual virtue cannot be defined in the same way I have just stated without circularity,"[11] and her subsequent adjustment to her definition resolves the problem of a formal circularity that has the potential to diminish the usefulness of the approach. "*An act of intellectual virtue A* is an act that arises from the motivational component of *A*, is something a person with virtue *A* would (probably) do in the circumstances, is successful in achieving the end of the *A* motivation, and is such that the agent acquires a true belief (cognitive contact with reality through these features of the act)."[12] Even in this more refined definition something more is necessary. How or why does virtue itself connect or anchor to reality? The failure to answer this question does not eliminate the useful employment of virtue theory in the epistemological endeavors, but it does require more for VR to stand on its own as a full replacement theory for a general conception of knowledge. Some understanding or anchoring of virtue that exists outside of

9. The ease of obtaining knowledge in this scenario is not that the practice of intellectual virtue is easy. By definition, the virtues are excellencies and require much from the agent to attain and practice them. Knowledge in this criticism becomes too easy by definition, not practice. Simply saying that knowledge is produced by virtue and virtue is only virtue if it produces knowledge makes the system too easy to label something knowledge by most reasonable epistemological standards.

10. Baehr, *Inquiring Mind*, loc. 185.

11. Zagzebski, *Virtues of the Mind*, 269.

12. Zagzebski, *Virtues of the Mind*, 269.

the knowledge circle whether it be in a metaphysical or theological manner remains unaddressed by Zagzebski's definition. For this definition to avoid the bootstrapping critique, there must be something which anchors the virtues and their connection to reality, but this is a metaphysical or theological dilemma as much as it is an epistemological one. The theological category of the Spirit's work is the connection that establishes the link but is not bound within its circle.

Specifically applied to VH, the problem of VE's circularity dilemma can be expressed in this way: if virtuous character traits are necessary to justify textual understanding, and virtuous character traits are only discernible as being the embodiment of textual, individual, or communal norms, ideals, or excellencies, then justification as an epistemological and hermeneutic concept can only be a well-developed and somewhat helpful form of self-justification (either individually or communally) with no metaphysical anchor allowing for any genuine "cognitive contact with reality" or textual meaning. Unless textual meaning can be encountered and engaged, and then either rejected, adapted, or integrated into the reader's broader system of understanding, VH offers nothing more than what current postmodern approaches offer. Instructive, transformative, or conversional readings are not possible in VH (or any hermeneutical system) if the virtues (or any justifying mechanism) exist solely as naturally-occurring ideals from discrete individuals, communities, or even some form of global human community (if that were even possible) with no transcendent anchoring to bridge, even in a limited manner, ultimate reality or meaning and the human perception of it. VE has developed its own answers to address this problem, but without the resources of a well-developed metaphysical or theological grounding to break the vicious circle, its answers remain, at best, pragmatic and prone to skepticism's critiques. The need for a metaphysical grounding to allow for contact with reality does not immediately address the capacity to understand this reality. Plantinga helps to bring us to the pneumatological key that answers the circularity in both the metaphysical and functional realms.

Plantinga is not formally a virtue epistemologist, but Roberts and Wood are correct in pointing out that his epistemological proper functionalism can be appropriately understood as

> an incipient virtues epistemology . . . He defines knowledge as warranted true belief and defines warrant in terms of the proper functioning of epistemic faculties in a congenial environment. The notion of proper function is reminiscent of the classical and

medieval understanding of virtues: virtues are bases of excellent human functioning, and epistemic virtues are bases of excellent epistemic function.[13]

This underlying compatibility between his reliabilism and VE affords a useful starting point for VE and VH to break the circularity of purely pragmatic or generalized versions of each discipline. Virtue theory is even more compatible to this idea of proper function and design plan than strict reliabilism and offers hope for more than the simplest form of knowledge.

His first premise for developing epistemological warrant is proper function (a concept that is compatible with virtue of either the faculty or character types). He immediately acknowledges that the notion of proper function is "inextricably bound with another: that of a design plan."[14] There can be no proper function if it is not first supposed that function is tied to design. While arguing that this premise need not be immediately transferred to the concept of a theistic positing of a creator/designer, his final argument expressed in *Warrant and Proper Function* leaves no mystery as to his resolution of this question. He argues that "Naturalism in epistemology can flourish only in the context of super-naturalism in metaphysics."[15]After exploring potential metaphysically naturalistic approaches to ground epistemological pursuits dependent on generally agreed-upon ideas of proper function, he concludes, "It is in fact impossible to give an account of proper function in naturalistic terms."[16] The idea of proper function, or in the case of VE/VH, intellectually virtuous functioning, is dependent upon some form of metaphysical reality expressed in the designer and in that which has been designed but also works to enable or restore proper function (or in this research, virtuous function) of the agent.

The most likely candidate in all of Scripture to fulfill this role is the Holy Spirit. The Spirit exemplifies this connection of the virtuous function of the natural world with the designer who fashioned existence in a way that makes the virtues virtuous (by which one means moral and epistemological excellencies fitted to work in the designed world). Of significance in the discussion to overcoming circularity, the Spirit as member of the triune God is self-existent apart from the agent and the agent's

13. Roberts and Wood, *Intellectual Virtues*, 7.

14. Plantinga, *Knowledge and Christian Belief*, 25.

15. Plantinga, *Warrant and Proper Function*, 194.

16. Plantinga, *Warrant and Proper Function*, 210.

community and, therefore, not bound within the closed circle of human cognitive endeavors. Yet, the Spirit is able to instill, inhabit, and express the transcendent divine influence within all realms of human agency and location in a way that demonstrates how the eternal, all-good, and all-knowing God who exists in a purity of being and knowledge beyond any human attainment can be engaged in all those seeking understanding (cognitive contact with reality).

When conceived of in this way, virtues are the most excellent dis-positions and workings of the agent embedded within a universe whose existence is attuned to these virtues and not simply agential, communal, or pragmatic projections. The importance of the Spirit to the epistemo-logical discussion is crucial, and when properly understood, allows for the Spirit to be engaged in *all* human knowing within the real world. While this engagement in human attempts to cognitively encounter real-ity can include a variety of expressions, both directly (immediate revela-tion) and indirectly (in the shaping and animating of the knowable world and the knower who inhabits it), it is the Spirit expressed as, "essential be-ing as the invisible Power (Energy) behind all that is, the creative Breath by which the living creature, indeed the whole universe is animated"[17] which aligns pneumatology and VE/VH. Properly expressed, this pneu-matological framework for the virtues permits and explains the presence of knowledge within all of humanity, not simple the regenerate, but it leaves room for the possibility that the regenerated mind may be able to understand and know things not accessible to all minds.[18]

The Spirit's presence not only allows a new metaphysical starting point for the generalized epistemology, which fits Plantinga's demand for a supernatural metaphysics to ground a natural epistemology, it also works within the epistemological system itself to secure and make avail-able the virtuous elements necessary to successfully engage in cognitive endeavors within creation. The Spirit's design plan instills meaning and continues to inhabit reality so that the virtues are efficacious and acces-sible to humanity in a way that is anchored beyond the purely individual or communal domains. In systematic and biblical theologies, the Spirit is active in both the metaphysical grounding as well as the epistemological functioning of all individual agents and communities. The creation narra-tive as well as several NT passages, most notably the Pentecost narrative,

17. Jewett, "God Is Personal Being," 274.
18. Isa 6:9–10; Matt 13:10–11; 1 Cor 2:6–16.

illustrate both the creational and ongoing sense of the Spirit's necessary place in VE and VH as an answer to endless circularity.

Two Archetypal Scriptural Passages on Pneumatological Breaking of Vicious Circularity

Genesis 1:2

While the full expression of the Spirit as the third person of the Trinity receives greater clarity in the NT record, students of biblical pneumatology do not wait long to be introduced to the mysterious presence of the רוּחַ אֱלֹהִים. As a necessary caution, Christian exegetes must be careful to not anachronistically import too much of the subsequent NT theology into these opening passages of Scripture, but should rather begin with a just and attentive reading that attempts to encounter the text where it is located at the head of the progressive revelation of the Canon. Even from this initial and most basic introduction to the Spirit, there is much within this passage which addresses the foundational epistemological matters of the comprehensibility of the agent-inhabited world and the Spirit's relationship to this ecosystem. It is beyond the scope of this project to fully exegete the place of Gen 1:2, but a brief evaluation of the text yields much insight as to the pneumatological element involved in the design of the material existence.

Genesis 1 is overwhelmingly focused on the detailing of the orderly and intelligible act of divine creation by a singular God using the schema of six days of creative action. The first two verses of the chapter serve as a separate prologue, giving direction to the entirety of the rest of the chapter and the first verses of chapter 2. In contrast to other competing creation stories with which the ancient Israelites would have been familiar, it is the orderliness of creation that stands out most vividly in the construction of the creation narrative of chapter 1. Creation narratives abounded in the Ancient Near East (ANE). These formulations often contained many of the same images in the biblical account, but the formation of the Genesis record used these images to convey a unique monotheistic and orderly cosmology.

Central to multiple ANE creation narratives is the idea of creation emerging from a great battle between a creator and some embodiment of chaos. This is seen in the Babylonian creation myth, *Enuma Elish*, in the battle between Marduk and Tiamat, or in the Ugaritic *Baal Cycle* from the *Ras Shamra* texts, involving Baal in combat with the chaotic force of Yam. Form critic Hermann Gunkel advanced the idea that this battle motif stood behind the biblical creation account even as he acknowledged, "The distinction between the Babylonian myth and Genesis 1 is so great in both the religious outlook and aesthetic coloration that they appear, at first glance, to have nothing in common."[19] Gunkel would have been better to have courageously left his conjecture at this first glance rather than unjustly and inattentively forcing the *Chaoskampf* motif as standing behind the biblical story. Cristina Sandulache effectively summarizes the biblical imagery in comparison to other ANE myths: "The similar elements are completely emptied of their original theological meaning, being used only as 'compatible vehicles' for illustration of the biblical Combat Story."[20] Both the encounter with the void and formless (תֹהוּ וָבֹהוּ) earth and the darkened deep (תְהוֹם) as well as the language of (רוּחַ) fit within the same technique of using the imagery and wording of the ANE stripped of previous theological significance as a vehicle to convey an entirely new understanding. Rather than describing a battle between two great foes (i.e., the creator and the monster of chaos), the prologue of Gen 1:1–2 borrows images but redefines the story. It is not a battle but an orderly bringing forth of creation according to divine purposes by the mediating and ordering presence of the *rûaḥ*. The *rûaḥ* mediates between the physical world, the intent of the Creator, and his effectual word by which he created it.

Although Ugaritic had the cognate word for the Hebrew *rûaḥ* (רוּחַ), it only possessed the meaning of wind. The Hebrews understandably borrowed this term in order to imbue it with a theological significance that metaphorically built upon the concept of the wind. "Wind is intangible, invisible. Just as the movement of the wind lay beyond the control of humankind, so also the coming of the spirit could only be awaited, never coerced."[21] When inscribed in the Gen 1:2 passage, the *rûaḥ* of God was "a *concept* that was found nowhere else in the Ancient Near East."[22] After the merism of v. 1 detailing God's all-encompassing act of creation, the first three days of creation are foreshadowed where the void is addressed in days one through three and the emptiness is resolved in

19. Gunkel, *Creation and Chaos*, 21.

20. Sandulache, "Yahweh`s Combat."

21. Neve, *Spirit of God in the Old Testament*, 1.

22. Neve, *Spirit of God in the Old Testament*, 1.

days four through six.[23] The empty and inhospitable-to-life earth of v. 2 is addressed by the creative act of day three. The pervasive darkness is resolved in the work of day one, and the hovering presence of the Spirit over the waters speaks to the separation of the waters into the heavenly and creaturely realms of day two. "Already in v. 2 the transformation starts of the *tĕhôm* into waters that no longer make creaturely life impossible, and this transformation is indicated by the presence of the *rûaḥ*. But simultaneously, the Spirit of God is related to the Word of God that will speak in the continuation of the story."[24] It is the Spirit whose presence over the deep which is then separated from the heavenly realm of divine dwelling and the earthly realm now made hospitable to all forms of life that is particularly significant. The Spirit is simultaneously hovering between both the heavenly realm of the divine dwelling and the emerging material realm designed for creaturely life.

"In the Old Testament literature *rûaḥ* is only used to express God's activity *as he relates himself* to his world, his creation, his people. It was Israel's way of describing God, not as he is in himself, but as he communicates to the world his power, his life, his anger, his will, his very presence."[25] This is the epistemological key that the pneumatology of the creation narrative furnishes. The Spirit is the divine agent that encounters an emerging creation that initially neither had the capacity to support life nor the structure to be sensibly encountered. It was void and empty, and the Spirit was hovering over the insensible deep. It is not a battle over chaos, but the systematic and progressive endowing or designing of the creation with an orderly sense of existence that allows the finite creaturely agents who will inhabit the creation the ability to perceive and engage with creation according the orderly purposes of God. "The passage is emphasizing the actual, powerful presence of God, who brings the spoken word into reality by the Spirit. Thus, the Spirit and the Word work together to present how the one God is responsible for all that is seen in the physical universe. That which was invisible became the material, physical world through the creatively active Spirit."[26] Not only does the creation become intelligible, its intelligibility is related to the agents' encounter with the orderly nature of creation ingrained by the

23. Hildebrandt, *Old Testament Theology of the Spirit*, 31.

24. Reeling Brouwer, "Work of the Spirit in Creation," 132.

25. Neve, *Spirit of God in the Old Testament*, 2.

26. Hildebrandt, *Old Testament Theology of the Spirit*, 35.

active Spirit of God, the *rûaḥ ' ĕlōhiym*. This is where the place of virtues becomes clearer, since the fabric of the creation reflects the nature of the designer, so those intellectual as well as moral character traits that reflect this underlying Spirit-endowed order allow for greater cognitive contact with reality.

The presence of the Spirit at this most foundational place of creation allows for the broadest application of this epistemological key that breaks the human-centered circularity that must exist if there is no supernatural metaphysical anchoring to the agent's encounter with the created world. The Spirit, in bringing order and meaning to creation, exists beyond purely soteriological dimensions but engages all agents who encounter the world that bears the imprint of its meaningful acts in creation. Because of the place of the Spirit in prelapsarian creation, theologians like Yong can explore the possibility of the Spirit's presence at work in a more broadly conceived "public theology" with other religious traditions, or what might be called a religious epistemology.[27] Justin Ukpong's description of the results of comparative religions studies could also be understood against this global pneumatological epistemology. "African traditional religion came to be seen as 'Africa's Old Testament.' African culture and religion came to be recognized as a *praeparatio evangelica* (a preparation for the gospel), that is, a fertile ground for the gospel."[28]

Acts 2

In developing a VH that begins with a robust pneumatological starting point, the implications of the Pentecost narrative of Acts are paradigmatic. Yong is at the forefront of developing what he describes as a *post-pentecost-al hermeneutic* (post-pentecost-al in the sense that it is a framework that commences after the events of the Acts 2 Pentecost event). In this approach, he uses the Pentecost narrative as the interpretive lens through which to approach biblical hermeneutics. "One might argue that the book of Acts provides the interpretive frame or point of entry into the biblical narrative as a whole."[29] While VH does not necessarily demand this singular lens, his approach shares several significant overlapping priorities with VH. First, he sees the epoch-making significance of the Pentecost

27. Yong, *Spirit Poured Out*, 235.

28. Ukpong, "Developments in Biblical Interpretation," 51.

29. Yong, *Hermeneutical Spirit*, loc. 1704.

narrative as it pertains to biblical interpretation. Second, he recognizes that the presence of the Spirit has epistemological implications and not just spiritual ramifications. It affirms that, "Meeting the living God by the Spirit transfigures human cognition precisely because it is wholly transformative of human knowing and perceiving in its multiple dimensions of tactility, affectivity, and emotions."[30] This holistic approach to epistemology shaped by the Spirit is central to VH. The primary divergence is the specific emphasis in VH on the mechanism of the Spirit's cultivation of virtues, both moral and intellectual, as the primary descriptive model of this transforming of human knowing, perceiving, feeling, desiring, and acting.

The story of the pouring out of the Holy Spirit on those gathered in the upper room addresses a host of significant realities, including important epistemological ones. If a primary criticism of VE and VH is both the metaphysical and practical forms of circularity, the former is addressed by the work of the Spirit in creation and the latter is engaged at Pentecost. Several theologically-sensitive epistemological motifs are engaged in the story: the reversal of the confusion of languages at Babel, the radical democratization of the Spirit's revelatory giftings to previously excluded socio-economic, gender, and age-restricted communities, and the transcendence of geographic and cultural limitations of the Spirit's illuminating work. Though each of these motifs was ontologically possible because of the Spirit's creative actions, it is at Pentecost that the public expression of a new era of understanding was inaugurated. Matthias Wenk is correct as he emphasizes that this new epoch that began at Pentecost is "the fulfillment of the eschatological renewal of God's people to be of pneumatic origin and with social-ethical consequences."[31] His explanation falls short in its failure to include the epistemological dimension of the Spirit's eschatological presence. The potentially destructive circularity that can be argued in a naturalistic form of VE which leaves no suprahuman context in which the virtues are anchored and experienced, especially in the domain of religious knowledge, is reversed by the revelation of the eschatological, pneumatically-focused age which commences at the Pentecost event of Acts 2.

Epistemology is concerned with both the knowledge-gathering faculties and their functioning, and the dramatic scene portrayed at

---

30. Yong, *Hermeneutical Spirit*, loc. 1733.

31. Wenk, "Acts," 117.

Pentecost is significant in its emphasis on the sensory nature of this in-breaking. F. F. Bruce summarizes the scene: "The Spirit's advent was visible as well as audible."[32] Yong further emphasizes this reality: "The Day of Pentecost narrative suggests that comprehension of the Spirit's presence is not just an intellectual task but is a perceptual one as well, one mediated through the full range of human senses."[33] The disciples *heard* a sound like a mighty rushing wind (Acts 2:2), *saw* tongues of fire (Acts 2:3), and experienced the *feeling* of being filled (Acts 2:4). The multitudes equally *heard* them speaking in their own languages (Acts 2:6) and *saw* the outpouring experience (Acts 2:33). Beyond the senses, the text further calls into the experience additional common cognitive processes: affections (Acts 2:37), reasoning (Acts 2:29–36), logic (Acts 2:15), and memory (Acts 2:22). Each cognitive element addressed is directly connected to the Spirit's presence and eschatological work as revolutionary and revelational knowledge was made accessible by the Spirit's work. In the narrative, no more important epistemological and hermeneutical statement is made than that each person declared, "We hear them telling in our own tongues the mighty works of God." The narrative makes clear that the ability to understand the message proclaimed that day was not merely the inherent cognitive capacities or senses of the people present, since some failed to understand what was happening and scoffed at it (Acts 2:13). It was the faculties, reasoning, and affections tuned to understand by the work of the Spirit. In this eschatological dawning of the pneumatological age, the Spirit engages all thinking agents (both the speakers and the hearers) with a transformational encounter that sharpens the cognitive processes in order to have contact with reality. The spiritual work breaks the purely human circularity by divine in-breaking. The ability of the multitudes to hear and comprehend the glossolalic messages is a fitting image of the dramatic influence of the Spirit within the hermeneutic realm.

The Noetic Condition

While the focus of this research is specifically addressed to the issue of textual interpretation, this endeavor exists within the broader realm of general human noetic functions. These noetic functions address holistic

32. Bruce, *Acts*, 50.
33. Yong, *Hermeneutical Spirit*, loc. 979.

discussions of the activities of the human mind. In his treatise on religious affections, Jonathan Edwards speaks of this function of the mind within two faculties of the human soul. One faculty is what he refers to as *understanding*, which is "capable of perception and speculation so that it can discern, see, and judge things," and the other is the *inclinations*, which are called the will when focused on actions, and the heart when addressing the function of the mind.[34] The division of the noetic function of the mind between those elements that produce and evaluate sensory and other forms of perceptions (e.g., memory, intuition, and possibly spiritual sense like Calvin's *sensus divinitatis*) and the strongest dispositions of the mind to this process and subsequent datum, which he calls *affections*, raises important questions as to how the human mind works best according to its design, its potential dysfunctions, and its ultimate hope for renewal.[35] The theological issue of the noetic effects of sin within these two domains and how this interacts with the concept of intellectual virtues under the tutelage of the Holy Spirit applies to epistemological matters, especially to the unique nature of textual understanding. As will be demonstrated, the destructive effects of sin on the affective matters of the will and heart as they impact textual interpretation is most benefitted by the ongoing presence of the Spirit within the framework of VH.

The creation narrative of Gen 1 and 2 frames the biblical expectation of a universe at harmony and functioning according to the willful design of its Creator. This primeval prologue of Scripture is central to understanding not only the moral nature of humanity but also its intellectual nature. In the crowning act of creation, God produces his image-bearer, and all of creation, including humanity, is declared to be "very good" (טוֹב מְאֹד) in Gen 1:31. In being "good," it was a declaration that it existed in harmony with the Creator's intents and purposes. In this state, various theologians have declared either perfection or innocence to be the prelapsarian state of humanity.[36] Both of these views seem insufficient, especially as it pertains to the concept of human knowing prior to the fall. If by "innocence" one means something akin to "a not fully developed condition,"[37] then it is difficult to discern how the act of the sin

---

34. Edwards, *Religious Affections*, 5–6.

35. Edwards's view of the soul as being understanding and inclination can be compared to Aristotle's description of the rational and appetitive.

36. Augustine is representative of those who speak of the perfection of humanity before the Fall. Irenaeus espoused a weaker view of moral innocence.

37. De Cruz and De Smedt, "Reformed and Evolutionary Epistemology," 61.

brought such cataclysmic ramifications to the ongoing noetic functioning of humanity. Conversely, equating the pre-fall existence of humanity with some form of perfection is also problematic in the epistemological realm, since this perfection in contemporary usage implies a sense of completeness that is not evident in the Genesis narrative. While not necessarily possessing error, knowledge in the garden was dramatically incomplete (seen in Adam's probable inability to provide cogent proofs in Euclidian geometry) and, even at some level, off-limits (consider the forbidden nature of the Tree of Knowledge).

If pre-fall knowledge in the garden is neither captured by the concepts of innocence or perfection, a more suitable description is necessary. Plantinga is helpful in this difficulty by defining the accruable nature of warrant as, "a property or quantity had by a belief if and only if that belief is produced by cognitive faculties functioning properly in a congenial epistemic environment according to a design plan successfully aimed at truth."[38] While this is central to his definition of knowledge in the current and less-than-ideal world of human experience, the Garden of Eden is the unparalleled epitome of this epistemological system. Both the faculties of humanity's progenitors and the environment in which they were placed had been deemed very good, or said another way, the exact expression of the designed plan by the Creator. While much knowledge was beyond human inculcation at this point of existence and development, pending growth and experience, the unhindered process of acquiring and utilizing knowledge as the fulfillment of the cultural mandate of Genesis 1:28 ("Be fruitful and multiply and fill the earth and subdue it, and have dominion over the fish of the sea and over the birds of the heavens and over every living thing that moves on the earth") lay fully open before the first man and woman. Rather than the designation of reliabilism, which suits a postlapsarian setting by reducing the epistemic fruitfulness of human beings and their environment, using Plantinga's conceptual basis, the epistemology of humanity in the garden could rightly be called certaintism.

With the entrance of sin, the harmonious function of Edward's concepts of understanding and inclining in a suitable environment was replaced with disorder and conflict bringing a calamitous end to certaintism. The end of harmony included humanity's relationship with its Creator (Gen 3:8–10), their environment (Gen 3:17b–19, 23–24), each

---

38. Plantinga, *Warranted Christian Belief*, 204.

other (Gen 3:12, 15–16, 16c), and themselves (Gen 2:17, 3:7, 16–17, 19). It would be inaccurate to say that the sensory faculties and even the inter-action of human reasoning with the embedded rationality of the created order was unaffected by the condition of sin. From a biblical view, this distortion of the Edenic condition initiates the process of death, disabil-ity, and suffering within the created order (Rom 8:19–21). The potential dysfunction of the senses (e.g., blindness, deafness, paralysis, etc.) is lo-cated within the original sin event. The implications for epistemology are obvious when the senses and reasoning skills are compromised along with an environment no longer harmoniously aligned with the know-ing agent's activities, but the greater disordering of the noetic functions resides in the impact upon the inclinations or affections of the mind. Calvin explains,

> We by no means condemn those appetites which God so im-planted in the mind of man at his first creation, that they can-not be eradicated without destroying human nature itself, but only the violent lawless movements which war with the order of God. But as, in consequence of the corruption of nature, all our faculties are so vitiated and corrupted, that a perpetual disorder and excess is apparent in all our actions, and as the appetites cannot be separated from this excess, we maintain that therefore they are vicious.[39]

Gratian Vandici summarizes Calvin's exposition of Gen 3 as it per-tains to the primary location of its noetic implications: "An overactive imagination in tandem with an unruly will frustrate human attempts at autonomy. The transition between the two [pre-fall and post-fall Eden] shows the incipient noetic effects of sin."[40] As it pertains to the func-tions of the mind, the two most prominent noetic effects of original sin are the "disordered lust for knowledge and the negative potential of our imagination."[41] Calvin, Edwards, and Plantinga all locate the most devastating impact on noetic function to be in the realm of the affec-tions, which include the will, passions, and motivations. "Sin is also and perhaps primarily an affective disorder or malfunction. Our affections are skewed, directed to the wrong objects; we love and hate the wrong

---

39. Calvin, *Institutes of the Christian Religion*, para. III.iii.12.
40. Vandici, "Reading the Rules of Knowledge," 181.
41. Vandici, "Reading the Rules of Knowledge," 179.

things."[42] Plantinga further explains the noetic problem: "The defect here is affective, not intellectual. Our affections are disordered; they no longer work as in God's original design plan for human beings. There is a failure of proper function, an affective disorder, a sort of madness of the will."[43] This conspiring of the affective dysfunction of the mind with a conflicted relationship with nature and other agents greatly diminishes, while not entirely eradicating, the entire epistemological capacity of humanity. Reinhold Neibuhr captures this internal and external noetic dysfunction: "The human reason remains a servant of the passions of nature within him and a victim of the caprices of nature about him."[44]

The location of the primary, but not exclusive, noetic impact of sin, within the affective realm, is central to the pneumatic emphasis of VH as a corrective aid to interpretive tasks. Just as would be expected in light of the affective nature of the noetic impairment of sin, Genesis records that the consequences and curses of the Fall, both ethically and cognitively, are most pronounced where agents engage in relational and cognitive exchange. "The noetic effects of sin are concentrated with respect to our knowledge of other people, of ourselves, and of God; they are less relevant (or relevant in a different way) to our knowledge of nature and the world."[45] Hermeneutics as a discipline is engaged in all three of these relationships: ourselves, God, and others. When seeking to understand and extend the meaning of a text, as has previously been discussed, the text and previous commentary can be recognized in the epistemological context of testimony. In reference to the biblical text, God is also included into this relational encounter through the text. When the affective nature of the postlapsarian mind is disordered in its desires, motivations, imagination, and will, the outcome is continual conflict in attaining meaning. Lewis speaks to the importance of these affective impulses as they pertain to the primary task of hermeneutics, that of discerning and extending meaning: "Reason is the natural organ of truth; but imagination is the organ of meaning. Imagination, producing new metaphors or revivifying old, is not the cause of truth, but its condition."[46] Being able to discern

---

42. Plantinga, *Warranted Christian Belief*, 208.
43. Plantinga, *Warranted Christian Belief*, 208.
44. Niebuhr, *Beyond Tragedy*, 102.
45. Plantinga, *Warranted Christian Belief*, 213.
46. Lewis, *Selected Literary Essays*, 265.

meaning and extend it into life and society requires the imaginative powers of a restored affective nature.

With the greatest noetic impact upon humanity being centered within the affective functions of the epistemic enterprise, it follows that the most impactful improvements to human knowing should explore those things that are most related to the areas of the will, emotions, and motivations. While assuredly not the neutral and objective things that Modernity hoped for, perception, proper inductive and deductive reasoning, and the nature of the natural world are not the fundamental problem in humanity's cognitive endeavors. Donald Bloesch carries the implications to a consistent conclusion: "Man in sin is not guided by the light of clear intelligence but gropes in the darkness of fear and resentment ... The structure of man's reason is not impaired, but the way in which he reasons is surely distorted by sin."[47] It is a lethargy to pursue deeper understanding; it is the conflictual dispositions of pride, selfishness, and envy that compel an agent to distort truth or attack dissenters. It is the fear to discover something which may conflict with the comfortability of the already-accepted ways of ordering one's world rather than poor eyesight in a darkened room that is the more likely culprit for much of the most important epistemic and interpretive failings of postlapsarian agents.

It is somewhat perplexing that Plantinga embraces the affective nature, including the will, emotions, and desires, as the most affected element of human knowing that impairs the pursuit of knowledge without embracing a more Responsibilist Virtue Epistemology approach. As he describes the cognitive impact of sin, he does not emphasize the failure of reliable faculties in conducive environments but on what could be called intellectual vices: "Because of hatred or distaste for some group of human beings, I may think them inferior, or less worth than I myself and my more accomplished friends. Because of hostility and resentment, I may misestimate or entirely misunderstand someone else's attitude toward me, suspecting them of trying to do me in, when in fact there is nothing to the suggestions."[48] Desires and emotions are not addressed by conversations concerning faculties and reliable processes. While the noetic effects of sin may not be fully curable by human initiative, that does not mean that they cannot be addressed by attentiveness to the affective element of the human noetic system. This is what a naturalized or general view of virtue theory

47. Bloesch, *Essentials of Evangelical Theology*, 102.
48. Plantinga, *Warranted Christian Belief*, 213.

attempts to do by identifying proper exemplars and practicing the most excellent human dispositions with the hopes of a deeper and more reliable habituating of these traits. Entire psychological approaches are built upon similar perspectives. The interrelated domains of the behavioral, affective, and cognitive elements of human beings are the underlying assumption of the Cognitive Behavioral Theory of psychotherapy, which seeks to address a full range of mental health issues by correcting dysfunctional thinking in the triad of behavior, affections, and cognition.[49]

The movement from a natural VE to a pneumatologically sensitive approach to VH recognizes the limitation of human ability to fully correct these underlying affective concerns by external influence (exemplars) or independent internal activity (addressing the will, emotions, and imagination). It is the unique place of the Spirit to address the entirety of the human condition. The Spirit is the guide who not only embedded the universe with knowability and the morality of knowledge as previously discussed, but also works to transform the noetic system that has become, at some level, dysfunctional because of sin. In cognitive tasks, especially those that place higher demands on the relational component to knowledge and understanding, the embodied and experiential nature of the Spirit's work opens the possibility of a fuller sense of virtue development and noetic transformation. Yong applies this particular encompassing sense of the Spirit to the task of hermeneutics: "The point is that the work of the Spirit is embodied, and the divine is not only read textually, but also encountered affectively and experienced perceptually."[50] Vanhoozer is the most explicit hermeneutician to link the pneumatological to the hermeneutical in the aretaic language.

> To what extent is understanding—of the Bible or of any other communicative action—genuinely possible, given human fallenness, without the aid of the Holy Spirit? Can readers avoid doing interpretive violence without the aid of the Spirit of peace, without that peculiarly Pentecostal (and perlocutionary) power that Barth called the 'Lord of hearing'? Postmodern interpreters who seek to do justice to the other—to the Word—must read in the right spirit. For good readers need to have the right desires, not simply the right devices—the right interpretive virtues, not merely the appropriate hermeneutical techniques.[51]

49. Beck, *Cognitive Therapy*, 29.
50. Yong, *Hermeneutical Spirit*, loc. 984.
51. Vanhoozer, *Is There a Meaning in This Text?*, 369.

It is the Spirit that applies the creational and the re-creational moral transformation to move beyond tinkering with the edges of the epistemological dysfunction of the fallen mind to afford agents the ability to embrace a more thoroughly virtuous hermeneutic. "He is the *Spiritus Creator*—the source of both our existence and our renovation."[52] With this understanding, the Spirit's work in illuminating the text is afforded a place beyond an exclusive limitation to only inspiring faith to believe or constant situated revealing of meaning as often as the text is read, but it allows for the illumining work to include the restoration of epistemic capacities dulled by sin.

The universality of the Spirit's work and the dulled, but not destroyed, image of God still present in every human agent, allows for those beyond the regenerate and confessing community to meaningfully participate in and contribute to the interpretive task within VH. As has been previously developed, understanding of the text is seen in its greater explanatory detail, and it is justified by the intellectual character of the agent acting as a virtuous agent would act. Although a weaker form of virtue theory than that which demands full possession of the virtues, the principle is significant. "An act is right because it is what a virtuous person might do."[53] If the Spirit is present within all of creation and engaged in all epistemic effort to pursue truth, then it is unnecessary and unwarranted to suppose that all understanding is beyond the range of human activity, even the pursuit of fallen humanity. This formulation acknowledges what is readily observable. An interpreter, who is interpreting in ways that a virtuous interpreter would, can accumulate significant levels of textual understanding, and this is still related to the Spirit's work in creation beyond the noetic effects of sin. Yet, it is still the contention of this research that full virtuosity is not possible by human effort alone. It requires the re-creative act of the Spirit. The interpretive effect of this re-creation is developed in the following section as a fresh understanding of illumination. At minimum, the Spirit's work within the noetic systems of fallen, but regenerate, agents involves the added capacity of faith, expectation of the fulfillment of the promises within the text, hope of truth and eternal meaning, and both the spiritual and experiential confirmation of the accumulated understanding. Even among the regenerate, the capacity for virtuosity does not necessarily imply attainment. The process of

---

52. Bloesch, *Holy Spirit*, 286.
53. Zagzebski, *Virtues of the Mind*, 16.

acquiring virtues, even within the pneumatological frame, still requires time, practice, habituation, and deep embedding of the motivations and behaviors commensurate with virtue attainment, but with the addition of the Spirit's work, there is the raising of potential, the addition of the Spirit as guide and exemplar, and the transforming work of the Spirit restoring the affective nature of the heart.

Paul's epistle to the church in Ephesus is relevant to understanding the impact of the Spirit upon the noetic structures and epistemological outcomes of fallen human agents. As in all of Paul's writings, the eschatological significance of the Spirit is at the essential core of his theological reflections. The Spirit seals believers. He is the down payment of their inheritance and the divine presence that unifies the diverse Christian community. As the Spirit accomplishes these primary tasks in the community, Ephesians reveals that a significant expression of this work is expressed in the domain considered epistemic or noetic. The Holy Spirit is directly mentioned in the letter twelve times, and at least five of the mentions are directly related to the relationship of the Spirit to epistemic matters.[54] Beyond the passages that specifically use the word *pneuma* (πνεῦμα), the context of the letter demonstrates Paul's further pneumatological emphasis in epistemic discussions that are more implicit. Two passages are important for our consideration of the significance of the Spirit in epistemic/interpretive contexts, one explicit (Eph 1:17–18) and the other implicit (4:17–18).

Ephesians 1:17–18

After extolling the Father for his manifest and manifold spiritual blessings in Christ as the believers await the final consummation of their inheritance of which the Spirit is the guarantee (1:3–14), the Apostle turns his attention to his prayer for the recipients of his letter. He establishes the reason for his thanksgiving and prayers for them as well as the nature of his remembrances of them. As for the specific request he was making on their behalf, the Spirit is central to his petition. Furthermore, in a long and clause laden sentence that continues from verse 15 through 19 in nearly all texts and a far as verse 23 in multiple other editors' evaluation, the request for the giving of the Spirit of wisdom (σοφίας) and revelation in the knowledge of him in verse 17 is the central verbal idea of the entire paragraph.

54. Eph 1:17; 3:5, 16; 4:30; 5:18.

Since he had already established the status of his recipients as being saints and believers (1:1), Paul's prayerful appeal for the Father to give to them the gift of the Spirit of wisdom and revelation is necessarily beyond a strictly soteriological nature. Fee describes this as Paul "praying that God will gift them with the Spirit yet once more, and that the Spirit in turn will supply the wisdom to understand what he also reveals to them about God and his ways."[55] Both of the ideas of wisdom and revelation fit within the context of epistemology and the impact that the presence of the Spirit has on the working of the mind of the regenerate. It appears to have special importance to the task of interpretation; it seems as though this epistemological bestowal of the Spirit grants a new and effective interpretive lens to properly understand God and his working internally and externally to the agent. Wisdom, in both its OT and non-canonical Second Temple Literature[56] expression have the idea of "prudent, considered, experienced and competent action" as applied to the world and the challenges of life within it.[57] Surely interpreting communication fits within this range of challenging circumstances that requires a divinely bestowed and humanly habituated wisdom. It is the Spirit who is bestowed in order to enlighten the eyes of the heart for believers in both knowledge of God and wisdom for life. In Pauline usage, the heart is the seat of all of life, especially the inner-life, including, the emotions (Phil 1:7), desires (Rom 1:24, 10:1), imagination (1 Cor 2:9), thoughts and reasoning (Rom 1:21, 10:6), and the will (1 Cor 7:37). In short, the entirety of the noetic system is included in the designation of the "eyes of your heart" with special emphasis on those categories identified as being part of the affective realm. Paul declares the need of believers to receive the help of the Spirit to heal or enlighten the function of these parts of

55. Fee, *God's Empowering Presence*, 676.

56. Sirach 39:1–6 details that the nature of wisdom and understanding is acquired through both careful attention and study, and supernatural filling. "He seeks out the wisdom of all the ancient and is concerned with prophecies; he preserves the sayings of the famous and penetrates the subtleties of parables; he seeks out the hidden meanings of proverbs and is at home with the obscurities of parables. He serves among the great and appears before rulers; he travels in foreign lands and learns what is good and evil in the human lot. He sets his heart to rise early to seek the Lord who made him, and to petition the Most High; he opens his mouth in prayer and asks pardon for his sins. If the great Lord is willing, he will be filled with the spirit of understanding; he will pour forth words of wisdom of his own and give thanks to the Lord in prayer. The Lord will direct his counsel and knowledge, as he meditates on his mysteries. He will show the wisdom of what he has learned, and will glory in the law of the Lord's covenant."

57. Wilckens and Fohrer. "Σοφία, Σοφός, Σοφίζω." *TDNT* 7:465–527.

the human mind. In light of this passage, Max Turner points out that it is the Spirit, "Who leads *all* believers deeper into the kind of relational knowledge of God that roots them in the new covenant life of salvation," and fuels their passionate devotion to God.[58]

Ephesians 4:17-24

As Paul transitions from the more theological discussion of chapters 1 through 3 to the parenetic materials that make up the balance of the letter, he directly addresses the noetic limitations of a mind attempting to function autonomously apart from pneumatological assistance. Throughout the text, the primary emphasis when speaking of the gentiles (ἔθνος) has been on the previously unexpected inclusion of non-Jewish individuals into the community of faith. This was accomplished by the work of Christ and affected by the work of the Spirit (2:11-22). The emphasis on the unity of all believers in Christ and the necessity of guarding this theological reality in practical expression in life is of primary importance in multiple segments of the epistle (as it is of many Pauline letters), but his usage of the term *gentiles* in chapter 4 speaks to the natural state of those outside of the community of faith apart from the work of the Holy Spirit rather than the miraculous inclusion of ethnic gentiles in full communion as the people of God.

While the non-Jewish members of the Christian community in Ephesus would have still been ethnically gentile, it is clear that Paul saw their present status in Christ as transforming their noetic and moral nature in a way disjunctive with their pre-Christian ethnic heritage. It is the Spirit who affected this transformation as is seen within the broader context of the letter. The contrast between the two ways of living is firstly premised upon the impact within their minds (4:17-24). "You must no longer walk as the gentiles do, in the futility of their minds."

The condition of the mind alienated and not functioning according to divine design is the described by Paul with vivid language. *Nous* is condemned to ultimate futility (ματαιότης) when left to its own resources. The Apostle draws on a long line of semantic emphasis as seen in the LXX when employing this term. Psalm 93:11 demonstrates that even the thoughts of the wise man are ultimately ματαιότης. Otto Bauernfeind summarizes the underlying significance of the word in the theological

58. Turner, "Ephesians," 192.

lineage Paul would have been employing, "In the NT there is no mitiga-
tion of the ruthless comprehensiveness of the LXX. It is a biblical truth
that even in the most favourable circumstances human reflection does
not escape μάταιον."[59] In contrast to the enlightening work of the Spirit
upon the eyes of the heart (1:18), the gentile mind has been darkened
(ἐσκοτωμένοι). Paul's use of the perfect tense emphasizes that the previously darkened mind continues to exert controlling influence upon those
who still think according to the pre-regenerate pseudo-autonomous condition. In a final flourish within the sentence describing the postlapsarian
noetic condition, Paul directly links the noetic limitations to a dysfunction within what has since been identified as being the affective element
of the noetic system. A persistent ignorance (ἄγνοιαν), or limitation to
knowing, is caused by dysfunction of the heart and corrupted desires
(4:22). The ultimate remedy to this noetic dysfunction within its affective
function is a renewal of the mind (4:23) so that it reflects the designed
parameters established by the Creator, which Paul refers to as true righteousness and holiness (4:24).

In exposing the NT perspective on the postlapsarian noetic condition, the impact of a Spirit affected transformation is clear. The area to be
addressed by the regenerated mind is not primarily in systems of logic,
reason, or historical analysis, but in the distorted affective elements of
humanity's epistemological workings. It is in the desires, will, motivations, and passions that hermeneutics encounters its most persistent and
pernicious challenges (as demonstrated in the example of Brutus). In
this way, it is a failure of the virtues of the mind in the highly conflicted
postlapsarian world which thwart human interpretive tasks. While virtue based philosophical frameworks, including Aristotle's *Nicomachean
Ethics*, nobly attempt to mitigate these noetic deficiencies by the development of virtue, the theological solution exposes that *full* virtue attainment is beyond humanity's best efforts apart from a pneumatologically
induced transformation.

The Analogy of Spirit-Led Morality and Epistemology

As previously established, understanding is an epistemological good
that possesses the capacity for ever-increasing richness and depth. In

59. Bauernfeind, "Μάταιος, Ματαιότης, Ματαιόω, Μάτην, Ματαιολογία,
Ματαιολόγος," *TDNT*, 4:519–24.

pursuing understanding, greater levels of explanatory data from diverse sources integrate with both standing and occurrent beliefs, emotions, and experiences in order to lend greater strength and plausibility to the overall epistemological system of an individual or community. Understanding cannot be bound by the artificial limitations of pure objectivity or a singular contributing source like reason, empirical considerations, or mystical spiritual perceptions. It welcomes active agents engaging the full range of human capacities, senses, and perceptions. When applied to textual interpretation, an understanding of a text that includes historical, sociological, grammatical, experiential, affective, and communal agreement with strong internal integration has a greater explanatory capacity than one that approaches the task exclusively from a single frame of reference. Consider a promise like Phil 4:7: "And the peace of God, which surpasses all understanding, will guard your hearts and your minds in Christ Jesus." The inclusion of Paul's experience as a prisoner at the time of the composition of this promise while also understanding the unique circumstances being faced by the Philippians contributes to understanding. When this information is combined with contextual, linguistic, and theological understanding of the concept of peace as used by Paul, the understanding is deepened. Finally, if a contemporary reader has prayed during a time of anxiety with the resultant internal experience of wholeness and peace, this adds an additional level of personal empirical understanding to the text. If this is true in reference to the engagement of texts in meaningful ways, it should also be true of the entire system.

The more integrated, explanatory, and comprehensive a hermeneutical approach is, the more likely it will fit within the category of understanding and increase its own plausibility and usefulness. While previous chapters made the argument for a generalized and philosophically supported view of VH, it can only increase support for the program if it can be demonstrated that its approach is seen in a biblical frame of reference and coheres with other biblical and theological concepts. Since the contemporary rise of virtue epistemology is directly related to the antecedent rise of virtue ethics, it is not surprising that a virtue approach to epistemology/interpretation is also reflected in the NT's approach to moral transformation. Both ethics and epistemology have been significantly impacted by the entrance of sin into the human condition and find remedy in the redemptive act of Christ. It lends greater support and understanding if it can be shown that both the ethical and epistemological domains are addressed from what may be seen as a virtue approach within the redemptive frame of the NT. This affinity between the systems has been longstanding and reflected in significant names in historic and contemporary contexts of both theology and philosophy (e.g., Thomas Aquinas, Stanley Hauerwas, L. Gregory Jones, Paul Wadell, Macintyre, and Zagzebski). The following discussion supports the correlation of a pneumatologically-directed approach to both moral and noetic functions.

It is an insufficient answer to equate NT teaching on morality with Aristotelian virtue theory. Neither Jesus nor Paul were Peripatetics. Kotva, who argues that "Aristotle's ethics are notably well-suited to the Christian moral life,"[60] is correct when he also acknowledges that it is not accurate to imply "that Matthew and Paul developed a virtue ethic or intentionally work from a virtue framework. They do not."[61] The Galilee of Jesus and the Tarsus and Jerusalem of Paul would have undoubtedly experienced significant exposure to Hellenistic influence, but it is important to carefully consider what Martin Hengel means when he says, "From about the middle of the third century BC all Judaism must really be designated 'Hellenistic Judaism.'"[62] It is incorrect to see this as a declaration that the underlying foundation for NT morality is simply the exchange of Jewish tradition for that of a Greek philosophical and literary point of view, but that by the time of Jesus, at the very least, the awareness of and engagement with the Hellenistic ethical tradition was widely known in Galilee and Jerusalem. Furthermore, much of the conversation within Judaism in the first century was the working out of the "tension between acceptance and rejection of the Hellenistic Zeitgeist."[63]

The language of virtue in the Greek context would not have been novel for Jewish teachers by the time of Jesus and Paul. Multiple apocryphal works dated to the Second Temple Period make this clear. The Wisdom of Solomon 8:7 presents Plato's four cardinal virtues (without formally citing Plato): "And if anyone loves righteousness, her labors are virtues; for she teaches self-control and prudence, justice and courage; nothing in life is more profitable for mortals than these." The combination of the primary Jewish concept of righteousness and the Greek concept of virtue is indicative of the interaction of the two systems. Fourth Maccabees 1:18 reproduces the same list of cardinal virtues with the specifically

60. Kotva, *Case for Virtue Ethics*, 41.

61. Kotva, *Case for Virtue Ethics*, loc. 1667.

62. Hengel, *Judaism and Hellenism*, 104.

63. Hengel, *Judaism and Hellenism*, 4.

Aristotelian emphasis on phronesis, declaring it to be the ruler or lord (*kýrios*) of all the virtues.[64] In the teaching of Jesus, and subsequently Paul, awareness and usage of vocabulary does not imply the absolute synonymity of the underlying philosophy. It is too much to say Jesus and Paul are simply redefining Judaism as Greek moral philosophy. It seems more plausible and accurate to say that they are expressing a New Covenant understanding of morality that is expressive of OT prophetic and eschatological expectations in the terms and literary styles that are relevant to their Hellenized milieu.[65] This could be likened to the manner in which OT writings employ the genres, vocabularies, and techniques of other Ancient Near Eastern cultures (e.g., Ugaritic poetry, Babylonian creation narratives, and Hittite covenant forms) while defining a radically different theological message within the literary forms. Virtue lists on the pages of the NT speak to this adoption of literary style to express the New Covenant understanding of moral transformation.[66] The similarity between some elements of the perspectives is less about borrowing or conflating as it is about an organic agreement in some matters and disagreement in others while employing culturally relevant methods of communication. The similarities include an emphasis on the internal sense of being, character, and motivations that precede external acts, the embodied and habitual nature of a virtuous agent's affections and behavior, the importance of exemplars, both systems' teleological focus, and the prioritization of inward transformation rather than the simple repudiation of all external rules. Differentiating between the two systems is clear when considering the fundamental problem of sin, the need for grace, the inescapable christologic/pneumatalogic center of Christian virtue thought, and the full democratization of the virtues.

Jesus's teaching on murder and adultery in Matt 5 are sufficient examples as to how Jesus's moral teaching is compatible with one element of virtue ethics. Using de Waal Dryden's acronym ARM (actions, reasons, and motivations) as a simplified template for wise and virtuous action, Jesus's teaching aligns well with the fundamental agenda of virtue theory. Right actions are necessary but are only one portion of the equation in

---

64. 4 Macc 1:18: Τῆς δὲ σοφίας εἰδέαι καθεστᾶσιν φρόνησις καὶ δικαιοσύνη καὶ ἀνδρία καὶ σωφροσύνη. 19 κυριωτάτη δὲ πάντων ἡ φρόνησις, ἐξ ἧς δὴ τῶν παθῶν ὁ λογισμὸς ἐπικρατεῖ.

65. Consider the internalization of the Law as prophesied in Jer 31:33 and Ezek 36:24–28 as prophetic precursors to NT moral teaching.

66. 1 Cor 13:13; Gal 5:22–23; Eph 4:2, Phil 4:8–9; Titus 1:8; Jas 3:17–18; 2 Pet 1:5–8.

being a morally upright person. In both of the cases addressed in the Sermon on the Mount, correct action is necessary but insufficient for the moral life of the kingdom of heaven. One cannot be deemed righteous simply by not consummating the physical actions of murder or adultery. The right external actions must be accompanied by the proper internally correct dispositions, affections, and motivations.[67] Failure to commit murder is not laudable if the internal desire motivated by anger is still present. In his interactions with the Pharisees, Jesus makes clear that external actions can be correct but fail to be righteous since they are sourced from entirely corrupted internal realities. This condition gave rise to his famous condemnation of his adversaries as being "whitewashed sepulchers," those who outwardly appear righteous to others but inwardly are full of hypocrisy and lawlessness. This is a break from rule-based or act-based forms of ethics that focus evaluation purely on external grounds. A morally upright person must act according to what de Waal Dryden expresses as right actions, for the right reasons, from the right motivations. Kotva explains the equivalent approach in virtue ethics: "Virtue theory sees a reciprocal or circular relationship existing between states of character (that is, virtues and vices, including feelings, tendencies, and dispositions) and actions. States of character inform, direct, and execute perceptions, choices, and actions. Conversely, actions express and help to develop states of character."[68]

The call for proper ethical action to arise from an inward ontological transformation is clear in Pauline theology but is also observable in the very structure of several of his epistles. Ephesians illustrates the point well. Chapters 1–3 employ the indicative case as the primary verbal mood. The emphasis is upon the current reality of the status and nature of the eschatological and pneumatically-sealed community of Ephesian believers. He is consistently describing who they are (ontological) or what is now true about them in Christ. Among other things, they are made alive with Christ, seated in heavenly places, saved by grace through faith, created in Christ Jesus for good works, brought near, made fellow citizens with the saints, built into a dwelling place for God by the Spirit, fellows heirs, members of the same body, and partakers of the promise in Christ Jesus. With the transition of his emphasis to parenetic concerns as expressed by his use of οὖν in 4:1, he shifts to the imperative mood,

---

67. Consider Jesus's teaching on giving, prayer, and fasting in Matt 6. The motivation to be seen for doing righteous acts disqualifies the actions from being truly righteous.

68. Kotva, *Case for Virtue Ethics*, loc. 1458.

which prescribes right actions and attitudes that express the previously recognized state of existence. They are now encouraged to walk in a manner worthy of the calling by which they were called, grow up in every way into him who is the head, put off their old self and be renewed in the spirit of their mind, put away falsehood, not sin in their anger, stop stealing, labor doing honest work in order to share with others in need, use their words to build up others, imitate God, walk in love, and walk as children of light. It is tempting to argue that the Apostle's ordering of the indicative preceding the imperative reflects a similar emphasis as seen in virtue theory that actions secondarily flow from the primary sense of being and internal character. While this possibility should not be ruled out entirely, it seems more prudent to simply acknowledge that there is a genuine connection and necessity for Christian ethics to reflect an emphasis on both internal matters of being and external matters of action in the establishment of righteous or moral individuals and communities.

The emphasis on habituated character as a way of expressing a truly moral life is seen in multiple metaphorical images employed in the NT. Matthew 7:15–20 draws a sharp distinction between the outward appearance of some who do not have a corresponding internal character. Jesus uses the imagery of wolves in sheep's clothing and of fruit-bearing plants. "Every healthy tree bears good fruit, but the diseased tree bears bad fruit . . . Thus you will recognize them by their fruits." The nature of people will ultimately be revealed in what they reliably produce. Jesus draws direct focus on the ultimate ingrained nature and character of agents as determining what they will ultimately do. Luke 6:43–45 expands on this teaching with the inclusion of the clause, "The good person out of the good treasure of his heart produces good, and the evil person out of his evil treasure produces evil, for out of the abundance of the heart his mouth speaks."

Paul employs the language of walking as a metaphor for the ongoing and habituated actions of the righteous. He, "like virtue theory, focuses less on specific acts and more on continuities and patterns of behavior."[69] The ongoing and progressive direction of an agent's life reflects the truest sense of their internal transformation. He speaks of walking in the footsteps of the faith of our father Abraham (Rom 4:12), walking in the newness of life (Rom 6:4), walking not according to the flesh but according to the Spirit (Rom 8:4), walking properly (Rom 13:13), walking in

---

69. Kotva, *Case for Virtue Ethics*, loc. 1725.

love (Rom 14:15), walking by faith (1 Cor 5:7), walk by the Spirit and not gratifying the desires of the flesh (Gal 5:16), walking in good works (Eph 2:10), walking in a manner worthy of the calling to which you have been called (Eph 4:1), walking as children of light (Eph 5:8), walking as wise not as unwise (Eph 5:15), walking in him [Christ Jesus the Lord] (Col 2:6), walking in wisdom (Col 4:5), and walking in a manner worthy of God (1 Thess 2:12). In using the image of walking, Paul emphasizes the ongoing, recognizable, and forward-moving character of the agent. It is not simply a moment or a single action considered in isolation from the ongoing conduct of their life that is important. "By itself, 'walking' does not imply moral growth or progress. But unlike many contemporary understandings of ethics, 'walking' envisions continuity and patterns of behavior. Instead of seeing morality primarily as discrete acts, judgments, and dilemmas, 'walking' or 'living' pictures morality as patterns of behavior and a continuous journey."[70]

Just as Aristotle's ethical system emphasized the necessity and influence of appropriate exemplars, the NT reflects an equally high place for this role. Rather than a purely rule- or act-based instructional approach that predicates transformation as resulting from an exclusively cognitive transfer between agents in developing Christian ethical and moral righteousness, the model of master with apprentice, rabbi with disciples, or exemplar with followers is the preferred method in the NT. The Apostle Paul regularly employs the language of the exemplar model of growth and understanding. "Brothers, join in imitating me, and keep your eyes on those who walk according to the example you have in us." The root word for "imitate" in this passage is μιμέομαι, which is the same word that Aristotle uses when speaking of following an exemplar in book 9, part 11: "But in all things one obviously ought to imitate (μιμέομαι) the better type of person."[71] Paul uses similar language of imitation in multiple passages to express the discipling process or to encourage future growth.[72] Beyond Pauline usage, Hebrews and 3 John also employ the language of mimesis as a way to grow in Christian character and conduct.[73] Other words fit this same concept, as when 2 Tim 1:13 encourages, "Follow the pattern of the sound words that you have heard from me, in the faith

---

70. Kotva, *Case for Virtue Ethics*, loc. 1710.

71. Aristotle, *Nicomachean Ethics*, loc. 3247.

72. 1 Cor 4:16, 11:1; Eph 5:1; 1 Thess 1:6, 2:14; 2 Thess 3:7, 8.

73. Heb 6:12, 13:7; 3 John 11.

and love that are in Christ Jesus," or the virtue-laden encouragement in 2 Tim 3:10, "You, however, have followed my teaching, my conduct, my aim in life, my faith, my patience, my love, my steadfastness . . ." In another text full of virtue concepts, Phil 4:8–9, Paul further summarizes the emphasis on following suitable exemplars in moral development: "Finally, brothers, whatever is true, whatever is honorable, whatever is just, whatever is pure, whatever is lovely, whatever is commendable, if there is any excellence, if there is anything worthy of praise, think about these things. What you have learned and received and heard and seen in me— practice these things, and the God of peace will be with you." For all the language of moral development through observing and imitating proper exemplars, the NT is unique in elevating Jesus as the ultimate archetype exemplar to which all subsequent demi-exemplars are first conformed. First Peter 2:21 describes Christ as having left an example: "so that you might follow in his steps." Paul predicates his potential as a suitable exemplar upon *his* following of Christ as an exemplar. "Be imitators of me, as I am of Christ."[74]

It is apparent in the Gospels that Jesus becomes the standard against which the rule- or act-based OT would now be evaluated. The laws of the Torah, apart from the agential embodiment in Christ, are not sufficient for true righteousness. Jack Kingsbury explains this transformation of viewing the Law through Jesus. "In the final analysis, therefore, what Jesus says about the law applies to it as something being authoritatively reinterpreted by his teaching. It is not the Mosaic law in and of itself that has normative and abiding character for the disciples, but the Mosaic law as it has passed through the crucible of Jesus's teaching."[75] Seen in this light, Matthew's Sermon on the Mount is a master class on Jesus as the embodied and ultimately authoritative exemplar of kingdom righteousness. Beginning in Matt 5:17 and continuing through 6:18, Jesus establishes himself as the living expression of God's righteousness. Nowhere is this more evident than in his formula, "You have heard that it was said . . . But I say to you."[76] In adopting the understanding, *telos*, affections, motivations, and pattern of Jesus's life, not in simply adhering to external rules, true righteousness is attained.

---

74. 1 Cor 11:1.

75. Kingsbury, *Matthew as Story* , 65.

76. Matt 5:21–22, 27–28, 33–34, 38–39, 43–44, and slight variation of the formula in 31–32, "It has been said . . . But I tell you."

Upon the departure of Jesus following his death, resurrection, and ascension, the absence of the embodied exemplar in Jesus posed a potential problem for a righteousness built upon his living example rather than on a strict letter of the Law. The NT solution to this dilemma is expressed in the continued presence of the Spirit. John 14:15–17 is a centerpiece passage in explaining the New Covenant transformation of the fallen human moral nature. "If you love me, you will keep my commandments. And I will ask the Father, and he will give you another Helper, to be with you forever, even the Spirit of truth, whom the world cannot receive, because it neither sees him nor knows him. You know him, for he dwells with you and will be in you." If, as has been argued, Jesus is the ultimate exemplar who embodies true righteousness, then the Spirit becomes the ongoing internal exemplar that dwells within the regenerate agent aligning beliefs, actions, reasons, affections, and motivations with righteousness. There is a continuity in embodied exemplars from Jesus to the Spirit within believers. In applying the word ἄλλον (other, another), it is clear that Jesus saw himself as the first who helped, or the first paráklētos, in the transformation of the moral and ethical character of his follower, and that the Spirit would then take residence within his followers as the subsequent paráklētos who would continue his work. This moral transformation at the hands of the ongoing work of the Spirit is expressed in Paul's theology in Gal 5:16–25. "But I say, walk by the Spirit, and you will not gratify the desires of the flesh . . . But if you are led by the Spirit, you are not under the law . . . If we live by the Spirit, let us also keep in step with the Spirit." It is not that Paul is dismissing the previously revealed moral dictates of the Law, but that the New Covenant expectation is that the internal transformation, the cognitive, affective, volitional, and motivational transformation, affected by the Spirit is not contrary to the Law but enables the disciple to grow to embrace it from the heart.[77] The extension of the Spirit's work to include both the moral and epistemological work as the internal exemplar for believers is evident in multiple NT passages.[78]

Both virtue theory and NT moral thought are teleological in their focus. For Aristotle, the end to be achieved was *eudaimonia*. *Happiness* is an often-used and simplified word to define the eudaimonistic end pursued by Aristotle's approach. Roberts and Wood expand it to a more likely

---

77. Rom 6:17: "But thanks be to God, that you who were once slaves of sin have become obedient from the heart to the standard of teaching to which you were committed."

78. John 16:13; 1 Cor 2:10; 1 John 2:20, 27.

richness in line with Aristotle's agenda by describing it as "the broadest and deepest human well-being."[79] The teleological direction of NT ethics is also apparent in Scripture even if it is not as succinctly expressed as Aristotle's *eudaimonia*. In thoroughly pneumatological language, Paul points toward a clear goal in Rom 8:23: "We ourselves, who have the first-fruits of the Spirit, groan inwardly as we wait eagerly for adoption as sons, the redemption of our bodies." Again, in the same chapter, he makes a further expression of this end, "For those whom he foreknew he also predestined to be conformed to the image of his son." The conforming of the redeemed to the pattern and image of Jesus implies both a moral and an epistemological end. This New Covenant experience of being conformed to the glorious image of the Lord is directly related to the Spirit's work in 2 Cor 3:18, "And we all, with unveiled face, beholding the glory of the Lord, are being transformed into the same image from one degree of glory to another. For this comes from the Lord who is the Spirit."

A final similarity between NT and virtue theory involves the relationship between the actions that flow from the seat of a transformed ontological center or the pneumatologically-enabled habituated character of the agent, and external laws or rules. It is erroneous to believe that either model is antinomian in orientation. J. A. Smith expresses Aristotle's approach in his introduction to *Nicomachean Ethics*: "The subject-matter of Human Conduct is not governed by necessary and uniform laws. But this does not mean that it is subject to no laws. There are general principles at work in it, and these can be formulated in 'rules,' which rules can be systematised or unified."[80] The important differentiation between act-based or rule-based approaches and the virtue/NT approach is not the rejection of external standards, expectations, and rules, but the manner in which they are truly fulfilled and applied into the vast diversity of human experience. Virtue/NT approaches emphasize the internal transformation of the individual on a fundamental and dispositional level so that rather than simply externally obeying imposed rules, the agent joyously and, in line with her transformed nature, naturally does what is right. Paul's multiple delineations of sins or works of the flesh,[81] as well as Jesus's clear affirmation of the righteousness of the Law[82] make clear that

---

79. Roberts and Wood, "Humility and Epistemic Goods," 158.

80. Smith, "Introduction," loc. 80.

81. Rom 1:28–32; Gal 5:19–21.

82. Matt 5:17.

they did not reject the dictates of the Law, but saw true righteousness as something which comes from a more fundamental transformation than discrete moral actions.

While the emphasis of this section is that there is an organic similarity between virtue theory and the NT's treatment of moral transformation which lends further cogency to a virtuous approach to epistemology and hermeneutics as well, it is important to acknowledge again that similarity and usefulness in descriptive terminology is not the same as complete synonymity. Each of the following points could be developed in a much fuller treatment, but since the focus is on the similarities, only a passing acknowledgment of the discontinuities is necessary for the purposes of this research. Aristotelian virtue theory brings the fundamental problem which demands moral education, as would be expected, to a very earthly focus. He seeks to know that one thing that is a good in itself, which he decides to be self-sufficient happiness, *eudaimonia*, and then finds fault with the insufficient and broken ways in which agents have tried to achieve it (e.g., pleasure, power, possessions, or talents). The problem from a biblical frame is far more sinister. It is sin which resulted from human overreach in attempting to assert both independence from and equality with God in an act of rebellion. These two starting points as to the initial problem with the moral and epistemological failings of human agents is vast. This difference naturally exposes the second primary problem in equating the two systems. Overcoming an insufficient approach to attaining the ideal of happiness is far different than traversing the gulf between a righteous and holy God and a rebellious and sinful humanity. While training, practice, exemplars, and habituation can, theoretically, fully resolve the former, only redemption, atonement, and grace can resolve the latter. A pneumatologically sensitive virtue approach cannot be conflated with any form of Pelagianism that makes true virtue attainment the achievement of human effort or will. This equating of virtue theory with works-based salvation remains the primary contemporary argument leveled against any form of Christian virtue theory, but this is a thorough misunderstanding and misstating of what is presented here as a pneumatologically sensitive virtue approach. Only the Christ event and subsequent Spirit transformation received solely by the gracious gift of God can lead to the redemptive and ultimate development of a maximally virtuous life. Having understood the inescapable divine initiative and activity to allow for the Spirit-actualized transformation, the acting and thinking agent must submit to the process and partner with the Spirit in living it out in moral and thinking contexts. In this way, Paul's encouragements to grow, mature, increase, and work out one's own salvation make sense. There is no Christian virtue theory apart from the redemptive work of Christ and the ongoing transforming presence of the Holy Spirit. A final difference worthy of discussion is the scope of virtue training and availability. Aristotle's ethic is one part of his broader ethical theory which includes his work *Politics*, and in this work, ethics is seen as the manner of moral education to train a proper citizenry for an ideal *pólis*. The focus in his Greek philosophy was on the virtue development of the moral elites. Since *eudaimonia* required some level of social and material status, true virtue acquisition was limited to a select portion of the population. His *polis* did not include "immigrants, outcasts, or anyone that might threaten the integrity of the city-state."[83] The gospel's call to redemption and transformation is distinctly democratized to include "everyone who calls on the name of the Lord."[84]

After considering both the similarities and differences between traditional virtue theory, epitomized in Aristotle's *Nicomachean Ethics*, and NT moral and epistemological expressions of redemptive and pneumatologically experienced transformation in both the realms of acting and thinking by human agents, the usefulness of virtue theory as a descriptive framework is well supported. Consequently, it lends greater weight to an approach of hermeneutical inquiry that takes seriously the transformation of the person and his mind as to how he engages with a text to understand it. All that remains is to align this process of renewing the mind by the Spirit to stabilize the pursuit and application of textually-expressed meaning and understanding from the Bible with the historic Christian doctrine of illumination.

Illumination as Virtuosity

If embedded virtue within the epistemological character of the interpreting agent is to be established as the significant matter that this research indicates, it seems surprising that two millennia of Christian hermeneutics should not have already developed the concept at some length. The failure to recognize the imprint of VH in Christian theology is attributable to the historic tendency to describe the fruit of VH by a more widely

83. Eberly and Mesimer, "Reforming Virtue Ethics."
84. Rom 10:13.

known theological moniker: illumination. As this chapter has detailed, a generalized virtue approach has some value and efficacy but also inescapable limitations in attempting to approach the biblical text, which is why the final development of the program demands a robust pneumatological understanding resulting in spiritual illumination.

Nineteenth century British biblical scholar, H. C. G. Moule, describes the unique role of the Holy Spirit in reference to the Scriptures: "We will remember that the blessed Spirit is not only the true Author of the written Word but also its supreme and true Expositor."[85] This description is hardly as clear as it first appears, and Moule is all too aware of this reality when he qualifies his statement within a page, "It may be well here, however, to say one word of caution as to the use made by the Christian of this truth of the Spirit's expository work. How may we expect Him normally to exercise for us this merciful function? Is it by direct illumination, such that this text or that passage shall be seen by the soul, in the way of supernatural intuition, to mean this or that?"[86] He concludes that a view of illumination that sees the Spirit's work in this way presumes "prophetic infallibility" and conflates interpretation with inspiration.[87] His caution and inconclusiveness is echoed through the subsequent century to the current day.

Multiple biblical texts are used to support the idea of illumination as a necessary attendant to hermeneutical endeavors. The most common passages are, John 16:12–15, 1 Cor 2:6–16, Eph 1:15–20, 1 John 2:26–27, and more obscurely in Ps 119:18, Luke 24:27–32, and 2 Tim 2:7. While these passages all point to the presence, and even necessity, of the Spirit's illumining work, the precise nature of the reasons, scope, manner, upon what faculties (i.e., noetic, spiritual, volitional, affective), and to exactly what end the Spirit accomplishes this task is a matter for great debate. Writing within the Pentecostal context, French Arrington describes much of the current understanding of illumination: "The Holy Spirit plays a definite role in the interpretation and understanding of Scripture, but rarely are the specifics of this role explained."[88]

A pneumatologically-attuned VH approach to textual interpretation helps to bring clarity to the often-misunderstood doctrine of illumination

85. Moule, *Veni Creator*, 63.

86. Moule, *Veni Creator*, 65.

87. Moule, *Veni Creator*, 65.

88. Arrington, "Use of the Bible by Pentecostals," 104.

and brings the preceding philosophical description of the program into agreement with a biblical and theological description. While the topic of illumination has been referenced by Christian teachers as recognizable as Origen, Augustine, Luther, and Calvin, a literature survey on the topic confirms Fred Klooster's description of the discipline: "Illumination of the Holy Spirit is regularly mentioned in theological literature; yet detailed discussion of this subject is rare."[89] All of the various strains of thought concerning illumination suffer from ardent polarization that is sufficiently resolved by the application of pneumatologically understood virtue theory. When interpreters are acting with virtue initiated by the Spirit's work and ingrained through guided practice and habituation, it is another way of saying that they are experiencing the fruit of illumination.

Contemporary Views of Illumination

Before addressing the variety of plausible and currently held understandings of illumination, several pseudo-illumination theories must be identified and dismissed. While each of these approaches seems to share some connection to the idea of illumination by the Holy Spirit, they all fail to meet the fundamental definition of the doctrine. For convenience, two broad categories of error can be identified. The first category references a key definitional difference between authoring and interpreting. The second category addresses the connection between the text and spiritual illumined meaning.

Firstly, illumination is not to be equated with inspiration. While both works are attributed to the Spirit in the canon, they differ in significant ways. In inspiration the Spirit moves upon an agent to produce a meaningful expression; in the case of Scripture, this expression is textual in nature. In the act of illumining, the Spirit works upon an agent to understand meaning already present. Stanley Grenz refers to this as the "twofold relationship between the Spirit and the Scripture. The Holy Spirit, evangelicals confess, is the agent in both the original composition of the biblical documents (inspiration) and the ongoing understanding of the truth in those documents (illumination)."[90] When this order is confused, then the categories of illumination and inspiration cease to have any biblical significance.

89. Klooster, "Role of the Holy Spirit," 451.
90. Grenz, *Revisioning Evangelical Theology*, 115.

Examples where this ordering is confused or conflated involve several hermeneutical systems. Reader-Response approaches that see the interpretive agent or community generating the meaning of the text are guilty of making the interpreter or the interpreter's community more of an author than an interpreter. Vanhoozer warns against this confusing of roles in Reader-Response: "It is important not to collapse the act of authoring (*logos*) into the church's act of reception (*pathos*). To suggest that the way the church receives the word determines what God is saying and doing in the Bible is to wreak havoc with the economy of divine discourse."[91] This usurping of the authorial role may sound spiritual, but as Bernard Ramm rightly observes, "it is a veiled egotism."[92] It is egotism in dismissing the unique originary role that the author alone possesses in formulating a text. While Reader-Response approaches to textual understanding originated in the broader academy from philosophical, linguistic, and literary disciplines, the same tendency to confuse authoring and interpreting have been observable in theological settings. The New Hermeneutic's focus on generating a new text by melding the first horizon of the author and the second horizon of the reader into a synthesized new meaning also crosses the wall between author and interpreter, albeit not as egregiously as Reader-Response approaches. As a more existentially attuned approach in the lineage of Heidegger and Bultmann, the New Hermeneutic focuses less on the interpreting of the text and more on the interpreting of the interpreter (not an entirely unworthy task, and one addressed by a virtue approach but separate from the function of textual interpretation).

The second pseudo-illumination theory shifts the attention from the creation of new meaning, which characterized the first error, to a view that creates a wedge between the text being interpreted and the meaning to be discovered. Illumination becomes less the creation of new meaning, as it does the illegitimate severing of meaning from the textual expression by the pursuit of a "spiritual meaning." Craig Keener addresses this failed view of illumination: "Divine illumination does not mean pretending away the textual nature of the biblical text; insofar as it is textual, Scripture by virtue of its textual form must be approached in the sorts of ways in which we must approach texts."[93]

91. Vanhoozer, *Drama of Doctrine*, 193.

92. Ramm, *Protestant Biblical Interpretation*, 17.

93. Keener, *Spirit Hermeneutics*, 12.

Origen's Alexandrian hermeneutics demonstrates this view of illumination. Daniel Fuller summarizes Origen's view: "He [the interpreter] will surely miss the text's meaning if he construes it merely from the way the writer used words."[94] For Origen, the failure to move beyond the text to the spiritual meanings hidden behind the text was a failure of true biblical interpretation and a sign of either simplicity or ignorance. The cause for erroneous apprehension of the Bible's message, according to Origin, "is no other than this, that the holy Scripture is not understood by them according to its spiritual, but according to its literal meaning."[95] While similar to the first error in that it sees illumination as a further form of revelation, it is different in that it believes the meaning is not created new but mystically hidden within the mysteries of the text by the Spirit and requires the Spirit to elucidate it. This gives rise to his allegorical approach, which seeks to express this "illumined" spiritual meaning of the text. Later descendants of this approach include the medieval Quadriga that placed the highest end of hermeneutic goods in the allegorical and analogical meanings hidden on a plane beyond the textual meaning. While certainly different in many ways, this need for new revelation to attain the true and relevant message of God is not entirely different than Neo-Orthodox approaches that see the text only as the occasion of revelatory meaning and not the carrier of it. Osborne addresses these types of views concerning illumination by observing that, "The Spirit . . . does not whisper to us the correct answer."[96] By illegitimately *spiritualizing* textual meaning in separation from the textual expression, the possibility exists of falling prey to Carl Trueman's warning, "Too much emphasis on illumination as providing the content of Christian belief can render biblical interpretation an essentially gnostic activity, which places the views of those who have been 'illuminated' beyond the criticism of those who have not."[97]

Having addressed these similar but insufficient views of illumination, there is still ample disagreement between contemporary scholars as to the range of the working of illumination in interpretive tasks. While all the following approaches are plausible within the biblical and theological range of concepts collected under the term *illumination*, there is impassioned disagreement as to how and in what element of human capacity

94. Fuller, "Holy Spirit's Role," 91.

95. Origen, *De Principii*, IV, n.d., 9.

96. Osborne, *Hermeneutical Spiral*, 341.

97. Trueman, "Illumination," 318.

the Spirit's work of illumining is active. The simplest and most agreeable expression of illumination, in distinction from inspiration which focuses on the original activity of writing, is the focus on the Spirit's work upon or within the contemporary reader or the reader's community to understand the biblical message. Clark Pinnock draws the focus upon the contemporaneity of the concern of Spirit illumination by asking the leading question, "Is it not naïve to think that one can master hermeneutics without paying attention to the Spirit and to the second horizon?"[98] The general neglect, confusion, and lack of consensus about the doctrine of illumination in contemporary conservative interpretive contexts is largely due to a reactive impulse against the liberal, post-liberal, and postmodern obsession with reader-driven interpretations, fears arising from the growing influence of Pentecostal and charismatic openness to non-canonical revelation,[99] concerns about the anti-intellectualism that some perceive as the inevitable result of allowing room for a pneumatological component in the epistemological domain, or the fear of illumination becoming a theological trump card to infallibilize any particular interpretation or excuse sloppy exegesis.

The primary approaches to understanding how illumination works are all attuned to different elements of the broadest conception of human noetic structures: cognitive, affective, and volitional. Of the three views prevalent in the contemporary theological climate, each view tends to emphasize the work of the Spirit in illumination as being concentrated in one of these specific areas, generally to the exclusion of the other two. This qualification of "generally" is necessary because of the imprecision of many formulations which sometimes leave the reader with the impression that a melding of more than one of these views is possible, even if that is not the seeming approach espoused. This imprecision is illustrated by the multiple ways in which the word *understand* can be construed.

In the first iteration of illumination, the Spirit acts within the reader's cognitive functions. "The mind is strongly influenced by one's evil will and by the sinful desires of the human heart. Desires such as pride, the

---

98. Pinnock, "Role of the Spirit," 491.

99. A. T. B. McGowan speaks to this issue: "Many evangelicals in the northern hemisphere, perhaps especially in my own Reformed tradition, have articulated their position in contradistinction to Pentecostalism and the charismatic movements and so have been wary of saying too much about the Holy Spirit lest they be regarded as having abandoned their cessationist position." McGowan, *Divine Authenticity of Scripture*, 23.

love of praise, and a love of sin cause a person not only to misunderstand the Scriptures but also to hate and deny them."[100] This is a meaning-based understanding of illumination. The foundational premise of this view is that human perceiving and cognition have been impacted by the effects of sin to a degree that the very truth and meaning of a text is nearly, if not entirely, inaccessible to those who read apart from the divine assistance of the Holy Spirit. Robert Plummer credits the Spirit with the ability to "enable us to perceive facts and judge the plausibility of arguments with greater clarity."[101] Millard Erickson is one of the strongest and most notable contemporary proponents of the cognitive view. In direct contradiction to the affective view of illumination, Erickson argues, "The problem, then, is not merely that natural man is unwilling to accept the gifts of wisdom of God, but that, without the help of the Holy Spirit, natural man is unable to understand them."[102] By this understanding, illumination affects the perceptive and reasoning elements of human interpretive acts so that the immediate, literal (which is generally defined by proponents as being a historical-grammatical understanding), and authoritative sense of the text is beyond the scope of the un-illumined mind.

Daniel Fuller redefines illumination as being focused on the affective dimension of the interpretive task. Fuller attempts to shift focus from illumination being necessary to discern meaning so that scholars, including unregenerate scholars, are viewed as being equally capable of discovering the meaning, especially in the textual and historical frame, as a regenerate interpreter since the work of the Spirit in interpretation is not in reference to meaning. His argument is predicated on the semantical differentiating between *lambáno* and *déchomai* in 1 Cor 2:14. Paul chooses to use the word *déchomai* which, as Fuller argues by reference to TDNT, "means to 'accept some requested offering willingly and with pleasure, either because it accepts it with gratefulness and eagerness for himself, or for the purpose of helping and supporting someone else.'"[103] When the Holy Spirit illumines an interpreter, he is transforming the interpreter's manner of receiving the text as being a good from God that should be welcomed and joyfully embraced. This affective transformation recognizes the meaning that is textually accessible to any interpreter

100. McKinley, "John Owen's View of Illumination," 98.
101. Plummer and Merkle, *40 Questions*, 146.
102. Erickson, *Christian Theology*, 248.
103. Fuller, "Holy Spirit's Role," 91.

as being divine in origin and receives it as such. In this way, "an agnostic or an atheist, whose concern is simply to set forth, say, a description of Pauline thought, can make a lasting contribution to this subject, if he has achieved a high degree of exegetical skill,"[104] even if the agnostic or atheist do not delight in or trust in God, or render him honor.[105] The reasoning capacities of humanity are less the problem in this view than the disordered loves that define the postlapsarian condition. The preference of sinful humanity to love themselves more than God, seek their own power ahead of submission to divine authority, and often indulge fundamentally narcissistic tendencies are what are transformed when the Spirit illumines a reader.

In the final approach to illumination, the Spirit's work is primarily volitional as seen in the empowering of the interpreter to translate the ancient meaning of the text into practical application, contemporization, and transformation by embracing the significance of the text. Douglas Kennard speaks of this view of the Spirit's work as not being "a hermeneutical promise for understanding the biblical text but rather a transformed life that can serve as the basis for evaluating everything in life."[106] Proponents of this view often use words like *significance*,[107] *dynamic*,[108] or *application* in expressing how they see the influence of the Spirit's work in reference to the interpreter. Vanhoozer uses speech-act theory to explain this sense of illumination: "The Spirit thus opens readers' hearts and minds so that the words can produce all their intended effects: effects of illocutionary understanding and effects of perlocutionary obedience."[109] This becomes illumination by the Spirit not in a cognitive sense, but in the manner in which the Spirit transforms and enables the sincere reader to carry out its instructions from the heart. Lee Anderson expresses the full application of this approach: "Only by the Holy Spirit's work in

---

104. Fuller, "Holy Spirit's Role," 92.

105. Fuller, "Holy Spirit's Role," 94.

106. Kennard, "Evangelical Views on Illumination," 802.

107. *Significance* is a technical term employed by E. D. Hirsch in his book, *Validity in Interpretation*, that "names a relationship between that meaning and a person, or a conception, or a situation, or indeed anything imaginable." This relationship to something else is generally considered application in biblical hermeneutics.

108. Klein et al. speak of "a dynamic comprehension of the significance of Scripture and its application to life," again drawing attention to the empowered and transformative experience of the text in the life of the interpreter.

109. Vanhoozer, *Is There a Meaning in This Text?*, 428.

illumination will the believer properly appropriate the truth of Scripture such that, ultimately, its teachings are accepted, its promises are depended on, and its commands are obeyed."[110]

While some of these views overlap in some treatments of illumination, generally, in contemporary dialogue, each view has a devoted following that dismisses alternative views as being improper understanding of pertinent texts. This is especially true for those who hold the cognitive view in contrast to either of the other two views. Those who argue against the cognitive work in illumination, both the affective and volitional camps, are adamant that interpretation is done by the proper employment of methods, skills, frameworks, and tools to attain the objective and theologically descriptive meaning of a text with no necessary reference to the confessional status of the interpreter. Conversely, those who argue for the Spirit's work in illumination as related to the special calling of the Spirit or regeneration are staunchly committed to the necessary renewal of the mind to even begin to perceive or comprehend the message of the biblical text. This polarization is not the only manner in which to understand the doctrine of illumination.

Puritan pastor and theologian, John Owen, saw a way in which the Holy Spirit bridged the gap that spans the distance between the extremes of rationalism and subjectivism, which David McKinley calls the notional and volitional divide (represented by the cognitive and affective/volitional in the preceding discussion).[111] Owen's approach acknowledged that illumination, while encompassing biblical interpretation, extended beyond merely textual employments in order to address sin's "profound, negative influence on the *human mind, will* and the *desires*. [emphasis added]"[112] Those who are familiar with virtue theory immediately recognize the underlying agreement in Owen's formulation. Using de Waal Dryden's acronym, ARM, the compatibility is obvious. Virtue ethics look to the transformation of the acting agent to have right actions, for the right reasons, from the right motivations. In virtue epistemology, it is true belief that arises from virtuous motivations. Owen even employs virtue and vice language when developing his understanding of illumination, condemning laziness, pride, and biases[113] while receiving from the Spirit humility, meek-

---

110. Anderson, "The Doctrine of Illumination," 233.

111. McKinley, "John Owen's View of Illumination," 97.

112. McKinley, "John Owen's View of Illumination," 97.

113. Owen, *Works of John Owen*, 186–87.

ness, and teachability. VH, as presented in this research with the pneu-matological emphasis of the final chapter, is the unifying approach that resolves the apparent divide between the competing views of illumination. Virtue epistemology as viewed from the theological perspective connects all the cognitive, affective, and volitional elements of illumination.

Pneumatological Virtue Hermeneutics as Answer to Contemporary Debates Concerning Illumination

It is unnecessary to redevelop the entire program of VH to demonstrate its connection to the doctrine of illumination, but several key elements of the program demonstrate how it answers the fundamental questions that are surfaced by contemporary struggles to understand illumination. In this way, VH resolves some of the current polarization but also aligns well with the necessary theological categories of the doctrine, but only when it is viewed from the lens of pneumatological initiative and contin-ued activity rather than a purely anthropological attainment. Failure to acknowledge the divine initiative and work of the Spirit in transforming the mind and heart of the interpreter condemns VH to the same anthro-pological center that plagued and, ultimately, was the undoing of Schlei-ermacher's approach. These important common elements between VH and illumination include its subjectivity, progressive nature, extension along a continuum of epistemological considerations, communal sense, and holistic nature.

While VE and hermeneutical realism both function from a perspec-tive of the existence of an objective reality, they both are emphatic in the subjective engagement of the cognizer or interpreter. There are those who would likely equate the discipline's subjective engagement with relativism or irreality. This is not the case in either virtue-focused discipline. The text and reality both exist but are inescapably encountered by subjects. Illumination is a subjective experience. It is the subject, the interpreter, who is illumined internally by the Holy Spirit rather than the text being illumined. The text meaningfully exists and can be encountered, but it is the interpreter who is in need of illumination on account of the spiritual nature of the message, the ontological limitations of the agents, and the noetic impact of sin. The Spirit guides the seeker into truth,[114] enlightens

---

114. John 16:13.

the eyes of the heart,[115] renews the mind.[116] Erickson describes the illumination process: "The objective word, the written Scripture, together with the subjective word, the inner illumination and conviction of the Holy Spirit, constitutes the authority for the Christian. The written word, correctly interpreted, is the objective basis of authority. The inward illuminating and persuading work of the Holy Spirit is the subjective dimension."[117] Just as VH is necessarily subjective in its justifying capacity beginning with the thoroughly virtuous character of the interpreter, so also illumination begins with the subjective work of the Spirit within the interpreter. This is more than correlation, but alignment. The Spirit illumines the mind, including the interpretive mind, by the reordering of the beliefs (cognition), motivations (affections), and will (volition).

While the Spirit can certainly act in dramatic and instantaneous ways in illumination, as in the opening of the eyes of the disciples heading toward Emmaus, it is not the exclusive, or even the primary, manner of illumination or virtue development. Illumination happens in the ongoing unfolding of understanding. Paul's rebuke to those who remained on a diet of milk rather than meat in reference to spiritual understanding in 1 Cor 3:1–3 is sufficient evidence that understanding can be a progressive work, just as is the renewing of the mind or behavior. This progressive and *telos*-oriented element is fundamental to the concept of virtue development. As a result, it is easy to see how the ongoing work of illumination in the interpreting agent is amenable to virtue conversations as their interpretive character becomes progressively more aligned with the embedded moral nature of the truth to be discovered and extended.

One argument against the doctrine of illumination in reference to biblical interpretation is the inability to definitively say that any of the passages in the NT that speak of illumination have textual consideration or a canonical corpus in view. The need for illumination, as those who see no application to biblical interpretation, speaks to a more basic spiritual awareness and understanding of the message of the gospel. While this is true, the epistemological nature of understanding would certainly extend to include textual inquiry, since it is a primary part of human cognition as well as Christian thought and history subsequent to the Apostolic Era. Furthermore, the existence of a broader view of illumination

---

115. Eph 1:18.

116. Rom 12:1–2.

117. Erickson, *Christian Theology*, 252.

cannot preclude the inclusion of a more limited subsection of the pursuit of truth in textual form. This extension of a continuum of illumination or intellectual virtue can also explain how non-confessing scholars can also engage productively in the hermeneutical dialogue. As discussed previously in this chapter, the Spirit, by virtue of its participation in creation, is directly involved in all knowledge, and this is extended in virtue theory by the embedding of virtues into the fabric of the universe. Agents who either imitate truly virtuous interpreters or practice a limited form of self-discipline in the interpretive virtues may very well gain some good fruit from interpretive endeavors. The Spirit is *generally* illumining any time any truth is discovered in any field; this equates with the broadest element of virtuous intellectual character. Further along the continuum, illumination is salvific in nature and possesses the dynamism to not only grasp, but also welcome, enact, extend into fresh settings, and embody the eternal truths of revelation.

"Writing, commitment of the word to space, enlarges the potentiality of language almost beyond measure."[118] The increase in vocabulary, abstract theorizing (seen in the realms of science, history, and philosophy), and the restructuring of thought patterns to include the idea of objectivity that writing instigates have added immeasurably to human society, but the move from orality to literacy has cost human understanding in several important ways as well. Ong demonstrates that writing is the first step of removing knowledge from a communal setting into a more individualistic experience. An interpreter is no longer experiencing the living expression of communication, but is able to retreat in solitude and quietness to individually encounter an objective text. As printed texts became more common, so did the "sense of personal privacy that marks modern society. It produced books smaller and more portable than those common in a manuscript culture, setting the stage psychologically for solo reading in a quiet corner, and eventually for completely silent reading."[119] This has almost eliminated the social aspect of reading, where one person reads to others in a group. Combined with the related increasing individualism of Western philosophy throughout the period of Modernity, the collective sense of illumination has nearly been lost.

Contemporary models of interpretation have attempted to readmit the reading community into the process of understanding (e.g., New

---

118. Ong, *Orality and Literacy*, loc. 521.

119. Ong, *Orality and Literacy*, loc. 2533.

Hermeneutic and Reader-Response). Unfortunately, this has come at the cost, in most of these systems, of the text bearing a meaning implanted by the author. VH offers a new and important place for the community to be part of the discerning and understanding process. The Spirit-filled community becomes a leading context for the exemplification and transmission of the values and virtues that shape the interpretive context of the reader. "The reader seldom approaches the text as an isolated individual cut off from the corporate life of the church because the expectations of readers are shaped by the community to which they belong."[120] Even if illumination does have a pronounced individual sense, "the context is still the Church because, even when we read the Bible alone, what we think about is not in abstraction from the traditions of our community."[121]

The Spirit-filled community shaping the intellect is different from some approaches that seem to highlight the same goal. For example, Kenneth Archer advances a "Pentecostal Hermeneutic" that emphasizes the Spirit, Scripture, and community in dialogue. While the terminology is similar to how this research engages the communal sense of interpreting, the foundational premise between the two makes these approaches irreconcilable. In VH, the community serves to exemplify and guide interpretive values in the pursuit of textual understanding. In Archer's model, the dialogue between the three participants is not to discover meaning by shaping the interpreter's virtuous approach to the text, but is seen "in producing meaning."[122] The community, also Spirit-filled in his model, is necessary to generate meaning, "because all written communication is indeterminate or, better, underdeterminate."[123] The guiding principle of this research is that the problem with understanding resides within the vicious or under-developed virtuous intellectual character of the interpreters not in the text itself or in the nature of texts generally. In the same way, illumination is not working upon the text, but upon the deficiency of the reader. Illumination is a subjective experience. This does create a critical place for the community in exemplifying and reinforcing the interpretive characteristics that afford the highest justifying ability to an interpretation, but this is fundamentally different from saying the community generates, at any level, the meaning of the text.

---

120. Pinnock, "Role of the Spirit in Interpretation," 495.

121. Pinnock, "Role of the Spirit in Interpretation," 495.

122. Archer, *Pentecostal Hermeneutic*, 213.

123. Archer, *Pentecostal Hermeneutic*, 213.

Finally, just like VE and VH are holistic, not limiting their frame of reference to strictly cognitive concerns, but including affective, experiential, and volitional realities, so too illumination extends to a much more holistic experience of Scripture. It involves the mental acuity to grasp the concepts presented, but also includes the realigning of emotions, passions, will, and actions. Klooster describes the experience as requiring "more than an intellectual grasp of the historical setting of the text or the literary structure of the passage . . . Heart-understanding demands the heart response in the totality of one's being to the living, triune God."[124] Calvin explores a similar sense of holistic illumination and understanding: "The heavenly doctrine proves to be useful and efficacious to us in so far as the Spirit both forms our minds to understand it and our hearts to submit to its yoke."[125] Whether viewed from the cognitive position of Erickson, the affective stance of Fuller, or the volitional perspective of Osborne, a pneumatologically-attuned sense of VH is aligned with the biblical view of illumination in its most holistic sense.

Conclusion

Though new in some sense of the terminology, the idea of a pneumatologically-attuned virtue approach to hermeneutics fully aligned with the most robust and holistic view of illumination. Illumination is a progressive subjective internal experience accomplished by the Holy Spirit, which transforms and elevates the agent's ability to understand meaning, order affections, and empower appropriate volitional action in all areas of life. This is especially true in reference to spiritual truth, which necessarily encompasses the experience of canonical readings. This definition is nearly identical to the previously-detailed program of VH that applies VE into textual studies with the necessary and sufficient addition of the divine initiative and activity through the effectual working of the Holy Spirit. Virtue development becomes a means by which the interpreter experiences the work of the Spirit in illumination. To be illumined is to be virtuous in understanding. In this declaration, no confusion between the source of illumination, *the divine*, the subject of the illumination, *the interpreter*, or the scope of the illumination, *cognitive, affective, and volitional transformation,* can be misconstrued to imply human autonomy or

---

124. Klooster, "Role of the Holy Spirit," 16.
125. Calvin, *Harmony of the Evangelists* , 225.

achievement. Yet, it does explain how even the non-regenerate can still attain some level of understanding of the text without doing harm to the salvific nature of the work of the Spirit.

Conclusion

For all the shared realities between biblical interpretation and the inter-pretation of any other text, there exists a qualitative difference between hermeneutics as a biblical discipline and all other literary forms of inter-pretation. A naturalized form of VH is able to address many areas in which biblical interpretation and other forms of textual literature overlap: textual-ity, communication, genre, grammar, historicity, social and anthropologi-cal concerns, as well as a long list of other categories, but it is insufficient to resolve the specific concerns of the biblical context without the addition of a suitable theological element. Grenz provides this element as he argues for a reassignment of bibliology from the prolegomena to theology to a place within pneumatology, since the Spirit is both the inspirer and illu-minator of the text.[126] As he explains, "Separating the doctrine of Scripture from its natural embedding in the doctrine of the Holy Spirit conceptually separates Scripture from the Spirit, whose vehicle of operation it is."[127] His emphasis on the thoroughly pneumatic nature of the scriptural revelation is a necessary reminder of the significance of the Spirit when speaking of anything to do with the Bible. From revelation, to inspired inscriptura-tion, canonical collection, preservation, illumination, interpretation, and application, the Spirit is at the center of the biblical experience of author-ing and interpreting the Christologically focused text from beginning to conclusion.[128] A pneumatological approach to hermeneutics argues even further that the Spirit establishes the entirety of the context of all human knowing and understanding. In this way, a pneumatologically-sensitive VH resolves the remaining challenges of a naturalized VH approach and also aligns with the classic doctrine of illumination.

The ubiquity of the Spirit in all of creation and human epistemo-logical endeavors resolves the persistent problem of circularity in existing

---

126. Grenz, *Revisioning Evangelical Theology*, 115.

127. Grenz, *Revisioning Evangelical Theology*, 115.

128. The emphasis in the research on the centrality of the Spirit's involvement in hermeneutics should not be construed to displace the Christological center of the message contained within the biblical text (John 15:26, 1 Pet 1:11).

forms of virtue thought. While virtue theory is useful and practical as a philosophical discipline, it continues to struggle to articulate a sufficient answer to its own circularity without a metaphysical anchoring. The Spirit as the active force in creation is this metaphysical solution. Beyond circularity, the problem of humanity's compromised noetic functions requires divine intervention to move beyond merely self-disciplined attempts at virtue acquisition. The power of the Spirit allows VH to hope for something beyond the permanent limitations of the postlapsarian condition.

In arguing for the cogency of a pneumatological form of VH, the case is further supported when the evidence for a spiritual expression of virtue ethics is as equally present within the New Covenant setting in the NT as is an epistemological virtue frame. The close connection between virtue ethics and virtue epistemology in philosophy is equally paralleled in the biblical context. While not a perfect analogue, the similarities are many, and the differences are resolved when understood against the biblical backdrop of human limitations, both ontologically and as a result of the Fall. Where naturalized virtue theory supposes human capacity to solve its vices by human effort alone, the biblical variety of virtue thought demonstrates the inability of human effort, apart from the divine initiative, action, and ongoing empowerment to bring the task to completion.

A final argument in favor of VH as a workable approach to biblical interpretation is made by understanding that a virtuous interpreter is an illumined interpreter. The commonalities in both categories support the claims of VH, but also resolve persistent difficulties in the church's formulation of the doctrine of illumination. In a comprehensive view, it allows for the place of skills, methods, and resources in interpretation while not eliminating the Spirit's continual presence and involvement in the process. It also allows for contribution from unregenerate interpreters, since the Spirit is not only present in the regenerate but within all of creation, but it also takes seriously the full range of impacts from the fall into sin on the entire noetic structure and function of humanity, individually and corporately (cognitively, affectively, and volitionally).

The Spirit is the essential contribution that renders VH more than a practically helpful approach to interpretation and transforms it into a necessary and sufficient system to gain hermeneutical goods. Further reflection on the intersection between pneumatology and hermeneutics is required, but this introduction makes way for the fields of theology and virtue theory to fruitfully move forward together in the contemporary discussions.

Conclusion

WHILE IT IS UNDENIABLY true that hermeneutics in any time period is a complicated and challenging task, it is not an unreasonable hope to believe that a justified understanding of a text that carries with it an increasingly more explanatory approximation of the text's meaning is possible even in an era of deep skepticism about these matters. Furthermore, the extension of this meaning into diverse settings in relevant ways is part of the understanding process, not an expendable or separate task. By applying the model of Responsibilist Virtue Epistemology (RVE) in an agent-centered approach, Virtue Hermeneutics (VH) provides legitimacy and stability to the hermeneutical realist's endeavors by honoring the unique place of the author and the text while admitting the subjective and communal sense of the interpreter's work. As it pertains to interpreting the Bible, the necessary inclusion of the pneumatological perspective shapes it to serve the Canon's unique nature as both an inspired and authoritative text.

In the preceding discussion, the reemergence of virtue theory in both ethical and epistemological settings demonstrates the awareness of the insufficiency of other contemporary models to resolve the aftermath of the decline of modernity's lofty goals of objectivity and certainty. RVE possess the necessary resources to address this deficiency that have been equally implanted into the field of hermeneutics. By developing a programmatic approach that emphasizes the development of the intellectual character of an interpreter as the means to bring justification to the full interpretive task that seeks deeper levels of understanding, the pneumatologically-attuned VH approach shows tremendous promise for the discipline.

In concluding this research, several potential areas for future reflection are obvious. While chapter 3 attempted to give expression to several

core interpretive virtues, this task is far from complete. Much more research on the possible inclusion of additional peripheral virtues and
further explication of those already detailed is greatly needed. Beyond
this task, the growing field of study that seeks to include extra-rational
contributions to the epistemological task is rapidly developing. Is there
such a thing as non-propositional knowledge? How can affections be
epistemological contributors? Virtue studies open the door to consider
other possible contributors to the broadest definition of knowledge, but
how this is done has yet to be fully developed. This is especially important in the realm of spiritual experience. More research must be done to
demonstrate the plausibility of spiritual knowledge and experience, and
specifically pneumatologically-initiated knowledge and experience, being
a justifiable epistemological contributor. Included in this category would
be further exploration of narratival knowledge. Smith has advocated for
this concept within pneumatological communities,[1] but absent the contribution of a more comprehensive epistemological framework with his
ideas, which VE could offer, the approach seems to lack a sufficient gravity
to remain relevant in the long term. Finding a way to anchor the approach
through a pneumatologically-attuned RVE may be, upon further research,
the necessary contribution to create a lasting sense to the approach.

---

1. Smith, *Thinking in Tongues.*

Bibliography

Alfano, Mark. *Character as Moral Fiction*. Cambridge, UK: Cambridge University Press, 2015.

Alston, William P. *Illocutionary Acts and Sentence Meaning*. Ithaca, NY: Cornell University Press, 2000.

Altman, Amnon. "The Role of the 'Historical Prologue' in the Hittite Vassal Treaties: An Early Experiment in Securing Treaty Compliance." *Journal of the History of International Law* 6 (2004) 43–63.

Anderson, Lee. "The Doctrine of Illumination and the Interpretation of Scripture: Considerations for Recent Creationists." *Creation Research Society Quarterly* 55 (2019) 223–34.

Annas, Julia. *Intelligent Virtue*. New York: Oxford University Press, 2011.

———. "The Structure of Virtue." In *Intellectual Virtue: Perspectives from Ethics and Epistemology*, edited by Michael R. DePaul and Linda Trinkaus Zagzebski, 15–33. Oxford: Clarendon, 2003.

Anscombe, G. E. M. "Modern Moral Philosophy." *Philosophy* 33 124 (January 1958) 1–19.

Anton, Audrey L., ed. *The Bright and the Good: The Connection between Intellectual and Moral Virtues*. Lanham, MD: Rowman & Littlefield International, 2018.

Aquinas, Thomas. *Summa Theologica*. Translated by Fathers of English Dominican Province. New York: Benziger Brothers, 2021. Kindle.

Archer, Kenneth J. *A Pentecostal Hermeneutic: Spirit, Scripture, and Community*. Cleveland, TN: CPT, 2009.

Aristotle. *Nicomachean Ethics*. Translated by D. P. Chase. N.d.: e-artnow, 2018. Kindle.

Arndt, William, et al., eds. *A Greek-English Lexicon of the New Testament and Other Early Christian Literature: A Translation and Adaptation of the Fourth Revised and Augmented Edition of Walter Bauer's Griechisch-Deutsches Wörterbuch Zu Den Schriften Des Neuen Testaments Und Der Übrigen Urchristlichen Literatur*. 2nd ed. Chicago: University of Chicago Press, 1979.

Arrington, French. "The Use of the Bible by Pentecostals." *Pneuma* 16 (1994) 101–7.

Audi, Robert. *Rational Belief: Structure, Grounds, and Intellectual Virtue*. New York: Oxford University Press, 2015.

Augustine. *On Christian Teaching*. Translated by R. P. H. Green. Oxford World's Classics. New York: Oxford University Press, 1999.

Austin, J. L. *How to Do Things with Words*. Edited by J. O. Urmson and Marina Sbisà. 2nd ed. Cambridge, MA: Harvard University Press, 1975.

Austin, Michael W., ed. *Virtues in Action: New Essays in Applied Virtue Ethics*. New York: Palgrave Macmillan, 2013.

Axtell, Guy. "Expanding Epistemology: A Responsibilist Approach." *Philosophical Papers* 37 (2008) 51–87.

———. "Introduction." In *Knowledge, Belief, and Character: Readings in Virtue Epistemology*, xi–xxiv. Lanham, MD: Rowman & Littlefield, 2000.

———, ed. *Knowledge, Belief, and Character: Readings in Virtue Epistemology*. Studies in Epistemology and Cognitive Theory. Lanham, MD: Rowman & Littlefield, 2000.

Baehr, Jason. "Character, Reliability and Virtue Epistemology." *Philosophical Quarterly* 56 (2006) 193–212.

———. *The Inquiring Mind: On Intellectual Virtues and Virtue Epistemology*. Oxford: Oxford University Press, 2011.

———. "Virtue Epistemology." *Internet Encyclopedia of Philosophy*. http://www.iep. utm.edu/virtueep/.

———, ed. *Intellectual Virtues and Education: Essays in Applied Virtue Epistemology*. New York: Routledge, 2017.

Bailey, Kenneth E. *Jesus Through Middle Eastern Eyes: Cultural Studies in the Gospels*. Downers Grove, IL: IVP Academic, 2009.

Barth, Karl. *Church Dogmatics, Vol. 4.1, Sections 57–59: The Doctrine of Reconciliation, Study Edition 21*. New York: Bloomsbury T. & T. Clark, 2010.

———. *The Epistle to the Romans*. Translated by Edwyn C. Hoskyns. 6th ed. London; New York: Oxford University Press, 1968.

Barthes, Roland. *The Rustle of Language*. Translated by Richard Howard. Berkeley: University of California Press, 1989.

Battaly, Heather. "Acquiring Epistemic Virtue: Emotions, Situations, and Education." n.d.

———. "Intellectual Perseverance." *Journal of Moral Philosophy* 14 (2017) 669–97.

———. *Virtue*. Malden, MA: Polity, 2015. Kindle.

———. *Virtue*. Malden, MA: Polity, 2015.

———, ed. *The Routledge Handbook of Virtue Epistemology*. New York: Routledge, 2018.

———, ed. *Virtue and Vice, Moral and Epistemic*. Malden, MA: Wiley-Blackwell, 2010.

Battaly, Heather, et al. *Virtue Epistemology: Contemporary Readings*. Edited by John Greco and John Turri. Cambridge, MA: The MIT Press, 2012.

Baur, Ferdinand Christian. *The Church History of the First Three Centuries, Volume I*. BiblioBazaar, 2009.

Baur, Ferdinand Christian, and Ferdinand Friedrich Baur. *Vorlesungen über neutestamentliche theologie*. Leipzig: Fues's (L.W. Reisland), 1864.

Bayer, Oswald. "Lutheran Pietism, or Oratio, Meditatio, Tentatio in August Hermann Francke." *Lutheran Quarterly* 25 (2011) 383–97.

Beck, Aaron T. *Cognitive Therapy and the Emotional Disorders*. Cognitive Therapy. New York: Plume, 1979.

Becker, Kelly. "Reliabilism." *Internet Encyclopedia of Philosophy*. https://www.iep.utm. edu/reliabil/#SH2b.

Bengel, Johann Albrecht, and Charlton T. Lewis. "Gnomon of the New Testament." https:// archive.org/stream/johnalbertbengeoobenggoog/johnalbertbengeoobenggoog_ djvu.txt.

Bernecker, Sven, and Duncan Pritchard, eds. *The Routledge Companion to Epistemology*. Routledge Philosophy Companions. New York: Routledge, 2011.

Bloesch, Donald G. *Essentials of Evangelical Theology Volume 1: God, Authority, and Salvation.* Peabody, MA: Prince/Hendrickson, 1998.

———. *The Holy Spirit: Works and Gifts.* Downers Grove, IL: InterVarsity, 2000.

Boden, Margaret A. *The Creative Mind: Myths and Mechanisms.* New York: Routledge, 2004.

BonJour, Laurence, and Ernest Sosa. *Epistemic Justification: Internalism vs. Externalism, Foundations vs. Virtues.* Malden, MA: Wiley-Blackwell, 2003.

Bowie, Andrew. "Hermeneutics and Modern Philosophy: The Art of Understanding." In *The Blackwell Companion to Hermeneutics*, edited by Niall Keane and Chris Lawn, 45–53. Chichester, UK: Wiley, 2016.

Brady, Michael, and Duncan Pritchard, eds. *Moral and Epistemic Virtues.* Malden, MA: Wiley-Blackwell, 2004.

Bray, Gerald L. *Biblical Interpretation: Past and Present.* Downers Grove, IL: IVP Academic, 2000.

Briggs, Richard. *The Virtuous Reader: Old Testament Narrative and Interpretive Virtue.* Studies in Theological Interpretation. Grand Rapids: Baker Academic, 2010.

Brink, David O., et al., eds. *Virtue, Happiness, Knowledge: Themes from the Work of Gail Fine and Terence Irwin.* Oxford: Oxford University Press, 2018.

Broadie, Sarah. *Ethics with Aristotle.* New York: Oxford University Press, 1993.

Broncano-Berrocal, Fernando. "A Robust Enough Virtue Epistemology." *Synthese* 194 (2017) 2147–74.

Brooks, David. *The Road to Character.* New York: Random, 2015.

Brown, Colin. *Philosophy and the Christian Faith: A Historical Sketch from the Middle Ages to the Present Day.* Downers Grove, IL: Inter Varsity, 1968.

Brown, Dale W. *Understanding Pietism.* Rev. ed. Nappanee, IN: Evangel, 1996.

Brown, Jeannine K. *Scripture as Communication: Introducing Biblical Hermeneutics.* Grand Rapids: Baker Academic, 2007.

Brown, Schuyler. *Text and Psyche: Experiencing Scripture Today.* Wilmette, IL: Chiron, 2003.

Bruce, F. F. *The Book of the Acts.* Rev. ed. Grand Rapids: Eerdmans, 1988.

Brunner, Daniel L., and Leah Payne. "Exploring Pietism as an Intermediary for Lutheran-Pentecostal Dialogue." *Dialog: A Journal of Theology* 55 (2016) 355–63.

Bultmann, Rudolf. *History of the Synoptic Tradition.* Translated by John Marsh. Oxford: Basil Blackwell, 1963.

———. "Jesus Christ and Mythology." In *Rudolf Bultmann Interpreting Faith for the Modern Era*, edited by Roger Johnson, 288–328. Minneapolis: Augsberg Fortress, 1991.

———. "Liberal Theology and the Latest Theological Movement." In *Rudolf Bultmann Interpreting Faith for the Modern Era*, edited by Roger Johnson, 65–78. Minneapolis: Augsberg Fortress, 1991.

———. *New Testament and Mythology.* Philadelphia: Fortress, 1984.

———. *The New Testament and Mythology and Other Basic Writings.* Philadelphia: Fortress, 1984.

———. "The Problem of a Theological Exegesis of the New Testament." In *Rudolf Bultmann Interpreting Faith for the Modern Era*, edited by Roger Johnson, 129–36. Minneapolis: Augsberg Fortress, 1991.

———. *Theology of the New Testament.* New York: Scribner, 1951.

Burke, Trevor J., and Keith Warrington, eds. *A Biblical Theology of the Holy Spirit.* Eugene, OR: Cascade, 2014.

Burnett, Richard E. *Karl Barth's Theological Exegesis: The Hermeneutical Principles of the Römerbrief Period*. Grand Rapids: Eerdmans, 2004.

Callahan, Laura Frances, and Timothy O'Connor, eds. *Religious Faith and Intellectual Virtue*. Oxford: Oxford University Press, 2014.

Calvin, John. *Commentary on a Harmony of the Evangelists, Vol. 3: Matthew, Mark, and Luke*. Forgotten Books, 2018.

―――. *Institutes of Christian Religion*. Bellingham, WA: Logos Bible Software, 1997.

―――. *The Institutes of the Christian Religion*. Translated by Henry Beveridge. Amazon Digital Services, 2021. Kindle.

―――. *The Institutes of the Christian Religion: The Four Books*. Translated by Thomas Norton. North Charleston: CreateSpace, 2017.

Cariño, Michael. *Reasonable Faith: The Role of Intellectual Virtues in the Justification of Religious Belief*. Independently published, 2017.

Carson, D. A. "Current Issues in Biblical Theology." *Bulletin for Biblical Research* 5 (1995) 17–41.

―――. *The Gagging of God*. Grand Rapids: Zondervan, 2002.

Caslib, Bernardo. "Why Intellectual Virtues Matter." *Kritike* 11 (2017) 93–103.

Chammas, Michael. "Wimbledon 2015: Nick Kyrgios Booed by Crowd Amid Tanking Accusations." *The Sydney Morning Herald*. https://www.smh.com.au/sport/tennis/ wimbledon-2015-nick-kyrgios-booed-by-crowd-amid-tanking-accusations-20150706-gi6h7x.html.

Charlesworth, James H., ed. "Introduction." In *The Old Testament Pseudepigrapha*, xxi– xxxiv. 1st ed. Garden City, NY: Doubleday, 1983.

Clem, Stewart. "The Epistemic Relevance of the Virtue of Justice." *Philosophia* 41 (2013) 301–11.

Code, Lorraine. *Epistemic Responsibility*. Hanover, NH: Published for Brown University Press by University Press of New England, 1987.

Cohen, Naomi G. "Philo Judaeus and the Torah True Library." *Tradition* 41 (2008) 31–48.

Coplan, Amy. "Feeling Without Thinking: Lessons from the Ancients on Emotion and Virtue-Acquisition." *Metaphilosophy* 41 (2010) 132.

Croce, Michel, and Maria Silvia Vaccarezza, eds. *Connecting Virtues: Advances in Ethics, Epistemology, and Political Philosophy*. Hoboken, NJ: Wiley, 2018.

Dalmiya, Vrinda. "Knowing People." In *Knowledge, Truth, and Duty: Essays on Epistemic Justification, Responsibility, and Virtue*, edited by Matthias Steup, 221–34. New York: Oxford University Press, 2001.

De Cruz, Helen, and Johan De Smedt. "Reformed and Evolutionary Epistemology and the Noetic Effects of Sin." *International Journal for Philosophy of Religion* 74 (2013) 49.

De La Torre, Miguel A. *Reading the Bible from the Margins*. Maryknoll, NY: ORBIS, 2013.

DePaul, Michael, and Linda Zagzebski, eds. *Intellectual Virtue: Perspectives from Ethics and Epistemology*. Oxford: Clarendon, 2007.

Derrida, Jacques. *Of Grammatology*. Translated by Gayatri Chakravorty Spivak. Baltimore: Johns Hopkins University Press, 2016.

Descartes, René. *Discourse on Method and Meditations of First Philosophy*. Translated by Elizabeth S. Haldane. Digireads.com, 2016.

―――. "Discourse on the Method of Rightly Conducting the Reason," In *Descartes and Spinoza*, translated by Elizabeth S. Haldane and G. R. T. Ross, 31:41–67. Great Books of the Western World. Chicag: Encyclopedia Britannica, 1952.

———. *Meditations and Other Metaphysical Writings*. Translated by Desmond M. Clarke. Penguin Classics. London: Penguin, 1998.

de Waal Dryden, J. *A Hermeneutic of Wisdom: Recovering the Formative Agency of Scripture*. Grand Rapids: Baker Academic, 2018.

Diller, Kevin. *Theology's Epistemological Dilemma: How Karl Barth and Alvin Plantinga Provide a Unified Response*. Downer's Grove, IL: IVP Academic, 2014.

Dilthey, Wilhelm. "Concluding Observations Concerning the Impossibility of a Metaphyscial Approach to Knowledge." In *Introduction to the Human Sciences*, edited by Rudolf A. Makkreel and Frithjof Rodi, 219–42. Selected Works. Princeton: Princeton University Press, 1991.

———. *Introduction to the Human Sciences*. Edited by Rudolf A. Makkreel and Frithjof Rodi. Selected works 1. Princeton: Princeton Univ. Press, 1991.

———. *Wilhelm Dilthey: Selected Works, Volume IV: Hermeneutics and the Study of History*. Edited by Rudolf A. Makkreel and Frijhthof Rodi. Princeton: Princeton University Press, 2010.

Dockery, David S. *Biblical Interpretation Then and Now: Contemporary Hermeneutics in the Light of the Early Church*. Grand Rapids: Baker, 1992.

Doris, John M. *Lack of Character: Personality and Moral Behavior*. New York: Cambridge University Press, 2002.

Driver, Julia. "Moral and Epistemic Virtue." In *Knowledge, Belief, and Character: Readings in Virtue Epistemology*, edited by Guy Axtell, 123–34. Lanham, MD: Rowman & Littlefield, 2000.

———. *Uneasy Virtue*. New York: Cambridge University Press, 2001.

Duvall, J. Scott, and J. Daniel Hays. *Grasping God's Word: A Hands-on Approach to Reading, Interpreting, and Applying the Bible*. 3rd ed. Grand Rapids: Zondervan, 2012.

Ebeling, Gerhard. *Word and Faith*. London: SCM, 1963.

Eberly, Brewer, and Brian Mesimer. "Reforming Virtue Ethics." *Mere Orthodoxy*. https://mereorthodoxy.com/reforming-virtue-ethics/.

Edwards, Jonathan. *Religious Affections: A Christian's Character before God*. Edited by J. M. Houston. Minneapolis: Bethany, 1996.

Emerson, Ralph Waldo. "Intellect." https://archive.vcu.edu/english/engweb/transcendentalism/authors/emerson/essays/intellect.html.

Erb, Peter C. *The Pietists: Selected Writings*. New York: Paulist, 1983.

Erickson, Millard J. *Christian Theology*. Grand Rapids: Baker, 1992.

Estep, James Riley. "Scripture and Spiritual Formation in the German Pietist Tradition." *Christian Education Journal* 9 (2012) S.

Ezekiel, Anna. "Novalis." *Internet Encyclopedia of Philosophy*. https://www.iep.utm.edu/novalis/.

Fairweather, Abrol. "Duhem-Quine Virtue Epistemology." *Synthese* 187 (2012) 673–92.

———, ed. *Virtue Epistemology Naturalized: Bridges Between Virtue Epistemology and Philosophy of Science*. New York: Springer, 2014.

Fairweather, Abrol, and Carlos Montemayor. *Knowledge, Dexterity, and Attention: A Theory of Epistemic Agency*. New York: Cambridge University Press, 2019.

Fairweather, Abrol, and Linda Zagzebski, eds. *Virtue Epistemology: Essays in Epistemic Virtue and Responsibility*. New York: Oxford University Press, 2001.

Fairweather, Abrol, and Owen Flanagan, eds. *Naturalizing Epistemic Virtue*. New York: Cambridge University Press, 2017.

Fatic, Aleksandar. *Virtue as Identity: Emotions and the Moral Personality*. New York: Rowman & Littlefield International, 2016.

Fee, Gordon D. *Gospel and Spirit: Issues in New Testament Hermeneutics*. Grand Rapids: Baker Academic, 1991.

———, ed. *God's Empowering Presence: The Holy Spirit in the Letters of Paul*. Peabody, MA: Hendrickson, 1994.

Fee, Gordon D., and Douglas Stuart. *How to Read the Bible for All It's Worth: Fourth Edition*. 4th ed. Grand Rapids: Zondervan, 2014.

Fish, Stanley. *Is There a Text in This Class?: The Authority of Interpretive Communities*. Cambridge, MA: Harvard University Press, 1980.

Fleischman, Manfred W. "August Hermann Francke's Short Course of Instructions on How Holy Scripture Ought to Be Read for One's True Edification." *Crux Mar 1989* (March 1, 1989).

Floriani, Peter J. *A Twenty-First Century Tree of Virtues*. N.d.: CreateSpace, 2014.

Fowl, Stephen E., and L. Gregory Jones. *Reading in Communion: Scripture and Ethics in Christian Life*. Eugene, OR: Wipf & Stock, 1998.

Frampton, Travis. "Spinoza and His Influence on Biblical Interpretation." In *A History of Biblical Interpretation: The Enlightenment through the Nineteenth Century*, edited by Alan J. Hauser and Duane Frederick Watson, 3:120–150. Grand Rapids: Eerdmans, 2003.

Franck, Augustus Herman. *A Guide to the Reading and Study of the Holy Scriptures*. Translated by William Jaques. Amazon Digital Services, 2021. Kindle.

Fuller, Daniel. "The Holy Spirit's Role in Biblical Hermeneutics." *International Journal of Frontier Missions* 14 (1997) 91–95.

Gadamer, Hans-Georg. *Truth and Method*. New York: Bloomsbury Academic, 2013.

Gartland, Dan. "Is the Earth Flat? Cavaliers PG Kyrie Irving Says Yes." *Sports Illustrated*, February 17, 2017. https://www.si.com/extra-mustard/2017/02/17/cavaliers-kyrie-irving-flat-earth.

Geisler, Norman L, and Paul D. Feinberg. *Introduction to Philosophy: A Christian Perspective*. Grand Rapids: Baker, 1992.

Gettier, Edmund L. "Is Justified True Belief Knowledge?" *Analysis* 23 (1963) 121–23.

Gjesdal, Kristin. "Georg Friedrich Philipp von Hardenberg [Novalis]." In *The Stanford Encyclopedia of Philosophy*, edited by Edward N. Zalta. Metaphysics Research Lab, Stanford University, 2014. https://plato.stanford.edu/archives/fall2014/entries/novalis/.

Goldman, Alvin. "Empathy, Mind, and Morals." *Proceedings and Addresses of the American Philosophical Association* 66 (1992) 17–41.

Goldman, Alvin, et al. *Knowledge, Belief, and Character*. Edited by Guy Axtell. Lanham, MD: Rowman & Littlefield, 2000.

Green, Adam. *The Social Contexts of Intellectual Virtue: Knowledge as a Team Achievement*. New York: Routledge, 2016.

Grenz, Stanley. *A Primer on Postmodernism*. Grand Rapids: Eerdmans, 1996.

———. *Revisioning Evangelical Theology*. Downers Grove, IL: IVP Academic, 1993.

Grimm, Stephen R. "Is Understanding a Species of Knowledge." *British Journal for the Philosophy of Science* 57 (2006) 515–35.

———. "Understanding." In *The Routledge Companion to Epistemology*, edited by Sven Bernecker and Duncan Pritchard, 84–94. Routledge Philosophy Companions. New York: Routledge, 2011.

Grudem, Wayne. "The Perspicuity of Scripture" Presented at the Tyndale Fellowship Conference: The John Wenham Lecture, Cambridge, England, July 8, 2009. http://

waynegrudem.com/wp-content/uploads/2012/04/Perspicuity-of-Scripture-for-Themelios-Word-97-93.pdf.

Gunkel, Hermann. *Creation and Chaos in the Primeval Era and the Eschaton: A Religio-Historical Study of Genesis 1 and Revelation 12.* Translated by K. William Whitney. Grand Rapids: Eerdmans-Lightning Source, 2006.

Gunkel, Hermann, and Mark E. Biddle, eds. *Genesis.* Mercer Library of Biblical Studies. Macon, GA: Mercer University Press, 1997.

Hardin, Michael. "The Authority of Scripture: A Pietist Perspective." *The Covenant Quarterly* 49 (1991) 3–12.

Hare, W., and T. Mclaughlin. "Four Anxieties about Open-Mindedness: Reassuring Peter Gardner." *Journal of Philosophy of Education* 32 (1998) 283.

Harman, Gilbert. "Moral Philosophy Meets Social Psychology: Virtue Ethics and the Fundamental Attribution Error." *Proceedings of the Aristotelian Society* 99 (1999) 315–31.

Harnack, Adolf von. *History of Dogma.* Vol. 1. Fili-Quarian Classics, 2010.

———. *What Is Christianity?* New York: Harper Torchbooks, 1957.

Hasselberger, William. "Knowing More than We Can Tell: Virtue, Perception, and Practical Skill." *Social Theory and Practice* 43 (2017) 775–803.

Hauerwas, Stanley. *A Community of Character: Toward a Constructive Christian Social Ethic.* South Bend, IN: University of Notre Dame Press, 1991.

Hauser, Alan J., and Duane Frederick Watson, eds. *A History of Biblical Interpretation: The Enlightenment through the Nineteenth Century.* Vol. 3. Grand Rapids: Eerdmans, 2003.

———, eds. *A History of Biblical Interpretation: The Medieval through the Reformation Periods.* Vol. 2. Grand Rapids: William B. Eerdmans, 2003.

———, eds. *The Enlightenment through the Nineteenth Century.* Grand Rapids: Eerdmans, 2017.

Heidegger, Martin. *Being and Time.* New York: Harper Perennial Modern Classics, 2008.

Helmbold, Andrew. "J. A. Bengel—'Full of Light.'" *Bulletin of the Evangelical Theological Society* 6 (1963) 73–81.

Hengel, Martin. *Judaism and Hellenism: Studies in Their Encounter in Palestine During the Early Hellenistic Period.* Eugene, OR: Wipf & Stock, 2003.

Henning, Tim, and David P. Schweikard, eds. *Knowledge, Virtue, and Action: Putting Epistemic Virtues to Work.* New York: Routledge, 2015.

Herman, Paul. "What Is a Scholarly Persona? Ten Theses on Virtues, Skills, and Desire." *History and Theory* 53 (2014) 348–71.

Hildebrandt, Wilf. *An Old Testament Theology of the Spirit of God.* Peabody, MA: Hendrickson, 1995.

Holland, Norman. "Unity Identity Text Self." *Publications of the Modern Language Association* 90 (1975) 813–22.

Homan, Matthew. "Continental Rationalism." *Internet Encyclopedia of Philosophy.* https://www.iep.utm.edu/cont-rat/.

———. "Rationalism, Continental." n.d. https://www.iep.utm.edu/cont-rat/.

Hookway, Christopher. "Cognitive Virtues and Epistemic Evaluations." *International Journal of Philosophical Studies* 2 (1994) 211–27.

———. "Epistemic Norms and Theoretical Deliberation." *Ratio* 12 (1999) 380.

Horowitz, Maryanne Cline. *Seeds of Virtue and Knowledge.* Princeton: Princeton University Press, 1997.

Hursthouse, Rosalind. *On Virtue Ethics*. New York: Oxford University Press, 1999.

Jacobsen, Douglas. *Thinking in the Spirit: Theologies of the Early Pentecostal Movement.* Bloomington, IN: Indiana University Press, 2003. Kindle.

James, William. *The Varieties of Religious Experience: A Study In Human Nature.* Lexington, KY: CreateSpace, 2009.

Jewett, P. K. "God Is Personal Being." In *Church, Word, and Spirit: Historical and Theological Essays in Honor of Geoffrey W. Bromiley*, edited by James E. Bradley and Richard A. Muller, 264–78. Grand Rapids: Eerdmans, 1987.

Johnson, Luke Timothy. *Living Jesus: Learning the Heart of the Gospel*. San Francisco: Harper, 1999.

Jones, L. Gregory. *Transformed Judgment: Toward a Trinitarian Account of the Moral Life*. Eugene, OR: Wipf & Stock, 2008.

Kant, Immanuel. *Kant's Critique of Judgement*. Translated by J. H. Bernard, n.d.

———. *Werkausgabe, Bd.3–4, Kritik der reinen Vernunft, 2 Bde.* Edited by Wilhelm Weischedel. Frankfurt am Main: Suhrkamp, 2002.

Kaufmann, Yehezkel. *The Religion of Israel, from Its Beginnings to the Babylonian Exile.* Translated by Moshe Greenberg. Chicago: University of Chicago Press, 1960.

Keane, Niall, and Chris Lawn, eds. *The Blackwell Companion to Hermeneutics.* Chichester, UK: Wiley, 2016.

Keener, Craig, and M. Daniel Carroll R. "Introduction." In *Global Voices: Reading the Bible in the Majority World*. Peabody, MA: Hendrickson, 2012.

Keener, Craig S. *Spirit Hermeneutics: Reading Scripture in Light of Pentecost.* Grand Rapids: Eerdmans, 2017.

Kelp, Christoph. "Extended Cognition and Robust Virtue Epistemology." *Erkenntnis* 78 (2013) 245–52.

———. *Good Thinking: A Knowledge First Virtue Epistemology.* New York: Routledge, 2018.

———. "Pritchard on Virtue Epistemology." *International Journal of Philosophical Studies* 17 (2009) 583–87.

Kennard, Douglas. "Evangelical Views on Illumination of Scripture and Critique." *Journal of Evangelical Theological Society* 49 (2006) 797–806.

Kennedy, George A. *New Testament Interpretation Through Rhetorical Criticism*. Chapel Hill, NC: The University of North Carolina Press, 1984.

Kidd, Ian James, et al., eds. *The Routledge Handbook of Epistemic Injustice.* New York: Routledge, 2017.

Kieran, Matthew. "Creativity as an Epistemic Virtue." In *The Routledge Handbook of Virtue Epistemology*, edited by Heather Battaly, 167–77. New York: Routledge, Taylor & Francis Group, 2019.

King, Nathan L. "Perseverance as an Intellectual Virtue." *Synthese* 191 (2014) 3501–23.

———. "Responsibilist Virtue Epistemology: A Reply to the Situationist Challenge." *The Philosophical Quarterly* 64 (2014) 243–53.

Kingsbury, Jack D. *Matthew as Story*. Philadelphia: Fortress, 1988.

Kittel, Gerhard, and Gerhard Friedrich, eds. *Theological Dictionary of the New Testament.* Translated by Geoffrey W. Bromiley. 10 vols. Grand Rapids: Eerdmans, 1977.

Klein, Peter. "Skepticism." In *The Stanford Encyclopedia of Philosophy*, edited by Edward N. Zalta. Summer 2015. Metaphysics Research Lab, Stanford University, 2015. https://plato.stanford.edu/archives/sum2015/entries/skepticism/.

Klein, William W., et al. *Introduction to Biblical Interpretation*. Rev. ed. Nashville: Thomas Nelson, 2004.

Kline, Meredith G. *The Structure of Biblical Authority*. 2nd ed. Eugene, OR: Wipf & Stock, 1997.

Klooster, Fred. "The Role of the Holy Spirit in the Hermeneutic Process: The Relationship of the Spirit's Illumination to Biblical Interpretation." In *Hermeneutics, Inerrancy, and the Bible: Papers from ICBI Summit II*, edited by Earl Radmacher and Robert Preus. Grand Rapids: Academie, 1984.

Koritensky, Andreas. *Glaube, Vernunft Und Charakter: Virtue Epistemology ALS Religionsphilosophische Erkenntnistheorie*. Stuttgart: Kohlhammer, 2017.

Kotva, Joseph. *The Christian Case for Virtue Ethics*. Washington DC: Georgetown University Press, 1996. Kindle.

Kotzee, Ben, ed. *Education and the Growth of Knowledge: Perspectives from Social and Virtue Epistemology*. Malden, MA: Wiley-Blackwell, 2013.

Kristjánsson, Kristján. "Justice and Desert-Based Emotions." *Philosophical Explorations* 8 (2005) 53–68.

———. "What Can Moralogy Teach Us About Moral-Exemplar Methodology? Comparisons With Approaches Old and New." *Journal of Character Education* 15 (2019) 25–38.

Kuhn, Thomas Samuel. *The Structure of Scientific Revolutions*. 2nd ed., enlarged. Vol. 2. International Encyclopedia of Unified Science Foundations of the Unity of Science. Chicago: Chicago University Press, 1994.

Kvanvig, Jonathan L. *The Intellectual Virtues and the Life of the Mind: On the Place of the Virtues in Epistemology*. Savage, MD: Rowman & Littlefield, 1992.

———. *The Value of Knowledge and the Pursuit of Understanding*. Kindle Edition. Cambridge Studies in Philosophy. Cambridge: Cambridge University Press, 2003.

Legaspi, Michael. "The Term 'Enlightenment' and Biblical Interpretation." In *A History of Biblical Interpretation: The Enlightenment through the Nineteenth Century*, edited by Alan J. Hauser and Duane Frederick Watson, 3:73–95. Grand Rapids: Eerdmans, 2003.

Lessing, Gotthold. "On the Proof of the Spirit and of Power." In *Lessing: Philosophical and Theological Writings*, edited by H. B. Nisbet, 83–88. 1st ed. Cambridge: Cambridge University Press, 2005.

Lewis, C. S. *Selected Literary Essays*. New York: Cambridge University Press, 2013.

———. *The Magician's Nephew*. New York: Harper Trophy, 2000.

Lipton, Peter. *Inference to the Best Explanation*. 2nd ed. International Library of Philosophy. New York: Routledge/Taylor and Francis Group, 2004.

Locke, John. *Of the Conduct of the Understanding*. Amazon Digital Services, 2011. Kindle.

Lott, Micah. "Situationism, Skill, and the Rarity of Virtue." *The Journal of Value Inquiry* 48 (2014) 387–401.

Lyotard, Jean-Francois, and Jean-Loup Thebaud. *Just Gaming*. Minneapolis: University of Minnesota Press, 1985.

Machen, J. Gresham. "Westminster Theological Seminary: Its Purpose and Plan." *Presbyterian* 99 (n.d.) 6–9.

MacIntyre, Alasdair. *After Virtue: A Study in Moral Theory, Third Edition*. 3rd ed. Notre Dame, IN: University of Notre Dame Press, 2007.

Mailloux, Steven. "Rhetorical Hermeneutics." *Critical Inquiry* 11 (1985) 620–41.

Makkreel, Rudolf. "Wilhelm Dilthey." In *The Stanford Encyclopedia of Philosophy*, edited by Edward N. Zalta. Metaphysics Research Lab, Stanford University, 2016. https://plato.stanford.edu/archives/fall2016/entries/dilthey/.

Maschke, Timothy. "Philipp Spener's Pia Desideria." *Lutheran Quarterly* 6 (1992) 187–204.

McDowell, John. "Virtue and Reason." *Monist* 62 (1979) 331–50.

McGowan, A. T. B. *The Divine Authenticity of Scripture: Retrieving an Evangelical Heritage*. Downers Grove, IL: IVP Academic, 2008.

McKim, Donald K., ed. *Dictionary of Major Biblical Interpreters*. Downers Grove, IL: IVP Academic, 2007.

McKinley, David J. "John Owen's View of Illumination: An Alternative to the Fuller-Erickson Dialogue." *Bibliotheca Sacra* 154 (1997) 93–104.

Mickelsen, A. Berkeley. *Interpreting the Bible*. Grand Rapids: Eerdmans, 1963.

Montmarquet, James. *Epistemic Virtue and Doxastic Responsibility*. Lanham, MD: Rowman & Littlefield, 1993.

———. "An 'Internalist' Conception of Epistemic Virtue." In *Knowledge, Belief, and Character: Readings in Virtue Epistemology*, edited by Guy Axtell, 135–50. Lanham, MD: Rowman & Littlefield, 2000.

Moser, Paul. "God and Epistemic Authority." *Journal for Cultural and Religious Theory* 14 (2015) 414–24.

Moule, Handley. *Veni Creator: Thoughts on the Person and Work of the Holy Spirit of Promise*. London: Hodder and Stoughton, 1890.

Napier, Stephen. *Virtue Epistemology: Motivation and Knowledge*. New York: Continuum, 2008.

Neill, Stephen, and N. T. Wright. *The Interpretation of the New Testament, 1861–1986*. 2nd ed. New York: Oxford University Press, 1988.

Neve, Lloyd R. *The Spirit of God in the Old Testament*. Cleveland, TN: CPT, 2011.

"Nick Kyrgios | Rankings History | ATP Tour | Tennis." *ATP Tour*. www.atptour.com/en/players/nick-kyrgios/ke17/overview.

Niebuhr, Reinhold. *Beyond Tragedy: Essays on the Christian Interpretation of Tragedy*. New York: Scribner, 1937.

Noel, Bradley Truman. *Pentecostal and Postmodern Hermeneutics: Comparisons and Contemporary Impact*. Eugene, OR: Wipf & Stock, 2010.

Ong, Walter J. *Orality and Literacy*. New York: Routledge, 2012.

Osborne, Grant R. *The Hermeneutical Spiral: A Comprehensive Introduction to Biblical Interpretation*. Downers Grove, IL: InterVarsity, 1991.

Owen, John. *The Works of John Owen*. Edited by William H. Goold. Vol. 4. Carlisle, PA: Banner of Truth, 1966.

Pascal, Blaise. *Pensées and Other Writings*. Edited by Anthony Levi. Translated by Honor Levi. New York: Oxford University Press, 2008.

Phillip Jakob Spener. *Pia Desideria*. Translated by Theodore G. Tappert. Minneapolis: Fortress, 2012. Kindle.

Pinnock, Clark. "The Role of the Spirit in Interpretation." *Journal of the Evangelical Theological Society* 36 (1993) 491–97.

Plantinga, Alvin. *Knowledge and Christian Belief*. Grand Rapids: Eerdmans, 2015.

———. *Warrant and Proper Function*. New York: Oxford University Press, 1993.

———. *Warrant: The Current Debate*. New York: Oxford University Press, 1993. Kindle.

———. *Warranted Christian Belief*. New York: Oxford University Press, 2000.

Plantinga, Carl. *Moving Viewers: American Film and the Spectator's Experience.* Berkeley: University of California Press, 2009.

Plato. *Theaetetus.* Translated by Benjamin Jowett. Amazon Digital Services, 2012. Kindle.

Plummer, Robert, and Benjamin Merkle. *40 Questions About Interpreting the Bible.* Grand Rapids: Kregel Academic & Professional, 2010.

Pomerleau, Wayne. "Western Theories of Justice." *Internet Encyclopedia of Philosophy.* https://www.iep.utm.edu/justwest/.

Ramm, Bernard L. *Protestant Biblical Interpretation: A Textbook of Hermeneutics.* Grand Rapids: Baker, 1970.

Reeling Brouwer, Rinse Herman. "The Work of the Spirit in Creation: According to Barth's Exegesis of the First Chapters of Genesis." *Zeitschrift für Dialektische Theologie* 34 (2018) 118–40.

Renic, Dalibor. *Ethical and Epistemic Normativity: Lonergan and Virtue Epistemology.* Milwaukee, WI: Marquette University Press, 2012.

Reventlow, Henning. *History of Biblical Interpretation: From the Enlightenment to the Twentieth Century.* Translated by Leo Perdue. Atlanta: Society of Biblical Literature, 2009.

———. *History of Biblical Interpretation: Renaissance, Reformation, Humanism.* Translated by James Duke. Atlanta: Society of Biblical Literature, 2009.

Richards, E. Randolph, and Brandon J. O'Brien. *Misreading Scripture with Western Eyes: Removing Cultural Blinders to Better Understand the Bible.* Downers Grove, IL: InterVarsity, 2012.

Ricœur, Paul. *Hermeneutics and the Human Sciences: Essays on Language, Action, and Interpretation.* Translated by John B. Thompson. New York: Cambridge University Press, 2016.

Riggs, Wayne D. "Open-Mindedness." *Metaphilosophy* 41 (2010) 172.

———. "Understanding 'Virtue' and the Virtue of Understanding." In *Intellectual Virtue: Perspectives from Ethics and Epistemology,* edited by Michael DePaul and Linda Zagzebski, 203–26. Oxford: Clarendon, 2007.

Roberts, Robert C., and W. Jay Wood. "Humility and Epistemic Goods." In *Intellectual Virtue: Perspectives from Ethics and Epistemology,* edited by Michael DePaul and Linda Zagzebski, 257–79. Oxford: Clarendon, 2007.

———. *Intellectual Virtues: An Essay in Regulative Epistemology.* Oxford: Oxford University Press, 2007.

Robinson, James M., and John Cobb, eds. *New Frontiers in Theology: The New Hermeneutic.* Vol. 2. New York: Harper & Row, 1964.

Rockmore, Tom. "Fichtean Epistemology and Contemporary Philosophy." *Philosophical Forum* 19 (1987/1988) 156–68.

Rosner, Brian S., et al., eds. *New Dictionary of Biblical Theology: Exploring the Unity and Diversity of Scripture.* Downers Grove, IL: IVP Academic, 2000.

Rothenfluch, Sruthi. "Virtue Epistemology and Tacit Cognitive Processes in High-Grade Knowledge." *Philosophical Explorations* 18 (2015) 393–405.

Russell, Gillian. *Truth in Virtue of Meaning: A Defence of the Analytic/Synthetic Distinction.* Reprint. Oxford: Oxford University Press, 2011.

Sakenfeld, Katharine D. *The Meaning of Hesed in the Hebrew Bible: A New Inquiry.* Eugene, OR: Wipf & Stock, 2002.

Sandulache, Cristina. "Yahweh`s Combat with the Sea: Echoes of a Ugaritic Chaoskampf Myth?" https://www.academia.edu/34223062/Yahwehs_Combat_with_the_Sea_ Echoes_of_a_Ugaritic_Chaoskampf_Myth.

Schleiermacher, Friedrich. *Hermeneutics and Criticism and Other Writings*. Edited by Andrew Bowie. Cambridge Texts in the History of Philosophy. New York: Cambridge University Press, 1998.

———. *Hermeneutik und Kritik mit besonderer Beziehung auf das Neue Testament*. Edited by Friedrich Lücke. Berlin: G. Reimer, 1838. http://archive.org/details/ hermeneutikundkrooschl.

Schonbaumsfeld, Genia. "Epistemic Angst, Intellectual Courage and Radical Scepticism." *International Journal for the Study of Skepticism* 9 (2019) 1–18.

Smith, J. A. "Introduction." In *Nicomachean Ethics*. N.d.: e-artnow, 2018. Kindle.

Smith, James K. A. "Storied Experience: A Pentecostal Epistemology." In *Thinking in Tongues: Pentecostal Contributions to Christian Philosophy*, 48–85. Grand Rapids: Eerdmans, 2010. Kindle.

———. *Thinking in Tongues: Pentecostal Contributions to Christian Philosophy*. Grand Rapids: Eerdmans, 2010. Kindle.

Sosa, Ernest. "'The Raft and the Pyramid: Coherence versus Foundations in the Theory of Knowledge." *Midwest Studies in Philosophy* 5 (1980) 3–26.

———. *A Virtue Epistemology: Apt Belief and Reflective Knowledge, Volume I*. New York: Oxford University Press, 2009.

———. *Virtue Epistemology: Oxford Bibliographies Online Research Guide*. New York: Oxford University Press, 2011.

Spinoza, Benedict de. "Ethics." In *Descartes and Spinoza*, translated by W. H. White, 31:355–463. Great Books of the Western World. Chicago: Encyclopedia Britannica, 1952.

———. *A Theologico-Political Treatise*. Translated by Robert Harvey Monro Elwes. Amazon Digital Services, 2011. Kindle.

Starling, David Ian. *Hermeneutics as Apprenticeship: How the Bible Shapes Our Interpretive Habits and Practices*. Grand Rapids: Baker Academic, 2016.

Stein, Robert H. "The Benefits of an Author-Oriented Approach to Hermeneutics." *Journal of the Evangelical Theological Society* 44 (2001) 451–66.

Stendahl, Krister. "The Apostle Paul and the Introspective Conscience of the West." In *Paul Among Jews and Gentiles and Other Essays*, 78–96. Philadelphia: Fortress, 1976.

Steup, Matthias. *An Introduction to Contemporary Epistemology*. Upper Saddle River, NJ: Prentice Hall, 1996.

———, ed. *Knowledge, Truth, and Duty: Essays on Epistemic Justification, Responsibility, and Virtue*. New York: Oxford University Press, 2001.

Steup, Matthias, and Linda Zagzebski, eds. "Recovering Understanding." In *Knowledge, Truth, and Duty: Essays on Epistemic Justification, Responsibility, and Virtue*, 235–51. New York: Oxford University Press, 2001.

Stichter, Matt. "Practical Skills and Practical Wisdom in Virtue." *Australasian Journal of Philosophy* 94 (2016) 435–48.

Sugirtharajah, R. S. "Postcolonial Biblical Interpretation." In *Voices from the Margin: Interpreting the Bible in the Third World*, edited by R. S. Sugirtharajah, 64–84. 3rd ed. Maryknoll, NY: Orbis, 2006.

Swanton, Christine. "The Notion of the Moral: The Relation between Virtue Ethics and Virtue Epistemology." *Philosophical Studies* 171 (2014) 121–34.

————. *Virtue Ethics: A Pluralistic View*. New York: Oxford University Press, 2003.

Tate, W. Randolph. *Handbook for Biblical Interpretation: An Essential Guide to Methods, Terms, and Concepts*. 2nd ed. Grand Rapids: Baker Academic, 2012.

Taylor, Mark. "Text as Victim." In *Deconstruction and Theology*, edited by Thomas J. J. Altizer et al., 58–78. New York: Crossroad, 1982.

Taylor, Rebecca M. "Open-Mindedness: An Epistemic Virtue Motivated by Love of Truth and Understanding." *Philosophy of Education Yearbook* (January 2013) 197–205.

Thiselton, Anthony. "The New Hermeneutic." In *A Guide to Contemporary Hermeneutics*, edited by Donald McKim, 78–107. Grand Rapids: Eerdmans, 1986.

————. *New Horizons in Hermeneutics*. Rev. ed. Grand Rapids: Zondervan, 1997.

Toland, John. *Christianity Not Mysterious, or, A Treatise Shewing That There Is Nothing in the Gospel Contrary to Reason, nor Above It and That No Christian Doctrine Can Be Properly Call'd a Mystery*. 2nd ed. London: Sam. Buckley, 1696. http://name.umdl.umich.edu/A62844.0001.001.

Treier, Daniel J. *Virtue and the Voice of God: Toward Theology as Wisdom*. Grand Rapids: Eerdmans, 2006.

Trible, Phyllis. *Rhetorical Criticism*. Philadelphia: Fortress, 1994.

Trueman, Carl. "Illumination." In *Dictionary for Theological Interpretation of the Bible*, edited by Kevin J. Vanhoozer et al., 316–18. Grand Rapids: Baker Academic, 2005.

Turner, Max. "Ephesians." In *A Biblical Theology of the Holy Spirit*, edited by Trevor J. Burke and Keith Warrington. Eugene, OR: Cascade, 2014.

Turri, John, et al. "Virtue Epistemology." *Stanford Encyclopedia of Philosophy*. https://plato.stanford.edu/entries/epistemology-virtue/.

Ukpong, Justin S. "Developments in Biblical Interpretation in Africa: Historical and Hermeneutical Directions." In *Voices from the Margin: Interpreting the Bible in the Third World*, 49–61. 3rd ed. Maryknoll, NY: Orbis, 2006.

Vainio, Olli-Pekka. *Virtue: An Introduction to Theory and Practice*. Eugene, OR: Cascade, 2016.

Van Til, Cornelius. *The Defense of Christianity & My Credo*. Philipsburg, NJ: Presbyterian and Reformed, 1971.

Vandici, Gratian. "Reading the Rules of Knowledge in the Story of the Fall: Calvin and Reformed Epistemology on the Noetic Effects of Original Sin." *Journal of Theological Interpretation* 10 (2016) 173–91.

Vanhoozer, Kevin J. *Biblical Authority after Babel: Retrieving the Solas in the Spirit of Mere Protestant Christianity*. Grand Rapids: Brazos, 2016.

————. *The Drama of Doctrine: A Canonical-Linguistic Approach to Christian Theology*. 1st ed. Louisville: Westminster John Knox, 2005.

————. "Imprisoned or Free? Text, Status, and Theological Interpretation in the Master/Slave Discourse of Philemon." In *Reading Scripture with the Church: Toward a Hermeneutic for Theological Interpretation*, by A. K. M. Adam et al., 51–94. Grand Rapids: Baker Academic, 2006.

————. *Is There a Meaning in This Text?: The Bible, the Reader, and the Morality of Literary Knowledge*. Grand Rapids: Zondervan, 1998.

Vondey, Wolfgang. *Beyond Pentecostalism: The Crisis of Global Christianity and the Renewal of the Theological Agenda*. Grand Rapids: Eerdmans, 2010. Kindle.

Wadell, Paul J. *Happiness and the Christian Moral Life: An Introduction to Christian Ethics*. 3rd ed. Lanham, MD: Rowman & Littlefield, 2016.

Wallace, James D. *Virtues and Vices.* Ithaca, NY: NCROL, 1978.

Warrington, Keith. *Discovering the Holy Spirit in the New Testament.* Peabody, MA: Hendrickson, 2005.

———. *Pentecostal Theology: A Theology of Encounter.* London: T. & T. Clark, 2008.

Weborg, John. "Bengel, Johann Albrecht." *Dictionary of Major Biblical Interpreters,* edited by Donald K. McKim, 184–88. Downers Grove, IL: IVP Academic;, 2007.

Wenk, Matthais. "Acts." In *A Biblical Theology of the Holy Spirit,* edited by Trevor J. Burke and Keith Warrington, 116–28. Eugene, OR: Cascade, 2014.

Whitcomb, Dennis, et al. "Intellectual Humility: Owning Our Limitations." *Philosophy and Phenomenological Research* 94 (2017) 509–39.

Witherington, Ben, III. *New Testament Rhetoric: An Introductory Guide to the Art of Persuasion in and of the New Testament.* Eugene, OR: Cascade, 2009.

Wolterstorff, Nicholas. *John Locke and the Ethics of Belief.* Cambridge Studies in Religion and Critical Thought 2. New York: Cambridge University Press, 1996.

Wood, W. Jay. *Epistemology: Becoming Intellectually Virtuous.* Contours of Christian Philosophy. Downers Grove, IL: InterVarsity, 1998. Kindle.

———. *Epistemology: Becoming Intellectually Virtuous.* Downer's Grove, IL: IVP Academic, 2009.

Wright, N. T. "Simply Lewis." *Touchstone: A Journal of Mere Christianity.* http://www.touchstonemag.com/archives/article.php?id=20-22-028-f.

Yarchin, William. *History of Biblical Interpretation: A Reader.* Grand Rapids: Baker Academic, 2011.

Yong, Amos. *The Hermeneutical Spirit: Theological Interpretation and Scriptural Imagination for the 21st Century,* 2017.

———. *The Spirit Poured Out on All Flesh: Pentecostalism and the Possibility of Global Theology.* Grand Rapids: Baker Academic, 2005.

Zagzebski, Linda. *Exemplarist Moral Theory.* New York: Oxford University Press, 2019.

———. "From Reliabilism to Virtue Epistemology." In *Knowledge, Belief, and Character: Readings in Virtue Epistemology,* edited by Guy Axtell, 113–22. Studies in Epistemology and Cognitive Theory. Lanham, MD: Rowman & Littlefield, 2000.

———. "Recovering Understanding." In *Knowledge, Truth, and Duty: Essays on Epistemic Justification, Responsibility, and Virtue,* edited by Matthias Steup, 235–51. New York: Oxford University Press, 2001.

———. "The Search for the Source of Epistemic Good." *Metaphilosophy* 34 (2003) 12–28.

———. *Virtues of the Mind: An Inquiry into the Nature of Virtue and the Ethical Foundations of Knowledge.* New York: Cambridge University Press, 1996.

Zimmermann, Jens. *Recovering Theological Hermeneutics: An Incarnational-Trinitarian Theory of Interpretation.* Grand Rapids: Baker Academic, 2004.